DEATH & TAXES

DEATH & TAXES

The Complete Guide to Family Inheritance Planning

Randell C. Doane & Rebecca G. Doane

SWALLOW PRESS

OHIO UNIVERSITY PRESS

Athens

Swallow Press/Ohio University Press, Athens, Ohio 45701
© 1998 by Randell C. Doane and Rebecca G. Doane
Printed in the United States of America
All rights reserved

Swallow Press/Ohio University Press books are printed on acid-free paper ⊗ ™

02 01 00 99 98   5 4 3 2 1

Book design by Chiquita Babb

Library of Congress Cataloging-in-Publication Data

Doane, Randell C.
    Death and taxes : the complete guide to family inheritance planning /
Randell C. Doane and Rebecca G. Doane.
      p. cm.
    Includes index.
    ISBN 0-8040-1010-2 (cloth : alk. paper). — ISBN 0-8040-1011-0
(pbk. : alk. paper)
    1. Estate planning—United States—Popular works. I. Doane,
Rebecca G. II. Title.
  KF750.Z9D63 1998
    343.7305'3—dc21   98-23963

Contents

Introduction

Estate planning is so vitally important to the security of your family, it simply cannot be ignored. Like saving for your children's education or preparing for retirement, estate planning is one of life's responsibilities that cannot be neglected for too long.

Estate planning is primarily concerned with protecting your assets—protecting them from taxes, from unnecessary interference by the probate court, from lawsuits, from divorces, and from the myriad of other disasters that can destroy your family's security. In its simplest terms, estate planning involves arranging your financial affairs so there will be minimum loss, minimum delay, minimum inconvenience, and minimum worry by your family at the time of your death or incapacity.

During the course of planning your estate you will need to consider several important issues and make a number of difficult decisions. The success of your plan will depend on how well you understand the various choices available to you. The primary role of the attorney in estate planning is to help educate the client so that he or she can make informed decisions concerning the available planning options and techniques. One aim of this book is to further that educational process.

After many years of advising and assisting people in connection with their estates, we have had ample opportunity to witness firsthand the results of a poorly conceived estate plan. Following is a sampling of some of the problems and unintended results that we have seen occur when the wrong estate plan or no estate plan has been established:

- You had a sizable estate, but over one-half was lost to the IRS instead of passing to your children.

- You left your entire estate to your daughter, but a few years after your death she divorced and a large portion of your estate was lost to her ex-husband.

- You left your entire estate to your surviving wife with the understanding that it would pass to your children at the time of her death. However, in her later years she suffered from diminished capacity, and most of your investments and other assets were lost to her final caretakers and others who took advantage of her condition.

- Your estate was sufficient to provide your son with a comfortable lifestyle for the remainder of his life. Unfortunately, all of your assets were lost to his business creditors.

- All of your assets were left to your surviving husband with the understanding that they would later pass to your children at the time of his death. However, most or all eventually passed to the second wife he married late in life.

- One-half of your estate was lost to taxes at the time of your death. Your children inherited the remaining one-half, but when they passed away many years later, one-half of that amount was also lost to taxes. As a result, the IRS received three-fourths of your property and your grandchildren received the remainder.

- Your mother became totally incapacitated during her later years. Because she had not properly planned for that possibility, it was necessary to establish a guardianship, which resulted in substantial expense annually for many years. It also meant that your mother's investments and other financial matters were controlled by a probate judge, rather than someone of her choosing.

- You left your estate to your son with the understanding that it would ultimately pass to your grandchildren. However, at the time of your son's death, your investments and property passed to your daughter-in-law, who later remarried. Your daughter-in-law's second husband was the ultimate recipient of your estate and your grandchildren received nothing.

- You had a simple will leaving all property to your wife if living, or to your children if your wife was not living. Unfortunately, that simple plan resulted in several hundred thousand dollars of additional estate tax that could have been easily avoided.

The above examples are just a few of the problems that we have routinely encountered during our combined thirty-plus years of advising people in connection with their family inheritance planning. Fortunately, none of those results need occur. Basic estate planning techniques will avoid those and many other unnecessary losses.

The primary purpose of estate planning is to assure that your assets will pass to your intended beneficiaries in the most economical and protected manner. Estate planning involves safeguarding your assets for the benefit of your surviving spouse, surviving children, or other beneficiaries. Because the biggest threat to many estates is the IRS, estate planning often involves analyzing your potential estate tax bill and choosing the best methods to reduce or eliminate the tax.

The following examples show that even the estates of the rich and famous can be decimated by taxes and administrative costs. The devastating results experienced by these estates were the result not of plans that failed, but of the failure to plan.

John D. Rockefeller, Sr., one of the most famous industrialists, spent his lifetime accumulating a vast fortune. However, he did not formulate a plan to preserve his estate.

Gross Estate	$26,905,182
Costs	<17,124,988>
Net Estate	$ 9,780,194>

64% shrinkage

Alta Rockefeller Prentice was the last surviving child of John D. Rockefeller, Sr. Her estate fared even worse than her father's.

Gross Estate	$12,775,531
Costs	< 8,672,315>
Net Estate	$ 4,103,216

68% shrinkage

Charles S. Woolworth was the founder of F. W. Woolworth Co. He was a brilliant businessman who developed the biggest retail empire of its time. Yet, he was not as successful in planning for the disposition of his estate.

Gross Estate	$16,788,702
Costs	<10,391,303>
Net Estate	$ 6,397,399

62% shrinkage

Alwin Charles Ernst was the founder and managing partner of a hugely successful accounting firm. Although his life was devoted to business planning and analysis, he failed to plan to protect his own estate.

Gross Estate	$12,642,431
Costs	< 7,124,112>
Net Estate	$ 5,518,319

56% shrinkage

There are many examples of successful and creative individuals who accumulated sizable estates, but who failed to plan adequately for the protection of those estates. A few more examples are as follows:

Individual	Gross Estate	Total Costs	Net Estate	Percent Shrinkage
J. P. Morgan	$17,121,48	$11,893,691	$ 5,227,791	69%
Frederick Vanderbilt	76,838,530	42,846,112	33,992,418	56%
Elvis Presley	10,165,434	7,374,635	2,790,799	73%
Marilyn Monroe	819,176	448,750	370,426	55%
Rock Hudson	8,600,000	4,673,712	3,926,288	54%

This book is designed so that you will need to read only those chapters that are relevant to your situation. As you read each chapter you will be referred to other chapters that may also be important for you to read.

- If you have a modest estate you may need to read only the chapters on wills, property ownership, and health care documents.
- If your estate is in excess of the exemption from estate and gift taxes, you will want to read the chapter on transfer taxes.
- If it is important to protect your estate for the benefit of your surviving spouse, children, or other beneficiaries, you should read the chapter on trusts.
- If it appears that your estate may be subject to substantial estate taxes, you will need to read the chapter on advanced planning techniques.
- If a large portion of your estate is invested in a closely held business, you should read the chapter on business succession planning.
- If you expect to inherit significant wealth or expect to serve as an executor of an estate, it will be important to read the chapter on postmortem planning.

- If you have significant life insurance coverage or are considering the purchase of a large policy, you should read the chapter on that subject.
- If you divide your time each year between two or more states, you should read the chapter on residency.
- If you may have a need to shelter assets from the reach of creditors, you should read the chapter on creditor protection planning.
- If you are establishing a trust or are considering serving as a trustee, you should read the chapters on trustees and on the funding of trusts.
- If you have a substantial IRA or other retirement plan, you should read the chapter on that subject.

When you die, your assets will pass from you to "others." Unfortunately, the voyage taken by your estate as it passes to those "others" can be uncertain and dangerous. In most cases a portion of your assets will pass to the IRS, a portion will pass to the lawyers and other professionals involved with the administration of your estate, and, hopefully, a portion will pass to your family. Fortunately, there are a number of planning opportunities that can significantly affect the outcome in favor of your family. The passage of your estate to your intended beneficiaries, like most important life events, is a case where a small amount of planning will be rewarded many times over. In the case of estate planning, it is your family that will reap the rewards.

For most people, estate planning is an unfamiliar subject with its own language and its own peculiar rules. Estate planning requires you to talk with lawyers, accountants, trust officers, insurance advisors, and other professionals and to pay them for the pleasure. Estate planning requires you to disclose private information concerning your family and your finances and to consider your own mortality. It is not surprising that most people's initial feelings about estate planning range from mild anxiety at best to fear and loathing at worst.

However, almost all clients who receive competent advice feel a great sense of relief, satisfaction, and comfort at the conclusion of the estate planning process. Knowing that you have established a plan to assure the safe and efficient passage of your estate can be one of your most rewarding lifetime endeavors.

The key to success for your estate plan is education. If you have a basic understanding of the purposes and objectives of estate planning and if you are aware of the opportunities and choices that are relevant to your situation, you will be able to establish a practical and efficient estate plan and you will find the experience to be one of your most rewarding undertakings. This book is intended to assist you in gaining the information and insight you need as you undertake one of life's most important responsibilities.

DEATH & TAXES

1

Wills

WHEN MOST PEOPLE think of estate planning they think first of wills. Wills have been around for a long time. The ancient Romans commonly used wills, and references to the will can be found in much older civilizations. Today, the will is still the most widely used estate planning tool.

There is a great variety of wills. Some are very simple, consisting of just a few paragraphs, and include only a single outright bequest of all property to a single beneficiary. Other wills are much more complex and may contain one or more specialized trusts and other advanced planning features designed to reduce taxes and better protect the inheritance.

The revocable living trust is the primary estate planning document in many modern estate plans. Even there, however, the will still plays an important secondary role.

Your will may govern the disposition of all of your property, some of your property, or none of your property. The manner in which your real estate, investments, and other property are titled or held will determine whether they will be governed by your will (see "Your Probate Estate," directly below). In many cases, one objective of an estate plan is to assure that no property will, in fact, be governed by your will.

If you die without a will, state law determines who inherits your property (see "Intestacy Rules," below). The law will almost certainly not be consistent with your wishes. Therefore, it is important for most people to prepare a formal will. Without a valid will your estate most likely will not pass to your intended beneficiaries.

Your spouse can usually veto the terms of your will if you leave him or her less than a "fair" share. What constitutes a fair share will be determined by the law of your particular state (see "Electing Against a Will," below).

Your Probate Estate

In general, your will governs only property titled individually in your name. For example, if you have a bank account, securities, real estate, or other asset titled individually in your own name, then it will pass to the beneficiaries designated in your will. But many of your assets may not be controlled by your will. In fact, through design or otherwise, your estate may have no asset that will be governed by your will.

> **Example:** If you own a bank account, real estate, or some other asset jointly with another person, with rights of survivorship, then upon your death that asset will pass to your co-owner regardless of the terms of your will. The asset is said to pass "by operation of law."

> **Example:** At the time of your death insurance proceeds will be paid to the beneficiary named in the insurance contract and will not pass in accordance with your will (unless the policy is payable to your estate).

> **Example:** IRAs and other retirement plans pass to the beneficiaries on file with the IRA or plan administrator regardless of the terms of your will.

Example: You have established a revocable living trust and have retitled all of your various assets in your name as trustee of that trust. Upon your death, those assets will pass to the beneficiaries designated in the living trust document. They will not pass through probate court proceedings and will not be governed by the terms of your will.

Probate court proceedings are generally the least efficient method of transferring property to your beneficiaries at the time of your death. Therefore, one goal of many estate plans is to avoid probate court proceedings. In small estates that is often accomplished through joint ownership. In the case of a medium or larger estate, that is usually best accomplished through the use of a revocable living trust.

Q: My husband recently passed away. Why must I commence probate proceedings if his will leaves everything to me?

A: Even though your husband's will leaves everything to you, you do not automatically acquire ownership of his assets. For example, you will not have access to a bank account, brokerage account, or other investment account that is titled solely in your husband's name without first initiating probate proceedings. A will speaks only through the probate court. Therefore, if your husband has any asset titled individually in his name, probate proceedings most likely will be required.

Intestacy Rules

If you die without a will, you are said to have died "intestate" and property titled individually in your name will pass in accordance with the "intestacy" rules. The intestacy rules vary significantly from state to state, but in many states they follow a similar pattern.

Example: In Florida, the intestacy rules provide, generally, as follows:
> If you leave a surviving spouse, but no living descendant, then your probate estate will pass 100% to your spouse.
> If you leave descendants, but no living spouse, your probate estate will pass 100% to your descendants, with the issue of a deceased descendant taking his or her deceased parent's share.
> If you are survived by a spouse and one or more children, then your

spouse receives one-half and your child or children the other one-half. The surviving spouse's share is increased by approximately $20,000 if all of the surviving children are also children of the surviving spouse.

If you have no surviving spouse or children, your probate estate passes to your parents.

If neither parent is living, your estate passes to your siblings, with the share for a deceased sibling passing to his or her descendants.

If you have no living sibling or descendant of a sibling, then to your grandparents.

If you have no living grandparent on one side of your family, then to your uncles and aunts or the descendants of a deceased uncle or aunt from that side.

Example: In California, if you have no will, your separate property will pass as follows:

Your spouse receives one-third of your separate property if you also leave two or more children.

Your surviving spouse receives one-half of your separate property if you have only one child or if you have no descendant, but have a living parent or descendant of a deceased parent.

Your surviving spouse receives all of your separate property if you leave no descendant, parent, or descendant of a parent.

If you leave no surviving spouse, all of your probate assets pass to your children or the descendants of a deceased child.

If you have no surviving spouse or descendants, then all probate assets pass to your parents.

If you have no surviving parent, remaining assets pass to your grandparents or the descendants of a deceased grandparent.

Example: In Massachusetts, the intestacy rules can be summarized as follows:

If you leave no blood relative, then all to your spouse.

If you leave one or more descendants, they take one-half and your spouse takes one-half.

If you leave no descendants, your spouse will receive the first $200,000 plus one-half of any additional estate and your closest relatives will receive the remainder.

Example: The intestacy rules in Illinois provide as follows:

If you have one or more descendants, then your surviving spouse takes one-half and your descendants take one-half.

If you have no surviving descendant, then your surviving spouse will take your entire estate.

If you have no surviving spouse, then all to your descendants.

If no surviving spouse or descendant, then your parents and siblings each receive an equal share (if one parent is deceased, the surviving parent receives a double share).

If no surviving parent or sibling, then to grandparents.

Q: I have only a small estate. Do I need a will?

A: Generally, yes. It is an unusual case where you will be satisfied with the intestacy provisions of your particular state. For example, if you have a small estate and a spouse and children, you may wish all property to pass to your surviving spouse so that he or she will have all available resources to adequately provide for the children, or in some cases you may wish to leave your estate just to your children. However, in most states, neither of those choices will be possible in the absence of a will.

Example: Assume that you have no will and that the intestacy rules of your state leave one-half to your surviving wife and one-half to your minor children. Generally, the one-half received by your minor children will not be available for their support. Your surviving wife will have the entire responsibility for their care without the availability of one-half of your estate. With a valid will you could have directed that all of your property pass to your surviving spouse if that is your desire.

Example: Assume that you have children from a prior marriage and that your second spouse has a substantial estate. Here you may wish to leave the majority of your property to your children. That generally will not occur in most states in the absence of a will.

It would be an unusual case if your wishes for your estate happened to coincide exactly with the intestacy laws of your state. Therefore, in almost all cases, it is important to have a will.

Electing Against a Will

Almost every state has enacted laws granting a surviving spouse a certain minimum share of the deceased spouse's estate. Therefore it is generally not possible to entirely disinherit your spouse simply by executing a will leaving everything to your children or to other individuals. Your surviving spouse will be able to *elect against* your will and receive a certain minimum share of your probate estate as specified by state law.

The minimum share to which a surviving spouse is entitled varies significantly from state to state. Depending on the state, the minimum share may be known as dower, elective share, courtesy, or by some other similar term. In many states the surviving spouse may have a choice of elections.

> **Example:** In Maine, a surviving spouse is entitled to one-third of the deceased spouse's estate regardless of the terms of his or her will. Florida provides an elective share to the surviving spouse equal to 30% of the net probate estate. In Michigan a surviving wife has a choice: a life estate in one-third of her deceased husband's real estate, or 50% of the amount that would have passed to her had her husband died without a will. A surviving husband in Michigan is limited to the second choice. Nearly all states have rules granting similar rights to surviving spouses, although the specifics of those rules vary greatly.

Because your surviving spouse will have a right to elect against the provisions of your will, it is generally not possible to disinherit him or her simply by executing a will leaving your property to individuals other than your surviving spouse. However, traditionally it has been rather easy to circumvent the election rules by arranging your affairs so that you will have no probate estate.

> **Example:** Assume that your insurance policies and IRA name your children from a prior marriage as beneficiaries. Assume that you own some assets jointly with rights of survivorship with your children and that the remainder of your property is held by a revocable trust created for the benefit of your children. Upon your death, all of your assets will pass to your children. If the law of your state grants to your surviving spouse the right to receive 50% of your probate estate only, then he or she will receive nothing, since all of your assets will pass outside of probate.

The elective share rules have traditionally applied only to the deceased spouse's probate estate as set forth in the above example. During the last several years, some states have changed their rules and now permit the surviving spouse to demand a share of nonprobate assets, such as property held in a revocable trust. In those states, it is more difficult to disinherit your spouse.

Executor, Administrator, or Personal Representative

Most states use the term "executor" to refer to the person named in a will to administer the estate. The term "administrator" generally refers to the person appointed by the judge to administer an intestate estate. In many states all such fiduciaries are referred to as personal representatives. In this book we generally use all of those terms interchangeably.

It is vitally important to have complete trust in the person you nominate as executor. Although the law will seek to hold the executor accountable if he or she abuses the position, that may not be helpful to your heirs if a dishonest or incompetent executor cannot be located or has no recoverable assets. As explained in the chapter on probate proceedings, the job of an executor may be difficult and time consuming. In some cases, it may also require considerable business, managerial, and financial experience. At the minimum, your intended executor should have sufficient common sense to consult and work with competent advisors.

The executor is responsible for the administration of the estate. The executor must locate and take control of all of the decedent's assets that comprise his or her probate estate. The executor must inventory and value the assets, liquidate assets where necessary, assure that creditors receive proper notice of the proceedings, pay valid claims, assure that required tax returns are filed and taxes paid, and distribute remaining assets to the beneficiaries entitled to them. In many cases, executors are also involved with nonprobate assets, such as the collection of life insurance proceeds or other death benefits, obtaining tax lien releases for survivorship property, assuring that IRA and annuity balances are paid to the proper person, and similar activities.

Most individuals who have not previously served as an executor are surprised at the amount of time and attention required for even a small and uneventful probate proceeding. Serving as an executor may become a major undertaking and a difficult and lengthy task if the estate encounters any unusual problem, such as:

- Litigation with creditors or debtors of the estate;
- A will contest between potential beneficiaries;
- Controversy with the IRS or state tax authorities; or
- The operation or liquidation of a closely held business.

An executor who does not proceed cautiously, or who does not receive competent advice, may become personally liable. The executor may become liable to beneficiaries who believe they received less than their fair share, to creditors who feel they were not properly satisfied, or to the IRS or state tax authorities who believe they did not receive their fair share. If an estate is at all complicated or extensive, the nomination of someone as an executor is not an honor, but a significant imposition.

In the majority of cases, family members are selected as executors. However, some individuals select a bank or trust company, or their attorney, accountant, or other trusted advisor. The selection of a third-party executor may be appropriate where there is no suitable family member or where the size or complexity of the estate indicates that a "professional" executor may be the better choice. The selection of a third-party executor may also be necessary where an impartial and dispassionate family member who has the requisite experience is unavailable.

When considering the appointment of an executor you may wish to refer to "Selecting a Trustee" in chapter 3. The same considerations in selecting a trustee apply to the selection of an executor. The candidate must have the necessary judgment, experience, temperament, and, above all, the highest degree of integrity.

Q: Who may serve as executor?

A: First priority is given to that executor nominated in your will. If there is no will, then the heirs are generally given preference.

Q: May I appoint whomever I wish as executor?

A: The rules vary from state to state. However, generally, you may appoint only an adult who is a blood relative or resides in the state of your residence.

Q: If someone appoints me as executor of his estate am I bound to serve?

A: Your selection as executor is not binding and you may always decline to serve.

Guardian of the Person for Minor Children

If you have a minor child or children, it is vitally important for your will to include the appointment of a guardian to raise your children in the event of your death. Your executor is concerned with settling the financial aspects of your estate. In contrast, the person you select as guardian of the person of your minor child will be a surrogate parent charged with raising your child. The guardian of the person is a parent substitute and is responsible for the health and safety of your minor children and for providing the love, teaching, discipline, inspiration, and all of the other qualities expected of a parent.

If you have children who are minors at the time of your death, the probate judge will ultimately appoint a guardian, but strong weight will be given to the nomination contained in your will. If possible, your will should nominate one or more successor guardians in case the first guardian cannot serve.

Q: If I nominate someone as guardian of my minor children, must they serve?

A: No. Assuming your nominee is appointed by the judge, your nominee may then choose to serve as guardian or not.

Q: I am leaving property in trust for my minor child. I will need to appoint a trustee and also a guardian. Should the same person be appointed to both positions, or should I attempt to find two different individuals?

A: The positions of trustee and guardian may or may not be best filled by the same individual. The two roles require much different skills or qualities, although some of the functions to be carried out by each may overlap. The trustee will be primarily concerned with investing trust assets and making distributions for the benefit of your child in accordance with the terms of the trust, your child's needs, and the resources available to your child. On the other hand, the guardian will be primarily responsible for raising your child and assuring that his or her physical, educational, and emotional needs are met. Obviously, one individual may or may not be best suited, or willing, to serve in both roles. In some cases, it may be more efficient to have one individual serve in a dual capacity. In other cases it may be important to have the "checks and balances" that will occur if two different individuals are involved with the well-being of your child.

Q: My husband and I have two minor children. Should I name my husband as the first choice for a guardian in the event of my death?

A: The surviving parent will automatically be the guardian (unless proven to be unfit). Therefore, you should nominate only third parties who will serve if both parents are deceased.

Q: Must I nominate the same guardian for all of my children?

A: There is no legal requirement that the same guardian be nominated for all children, but that is the usual case since you will generally want the children to be raised together.

Q: Can I nominate two people to serve together as guardians?

A: Although you may name co-guardians to serve concurrently, it is often better to name a single guardian in case the co-guardians become separated or cannot agree.

Q: Should I leave property to my nominated guardians so they will have additional resources to help raise the children?

A: Your children's inheritance should be left directly to them or, better yet, in trust for them. Your guardian will have access to the income or principal of your children's inheritance as needed by your children. A token bequest directly to the guardian may be appropriate in some cases. However, your children's inheritance should be left directly to your children, or in trust for them, and not to the nominated guardian.

Q: I am divorced from my wife and I have been awarded sole custody of our children. I do not believe that my wife would be a suitable guardian. Can I appoint someone other than her to serve as guardian?

A: The surviving parent will almost always gain custody of the children unless it can be proven that he or she is unfit as a parent. Unfortunately, there is very little that you can do to affect that situation other than to develop and document the facts to support your belief that your wife is not a suitable custodian.

Guardian of the Property for Minor Children

If you have minor children it will also be necessary to nominate a guardian of the property for them. Minors are not permitted to own property of any significant value. The amount of property that a minor may own depends on state law and is usually in the range of $2,000 to $5,000. Therefore, if you intend to leave any significant amount of property to a minor child it will be necessary to appoint an adult guardian of the property to hold and administer the property for the benefit of the child.

If you leave real estate, investments, or other property outright to a minor child, it will be held and administered by the child's guardian. However, in most cases it is much better to leave property in trust for children (see chapter 2). A trust offers several advantages over a guardianship of the property:

- A guardian holding property for your minor child will be required to account to the court each year and such accountings can be expensive to prepare and usually require the assistance of an attorney. Trusts typically operate free of the probate court.
- Under the law of most states, guardians are much more restricted as to the use of the guardianship property for the child's benefit. On the other hand, trusts can be much more flexible and therefore serve the needs of the child much more effectively.
- In the case of a guardianship, all remaining assets must be distributed outright to the child when he or she attains the age of eighteen in most states. That is often much too young for a child to receive substantial assets. Alternatively, a trust may be designed to remain in effect until the child has attained a more mature age, or it may stay in effect throughout the child's lifetime in order to better protect and conserve the trust resources.
- Trusts for children can be very flexible and can be designed to accomplish a number of important objectives. Trusts for children are discussed in detail in chapter 2.

Q: If my will includes a trust to manage my children's inheritance, do I still need to nominate a guardian of the property?

A: It is important to choose a guardian of the property for your children in case they directly receive any property from other sources. Also, if your children are minors, a guardian may be needed to receive distributions from the trust.

Example: Assume you have a will stating that your investments and other property will be held in trust for the benefit of your minor children. In that event, all of your probate assets (see "Your Probate Estate," above) will pass to the trust to be held in accordance with its provisions. However, assume that you also have a sizable insurance policy payable to your children and an IRA that names them as the beneficiary. In that event, the insurance proceeds and IRA balance will not pass to the trust established in your will. Rather, those assets will pass directly to your children. Therefore, it would be important to have nominated a guardian of the property for their benefit.

Q: I understand that my probate assets may be left in trust for the benefit of my minor children. However, a sizable portion of my total estate consists of life insurance and a retirement plan that are payable directly to my children. How can I cause those assets to be held in the trust rather than being held by a guardian with all of the disadvantages of a guardianship?

A: The simple solution is to name your estate as the beneficiary of your life insurance, retirement plans, and other assets that permit a beneficiary designation. Those assets will then become part of your probate estate and will be added to the trust along with your other probate assets. In most cases a better arrangement would be to establish a revocable living trust that would be named as beneficiary of your insurance, retirement plans, and other beneficiary type assets. It should be noted that naming your estate or trust as beneficiary of your qualified retirement plan will often cause your heirs to lose the advantage of continued income tax deferral (see "Minimum Distribution Rules" in chapter 9).

Q: Whom should I nominate as guardian of the property for my minor children?

A: Generally, the guardian of the property should be the person who serves as trustee of the trust established for your children. However, in some cases the guardian of the person may also be the best choice for guardian of the property, and a second person or trust company may be nominated as trustee.

Q: My husband and I have two minor children and we are divorced. If I were to die before him I would not want him to have control over the property I left for my children. Will he automatically be appointed as the guardian of the property for my children?

A: Unlike the guardian of the person, the surviving parent will not necessarily be appointed as guardian of the property. Therefore, you should nominate a guardian of the property of your choosing. But a much better approach would be to provide a trust for your children, nominate a trustee of your choosing, and assure that all of your property, life insurance, retirement plans, and other assets are structured so that they will be included in the trust to be administered in accordance with your wishes and by the trustee of your choosing.

Q: I understand that my life insurance, IRAs, and other assets should be payable to my estate so that they will be included in the trust established in my will. However, that will result in my having a substantial probate estate with the costs and delays associated with that. Is there any alternative idea?

A: Your heirs would probably be better served by the establishment of a living trust. Life insurance, IRAs, and similar assets could then be made payable to the living trust and would, therefore, pass to the trust at the time of your death without adding to your probate estate. In fact, if your individually owned assets were also transferred to the living revocable trust, then it is likely that no probate proceedings would be required (see "Revocable Living Trust (RLT)" in chapter 2).

Other Purposes of a Will

Your will can also serve to accomplish important tax planning. There are a number of taxation choices or elections that can be made via your will. Also, your will can establish a credit bypass trust (see chapter 2) so that an additional $625,000 can be exempted from the estate tax ($1.0 million after 2005).

Your will can empower your personal representative to transact certain matters without the delay and expense of securing court approval. For example, in the absence of an express grant of authority, your personal representative generally cannot sell real estate without securing prior court approval.

In addition, your will can authorize your personal representative to proceed without the need to post a bond. The ultimate decision as to whether a bond will be required and its amount will be made by the judge, who will not be bound by the recommendation contained in your will; however, it is more likely that the judge will not order the posting of a bond, or will require a smaller bond, where it has been waived in your will.

Q: Should my burial instructions be contained in my will?

A: It is permissible to record your wishes concerning burial, cremation, funeral services, and related matters in your will. However, as a practical matter, it is most likely your remains will be disposed of long before your will is located, read, and acted upon. It is much preferable to express your wishes concerning such matters in a separate letter and to give copies of the letter to your family or other loved ones and discuss those matters with them to be sure they understand your desires.

Q: May I leave money to my pet for his care?

A: Although we often think of our pets as people, they legally are not people and cannot own cash or other property. Therefore, a bequest to a pet would be ineffectual. However, you can leave your pet to a human beneficiary and you can leave a bequest to the human to help cover the cost of maintaining your pet.

Q: Should I sign multiple copies of my will?

A: Almost all experts advise against signing more than one copy of your will. If you later decide to revoke or amend your will it would be necessary to locate each of the signed originals.

Execution of a Will

Although not complicated or difficult, the rules concerning the execution of a will are very precise and unforgiving. A will that is not executed with the exact required formalities will be invalid. It is not enough to "substantially comply" with the rules or to be "close but not perfect." The rules are harsh and if the exact formalities are not satisfied, the will cannot be admitted to probate.

The requirements of a valid will vary from state to state. It is, therefore, important to have a will drafted by an attorney knowledgeable of the rules of that particular state. Furthermore, the actual execution of the will also should be supervised by someone knowledgeable of the rules.

In most states, a will is generally valid if it is signed by the testator in the presence of two or more witnesses who swear and acknowledge the signature in the presence of each other and in the presence of the testator. Although those rules appear simple, the law is full of cases involving improperly executed wills that were determined to be invalid. Great care must be taken in the execution of a will.

Q: If I move to a different state, will I need to have a new will prepared in that state?

A: Not necessarily. Most states have a saving statute, which says, in effect, if a will was validly executed under the laws of the state where you resided at that time, then it will be valid when you move to the new state. However, when you move to a new state, you should have your will and other estate plan documents reviewed by someone knowledgeable of estate planning in that state.

Q: Who should *not* serve as a witness?

A: A beneficiary of the will should never serve as a witness. Although it may be technically permissible in some states, it is never a good idea to have a beneficiary witness the will.

Q: Where should my will be kept?

A: Most attorneys advise that only one copy of your will be executed. Therefore, it is critically important to properly safeguard that one copy. Many individuals prefer to leave the original copy of their will with the attorney who drafted it to be safeguarded in the attorney's will vault. A fireproof safe in your home or your safe deposit box are other alternatives. In some states, however, safe deposit boxes are automatically sealed upon the death of the owner, which may result in additional expense and delay because a court order will be required to open the box to obtain the will.

Amending or Revoking a Will

When a new will is executed, it will generally state that all former wills or codicils are revoked. However, a new will can revoke a former will only if the new will or codicil is signed with the requisite formalities required of wills.

It is possible to revoke a will by destroying or obliterating all original copies of the will with the intention of revoking the will; however, revocation through physical act can be highly uncertain and is not recommended. When you tore up your will, did you do so with the intention of revoking it or not? Did you intend to die without a will or was your intention to reinstate a former will? The questions raised by the physical destruction of a will can be difficult to resolve. There are countless court cases concerning the purported revocation of a will. Suffice it to say that the same deliberation and care should go into the revoking of a will as into the execution of a new will.

Q: I wish to make only minor changes to the terms of my will. Can I simply cross out an old provision of my will and write in a new one?

A: You should never attempt to amend a will by crossing out an old provision and writing in a new one. The result is highly uncertain and will most likely result in litigation. The cross-out may have no effect since it was not accomplished with the testamentary formalities described above. On the other hand, it may be interpreted as a partial revocation of your will. There are other possible interpretations as well. All amendments of a will must be accomplished through a duly executed new will or codicil.

A codicil is simply an amendment to a will. It must be signed with the same formalities required of a valid will. In some cases a codicil may not be located after your death, with the result that it will be of no effect. Therefore, in many situations, it will be preferable to simply restate the will rather than to have a will and one or more codicils.

Q: If I sign a will leaving property to my children and later have an additional child, will that additional child be included?

A: You should review your will and other estate plan documents after any significant financial or family event, such as the birth of a child. In some cases the language contained in your will may automatically include additional children; however, in some cases the particular language in the will includes only children living at the time the will was signed. Most states have a statute granting a certain percentage of your estate to children born after your will was signed.

Q: If my wife and I are divorced, should I prepare a new will?

A: Many, but not all, states have a statute providing that subsequent divorce revokes the provisions in a will in favor of the former spouse. However, even if your state has such a statute, you should not rely upon it to accomplish your purpose. Rather, you should sign a new will.

Q: How often should I update my will?

A: You should review your will every two or three years. It should be updated if there has been a major change in your life or financial situation, such as marriage, divorce, birth of children, death of relatives, or a significant increase or decrease in your income or estate.

Q: If I execute a new will, should I destroy all copies of my old will?

A: In most cases, old wills should be destroyed to safeguard against the possibility of someone discovering only your old will at the time of your death and not finding the amended version. However, in some cases it may be important to retain old wills if a will contest is anticipated (see "Will Contests," below).

Q: I have a bank account, a money market account, and a bond fund. Each of the accounts are worth approximately the same amount. Since I have three children, should I simply leave one of the accounts to each of the children?

A: It is generally not a good idea to leave specific assets to specified individuals. If, during the years to come, one account declines in value or another increases in value, your children will not be treated equally. Rather than constantly monitoring the value of each specific asset, you would be much better advised to simply state that each child will receive one-third of your total estate, without reference to specific assets.

Will Contests

Heirs who receive no share of an estate or a share they believe to be unfairly small may contest the validity of the will. Such will contests are quite common and may be based on one or more theories:

Forgery—The will contestant claims the purported will was not actually signed by the decedent. Howard Hughes provided us with one of the more famous will forgery cases.

Improper execution—The will contestant claims that the requisite formalities of a valid will were not followed.

Mental incapacity—It is claimed that the testator lacked the necessary mental capacity to make a valid will. (This is the most common basis for a will contest.)

Undue influence—It is claimed that someone in a position of trust unduly influenced the testator to the point that the terms of the will do not represent his or her true intentions. (Undue influence is a relatively common basis for will contests.)

Mistake—The claimed mistake can relate to a particular term of the will or to the will in its entirety.

Revocation—It is claimed that the testator revoked the will in question.

Although it is true that only a small percentage of wills are contested and that most of the contests are unsuccessful, when a will contest does arise, the results can be disastrous to the estate. In many cases, a will contest takes several years to resolve and consumes a large portion of the value of the estate. In some cases, will contests with no real basis are initiated for their nuisance value and the hope of obtaining a compromise settlement.

In many cases, a will contest can be anticipated in advance. If one child is omitted or receives a disproportionately small share, a will contest may arise.

In some cases, additional steps are taken during the execution of the will to help establish that the testator is competent and free of undue influence. Often the testator will be engaged in conversation so that witnesses have a basis to later testify that he or she appeared competent. Sometimes the execution of the will, as well as discussions before and after, are videotaped for later use should a will contest arise. Additional language may be added to a will or other estate planning document to clarify the testator's intentions and the reasons for favoring or disfavoring a particular beneficiary.

Q: If a court determines that my will is invalid, who will receive my property?

A: Most wills state that all former wills are revoked. Therefore, if your final will is declared invalid, it will generally reinstate your former will, which will then govern the disposition of your estate. If you had no prior will, then the intestacy laws of your state will control.

Q: I want to disinherit my son. May I include a provision in my will leaving him a modest bequest and further providing that he will lose even that bequest if he contests my will?

A: You are referring to an "in terrorem" clause which supposedly puts the heir "in terror" of contesting the will. In terrorem clauses are invalid in many states and significantly limited in others. Where they are permitted, they may be a useful device to avoid a will contest.

Q: I wish to disinherit my youngest daughter. Is it necessary to leave her a token amount such as $1 or $10?

A: If you intend to omit one of your children from your will it would be important to state your intention specifically so she cannot later claim that she was omitted through inadvertence. However, it is neither necessary nor helpful to leave a token sum. In fact, it will cause your executor unnecessary time and effort to track down your omitted daughter in order to pay her the $1 or $10.

Testamentary Trusts

Your will can leave property outright to one or more named beneficiaries. Alternatively, your will can specify that all or a portion of your property will be held in trust for the intended beneficiary, rather than distributed outright. A trust specified in your will is known as a testamentary trust and is created at the time of your death. A testamentary trust may be useful in a variety of situations:

- Your intended beneficiary may be young, incapacitated, or otherwise incapable of safely managing significant assets. It may, therefore, be appropriate to leave his or her share in trust and delegate investment and administrative authority to a trustee.
- It may be important to segregate your unified credit equivalent (currently $625,000, increasing to $1.0 million in 2006) in a trust so that it is excluded from your surviving spouse's estate. See "Credit Bypass Trust" in chapter 2.
- You may wish two or more people to enjoy your estate in succession.

For example, you may wish your surviving spouse to have the income from your estate, but you may also want to assure that the remaining principal will pass to your children at your spouse's death. That can be accomplished through the use of a testamentary trust.

- You may wish to protect your child's inheritance in the event of the child's divorce, creditor problem, or other misfortune.
- You may wish to leave property in a trust, so that your child will have the use and benefit of the property during his or her lifetime, without making the property subject to estate tax again at the time of your child's death.

There are numerous other uses for testamentary trusts, many of which are discussed in the following chapter. However, it must be remembered that a testamentary trust will not avert probate proceedings. In fact, it will become operative only after your assets have passed through probate and into the testamentary trust. Living trusts are often used instead of testamentary trusts in order to avoid probate.

Pour-over Wills

A will that contains a bequest to a trust, rather than to a person directly, is said to "pour over" to the trust. It is known as a pour-over will.

You may establish a revocable living trust and transfer your assets to the trust so that they will avoid probate in the event of your death. However, even if you believe that all of your assets have been transferred to the revocable trust, a pour-over will is important as a safety measure in the event that an asset titled in your own name is discovered at the time of your death.

2

Trusts

Revocable Living Trust (RLT)
Trusts for Children
Sprinkle Trust
Generation-Skipping Trust (GST)
Dynasty Trust
Trust for Surviving Spouse
Credit Bypass Trust
Marital Deduction or QTIP Trust
"A-B" Trust
"A-B-C" Trust
Spendthrift Trust
Insurance Trust
Educational Trust
Lifetime Gift Trust
Trust for a Disabled Beneficiary
Trust for an Elderly Parent
Charitable Trust
Qualified Personal Residence Trust (QPRT)
Qualified Domestic Trust (QDT)
Medicaid Trust
S Corporation Trust
Blind Trust
Rabbi Trust
Intentionally Defective Trust
Land Trust
Totten Trust
Powers of Appointment

Trusts are not new. They were used by the ancient Romans and by prior civilizations and have been a major part of English law since early times. Over the last twenty or thirty years, there has been a great increase in the use of trusts. Most estate plans now employ one or more trusts.

Trusts are highly versatile tools. They can be used in a variety of situations to solve a number of problems. They can be used to better protect and administer property and they can be used to reduce or eliminate various taxes.

A trust, like a corporation or a partnership, is a separate legal entity. A trust consists of three individuals or entities:

The grantor (also known as settlor or trustor)—the person who establishes the trust and transfers property to the trust;

The beneficiary—the person for whom the trust was created and for whose benefit income or principal may be distributed; and

The trustee—the person who holds legal title to the trust assets and is charged with the responsibility of administering, investing, and otherwise protecting the trust assets for the benefit of the beneficiary.

A trust may have more than one grantor. Such a trust is generally known as a joint trust. Joint revocable living trusts are often used by married couples whose combined gross estates are less than the lifetime exemption from estate tax but who wish to avoid probate proceedings in the event of their deaths and also to avoid the imposition of a guardianship in the event of incapacitation of one or both.

A trust may have more than one beneficiary. Multiple beneficiaries may enjoy the trust income or principal concurrently or in succession. For example, you may create a trust for the benefit of your three children, all of whom will enjoy the income or principal of the trust concurrently. Or, as an example of successive beneficiaries, you may leave property in trust to benefit your surviving spouse and, upon his or her death, to then benefit your children or other descendants.

A trust may have more than one trustee. When two or more individuals serve concurrently, they are known as co-trustees.

One person may serve in more than one capacity. If you established a trust, you would be the grantor. If the trust was intended to benefit yourself, you would also be the beneficiary. If you also named yourself as trustee, then you would occupy all three positions. In fact, that is the most common arrangement in the case of a "revocable living trust."

Although all trusts have the same basic elements described above, there is a great variety of trusts and many different applications for trusts. Trusts are highly flexible and can accomplish a number of important goals.

All trusts can be classified as either revocable or irrevocable. A revocable trust, as the name implies, may be revoked or amended by the grantor at any time. On the other hand, once an irrevocable trust is established, it is not easily cancelled or amended.

Q: I established an irrevocable trust several years ago, but now I am dissatisfied with some of its provisions. Is there anything that can be done?

A: Although it is not easy to amend or revoke an irrevocable trust, it may be possible to do so if all of the interested parties are in agreement. In some cases it may be necessary to petition the probate court to make a change to an irrevocable trust. In all cases, care must be taken to assure that no unfavorable tax result will follow from the amendment or cancellation of an irrevocable trust.

Trusts can also be classified as either testamentary or living. Testamentary trusts are set forth in your will and do not become effective until your death. Living trusts are established during your lifetime and have legal significance before your death. Although living trusts may be either revocable or irrevocable, the term "living trust" generally refers to a revocable living trust.

Revocable Living Trust (RLT)

The revocable living trust (often simply referred to as a living trust), or RLT, is one of the most commonly used trusts. The revocable living trust replaces the traditional will and forms the basic foundation for many modern estate plans. Revocable living trusts are used primarily to avoid probate in the event of death and to avoid the establishment of a guardianship in the event of incapacity.

Most revocable living trusts contain multiple specialized subtrusts. Many of the other trusts discussed in this chapter are often placed within a revocable living trust.

> **Example:** Assume that you and your wife have two children and that you have decided to establish a revocable living trust. At a minimum, your RLT will probably include three subtrusts: a trust for your benefit, a trust for your wife, and a trust for your children. It might also contain one or more additional specialized subtrusts. One possible way in which your revocable living trust could be designed is summarized as follows:
>
> > During your lifetime—You would be the trustee or you and your wife would be co-trustees. One or more successor trustees would be named. You can amend or revoke the trust at any time and you may add property to the trust or remove property from the trust at any time. If you are incapacitated, the successor trustee may use the trust income or principal for your needs and possibly also for your wife's and children's needs if that is specified in the trust agreement. Upon your death, all remaining trust principal and income will be held in a trust for the benefit of your wife if she survives you.
> >
> > After you are deceased, with your wife surviving—All remaining assets will be held for her primary benefit. She will be appointed as the sole trustee of the trust for her benefit if that is your wish. The trust will distribute income and principal as needed for her health, maintenance, and support. Upon her death the remaining trust principal will be held for the benefit of your children. The trust or trusts established for your wife's benefit after you are deceased can be structured in a number of ways. (See "Trust for Surviving Spouse" in this chapter.)
> >
> > After you and your wife are both deceased—The remaining assets will then be held for the benefit of your children. The trust for their benefit can be structured in a number of different ways. (See "Trusts for Children," immediately below.)

The above example summarizes a common basic structure for a revocable living trust. It contains a trust for your benefit to manage your affairs, free of a guardianship, in the event of your incapacity. It may also be designed to provide income or principal to your surviving spouse and children in the event of your incapacity. It will permit you to name the individual or trust company you wish to step into your shoes and manage your financial affairs if you are ever seriously disabled.

Your revocable living trust will include a trust for your surviving spouse, if any, after you are deceased. The design of trusts for surviving spouses is discussed later in this chapter. The trust for your spouse will typically be divided into a credit bypass trust and a marital deduction or QTIP trust, as discussed later in this chapter.

The trust for your surviving children can also be structured in a number of different ways. Trusts for children will often be designed as spendthrift trusts. Trusts for children are also often designed as generation-skipping trusts. Trusts for children may also include one or more other types of trusts.

A revocable living trust is established by executing a trust document. That document will specify the rights of the various beneficiaries during your lifetime, during the lifetime of your spouse surviving you, and during your children's lifetimes after you and your spouse are both deceased. After you have established your RLT, it will generally be important to transfer some or all of your property to the trust. Assets not transferred to the RLT during your lifetime will be subject to probate at the time of your death, thus negating one benefit of the RLT. The funding of trusts is discussed in chapter 4.

The above example illustrates one possible structure for a revocable living trust, assuming that you are married and have children. If you are not married, but have children, then your RLT might be similar to the one illustrated above, except that it would not include the trust for your spouse. If you are married, but have no children and do not expect to have any children, then your RLT might be structured similar to the above example, except that it would not contain a trust for your children. Instead, it might provide that after you and your spouse are both deceased remaining assets will be distributed outright to one or more named beneficiaries. However, if one or more of such beneficiaries were children, then your RLT would likely contain a trust for them.

Q: If I establish a revocable living trust and transfer my assets to the trust, will they be protected from the reach of my creditors?

A: Your RLT will provide no creditor protection for you during your lifetime; however, it may provide substantial protection from creditors for your surviving family or other beneficiaries after you are deceased.

Q: If I transfer my property to my RLT will I lose any control over it?

A: You will not lose any control over assets transferred to your RLT. Assets in your RLT can be easily and quickly transferred back to your name individually if that is ever desired.

Q: Will it be necessary to file a separate income tax return for my revocable living trust?

A: RLTs are ignored for income tax purposes. If any interest, dividends, or other income is earned by your RLT, that income will be reported on your individual income tax return as though the RLT did not exist. Therefore, no income tax return is required for your RLT during your lifetime.

Q: Will my revocable living trust cause any administrative problems?

A: RLTs generally require no additional record keeping or other administration. There should be no significant change in your finances after the RLT is established and funded.

Q: The above illustration of a revocable living trust includes a subtrust for the benefit of the children. What choices or options exist when designing the subtrust for children?

A: Options for the subtrust for children include the following: At what ages the child may receive income/principal without the trustee's consent. Whether the trust should include generation-skipping provisions. Whether an adult child should be his or her own trustee or cotrustee. Whether assets should be held in a single sprinkle trust or whether they should be segregated into separate trust shares for each child. Whether remaining assets in the trust when the child passes away should automatically pass to grandchildren or other specified beneficiaries or whether your child should have a power of appointment so that he or she may specify the beneficiaries to receive the remainder interest after the child passes away. These options and choices and several others are discussed later in this chapter.

Q: The above illustration of a revocable living trust includes a trust for the surviving spouse. What choices or options are available in connection with that trust?

A: A major consideration will be whether the trust for your surviving spouse should be designed to qualify for the marital deduction or whether it should be a credit bypass trust. Another issue is whether upon your spouse's death the remaining assets should automatically pass equally to the children or whether your spouse should have a power to appoint remaining assets to any one or more of your descendants in any proportions, and whether he or she should have the power to appoint to individuals other than your descendants. Another issue is whether your surviving spouse should be his or her own trustee or co-trustee, or not serve as a trustee in any capacity. Another issue is the degree of access to principal that your spouse should have. These and many other concerns are discussed below.

Trusts for Children

It is often thought that real estate, investments, and other property should be left in trust for children only if the children are young or are otherwise unable to manage or conserve their inheritance. The modern trend, however, is to leave property in trust for children in most cases, even where the children are adult, mature, and responsible. Property is often left in trust for mature, responsible children so that it will be better protected from potential divorces, creditor problems, and additional taxes. A properly designed trust can protect your child's inheritance from a variety of possible misfortunes and yet provide the child with virtually unrestricted access to, and control over, his or her inheritance.

Estate planning often involves planning for the transfer of assets to children while assuring that there will be proper management and administration of those assets for the children's benefit. Trusts are frequently used to assure the proper management and administration of the assets and to assure that the child will ultimately receive the income and principal at the appropriate time and in the appropriate manner.

If children are young it is obviously better to leave their inheritance to them in a trust. If property is left outright to a minor child, it will be held by the child's appointed guardian and will be distributed outright to the child at age 18 in most states. Leaving significant property to a child to be received at age 18 or even at age 21 may be a great disservice to the child and may cause more harm than benefit, especially for a child who is not accustomed to having significant income or wealth and who suddenly receives substantial assets. Most of us have known of someone who received "too much too soon." Such children often suffer serious developmental problems and may never acquire a satisfactory level of maturity or responsibility. In most cases it is preferable to leave property in trust for children so that the property will be properly managed and administered for their benefit and will ultimately pass to them at a more mature stage of their lives.

When designing a trust for a child, it is often desirable to focus separately on the principal of the trust and the expected income from the trust. A common trust arrangement for a child might be as follows:

- When the child is young, the trustee will make all decisions regarding the use of income or principal for the child's health, education, maintenance, and support.

- After the child reaches age 25 (or some other specified age), all income from the child's trust will be distributed currently regardless of the child's needs. The idea is to begin to give the child some sense of responsibility. The child will receive all income from his or her separate trust, but still must obtain the trustee's approval before principal may be expended.

- Finally, remaining principal will be distributed to the child in stages. For example, one-third at age 30, one-third at age 35, and the remaining one-third at age 40. Here, the idea is to distribute principal in stages so that if the child is wasteful or otherwise imprudent with the first partial distribution, hopefully he or she will have acquired some additional maturity by the time the next partial distribution is made.

The above example provides that all income will be distributed regardless of need starting at age 25. You may wish to select an earlier or a later age. That will depend on the amount of trust income anticipated, the apparent maturity level of the child (if that can be judged), and your particular philosophy concerning financial matters as they affect a young person's development. Similarly, where the above example distributes one-third of remaining principal at ages 30, 35, and 40, you may select earlier or later ages depending on the same factors. As discussed below, there are significant advantages in, and a growing trend toward, eliminating mandatory distributions at specified ages and permitting the child to receive the benefits of the trust throughout his or her lifetime. See "Generation-Skipping Trust (GST)" in this chapter.

There are a great number of additional terms and provisions that can be included in a trust created for a child to better serve the child's needs in a given situation.

Example: The trust can be used to positively motivate the child. You may wish to provide that the child will start to receive all of the income from the trust (without trustee approval) starting at the earlier of (1) attaining a baccalaureate degree or (2) age 30. That may give the child some incentive to promptly complete his or her education. Of course, the mandatory distribution of all income without trustee discretion could be tied to attainment of a higher degree or to some other important achievement.

Example: The trust might provide that income will be distributed as needed for the child's health, education, maintenance, and support, but at a minimum, income will be distributed in an amount at least equal to the child's personal earnings for that year. So, for example, if the child earns $30,000 in a given year, then the trustee will distribute at least $30,000 of trust income to the child. Naturally, that will tend to encourage the child to be more serious about establishing a career and earning an appropriate livelihood.

Example: The child's trust may provide that at a specified age the child will become the co-trustee of his or her separate trust fund. That technique is intended to instill and develop a sense of responsibility and afford the child some real-life experience in managing and administering significant assets.

Another factor to consider is the degree of access to principal to be enjoyed by the child. The child's trust may be established only for his or her education, or it may be established for the child's health needs or maintenance and support, or for a combination of those purposes. The trust may or may not permit income or principal to be used for other purposes such as travel, expenses incident to marriage, the purchase of a home, the establishment of a business or a professional practice, or other important purposes. Obviously, the age and maturity of the child, the size of the trust fund, and other relevant factors must be considered.

In some situations it may be appropriate to provide that no principal is to be distributed during the child's lifetime. The inclination of the child, the size of the trust fund, and your particular goals may indicate that an "income only" trust is appropriate. For example, if the trust fund is modest in size and your strong desire is to assure at least a minimal income to supplement your child's own earnings throughout his or her lifetime, it may be appropriate to provide for income only. If principal invasion is permitted in the case of a modest trust fund, the possibility exists that the principal will be eroded so that the trust will not provide the minimal level of supplemental income you had wished to provide. A compromise position that is occasionally used is to permit invasions of principal only in the event of a "medical emergency," a "financial emergency," a significant decline in the child's standard of living," or some other similar standard. Great care can be taken to control and limit access to principal, but the possibility will exist that principal will be significantly depleted. Obviously, the philosophy of your chosen trustee, your ability to communicate your wishes to the trustee, and his or her ability to carry out your wishes will also have a bearing on the principal access issue. Unfortunately, if your overriding purpose is to provide a basic "safety net" in the form of a minimal standard of living for the duration of your child's lifetime, you are necessarily looking many years into the future, and the identity and ability of successor trustees at that time may not be known. Also, if your philosophy and intention regarding access to principal cannot be objectively stated and administered, a corporate trustee may not be willing to undertake the responsibility.

Another factor to consider is who should receive the remaining trust assets in the event of a child's death. There are numerous options that may be appropriate. A common approach is to provide that remaining assets will be held for the benefit of the deceased child's children (your grandchildren). Or, if the deceased child had no living descendant, then remaining trust assets would be added to the shares created for your other children or the descendants of a deceased child. This approach assures that trust assets will remain in your bloodline and will be used only for the benefit of your children and other descendants. It prevents trust assets from being diverted to sons-in-law, daughters-in-law, and other third parties.

Another common approach is to grant the child a "power of appointment," which permits the child to specify by will who is to receive the remainder of the child's trust at the time of the child's death. It is often difficult to decide whether to grant the child a power of appointment or to require that remaining assets will pass to grandchildren at the child's death. Your first inclination may be to place the least restrictions on the trust and permit your child to designate the ultimate beneficiary. However, that often means that your trust property ultimately will be left to your child's spouse rather than your grandchildren. Even though you may love your daughter-in-law or son-in-law, you may feel a greater duty to protect and provide for your grandchildren. Therefore, you may decide to omit a power of appointment and simply require that remaining trust property at your child's death will pass to grandchildren.

A compromise position that is occasionally used is to grant your child a limited power of appointment. For example, you may permit your child to specify which of the grandchildren will receive the remainder interest in the trust and in what proportions. Your child can designate that remaining assets will pass to any one or more of the grandchildren or other descendants. In that way, your child can direct remaining trust assets among the descendants to where they are most needed or where the greatest overall tax benefit will accrue to the family as a whole. Of course, the class of beneficiaries to whom your child may appoint remaining principal may include other family members, charities, or any other individuals or institutions you may wish to benefit.

Q: My children are mature and responsible adults and I have complete confidence in their ability to handle money. Why would I want to leave their inheritances to them in trust?

A: As explained below, assets left in trust are much better protected than are assets left outright. If your children are mature and responsible, you will likely want to make them their own trustees. However, if the trust is properly designed, it will add a significant level of protection for your children's inheritance.

Q: I intend to leave my son's inheritance in trust for him so that it will be better protected. I have conflicting feelings as to the disposition of the remainder interest after my son is deceased. On the one hand, I want to afford him the greatest flexibility and control and would therefore wish him to have a power to appoint the remainder to his wife or other beneficiary that he might choose. On the other hand, I want to assure that significant assets will eventually pass to my grandchildren for their security and benefit. Are there any solutions to this dilemma?

A: One possibility is to grant your son a power to appoint a percentage of the remaining principal of the trust. You could provide that 25%, 50%, or some other amount may be appointed by him to the beneficiary of his choosing, but that the remaining portion of his inheritance will automatically pass to your grandchildren. Another approach might be to permit your son to appoint the remainder (or a fraction thereof) of his inheritance to his spouse in a trust that will provide only income to her with the remainder passing to your grandchildren at the time of her death. There are several other possible arrangements that may be helpful in certain circumstances.

Trusts are highly flexible tools that may be designed to fit any particular set of circumstances. When designing a trust for your child, a great number of choices are available. The following examples are intended to show some of the types of trusts that may be created for children.

Example: The child is named as his own trustee. He may withdraw all income and has very liberal access to principal. At the child's death remaining trust assets will pass as directed by the child.—This is a typical structure for a mature and responsible child. He will have virtually unrestricted access to trust assets and yet the assets may be highly protected if the trust is properly designed. In addition, significant additional estate taxes may be avoided. See "Generation-Skipping Trust (GST)" below.

Example: Assume the same facts as above, liberal access to principal, own trustee, etc. In this case, however, the child does not have the right to name who will receive the remainder at the time of his death.—Again, this trust is for the mature and responsible child, but the parent wishes to assure that trust assets will remain in the bloodline, benefitting grandchildren after the death of the child, rather than being diverted to a daughter-in-law or other beneficiary.

Example: Assume the child is designated as her own trustee and receives all income, but may not withdraw principal or has very limited access to principal.—This trust is for an honest child who can be relied upon to follow the terms of the trust and is, therefore, named as her own trustee. However, based on the limited size of the trust or because of the child's spending habits, it was decided that principal should be conserved. This might be the trust for a dependable and responsible child who may be subject to pressure from his or her spendthrift spouse. Your child will be fully in control of the trust, but will be able to say to her spouse, "Sorry, although we enjoy the income from my parents' trust, we are not permitted to withdraw principal."

Example: A trust can provide that all income shall be distributed to the child and that principal also may be distributed liberally for his health, education, maintenance, and support, but with a bank or other third party designated as trustee.—This is likely a trust for a child who is not responsible in financial matters. The parent does not feel comfortable naming him as his own trustee. Based on the size of the trust it is appropriate to permit liberal distributions of principal as long as a dispassionate third party is overseeing such distributions.

Example: This trust provides for distributions of income only, with no access to principal, and specifies a bank or other third party trustee.—This might be for a highly irresponsible child who cannot serve as his own trustee. In addition, the parent may feel that any access to principal may be abused by the child and could eventually result in a significant depletion of limited trust assets.

The above examples illustrate only a few of the possible trusts that can be created for a child. There are numerous additional provisions that can be included or variations of the above provisions that can be used to fine tune the trust to meet your family's particular circumstances and needs.

Sprinkle Trust

A sprinkle trust is one that permits the trustee to allocate or "sprinkle" trust income or principal among the members of a specified class. A sprinkle trust is frequently used in cases where there are young children and modest trust assets. The sprinkle trust would permit the trustee to distribute income or principal as needed by any one or more of the children. There would be no requirement that the children be treated equally. The idea is to permit the trustee to respond more as a true parent would.

Although parents generally wish to treat their children equally, they often pay greater attention to each child's individual needs. A child who has a greater medical or educational need may receive more of the family's resources. The sprinkle trust permits the trustee that discretion.

A sprinkle trust is often most appropriate where trust resources are limited and children are young.

> **Example:** You have three children ages 4 through 8 and you will be able to provide them a total inheritance of $300,000. If the $300,000 is divided equally into three separate trust funds at the time of your death, then each child will have a $100,000 fund. It is possible that one child could suffer a medical or other misfortune that would require substantially more than $100,000. You may also have a gifted child who qualifies for scholarships or has other available resources and does not need his full share. If the trust is divided into separate trust funds, the trustee will not be able to shift resources among the children in accordance with their relative needs.

> **Example:** The $300,000 is left in a single trust for the benefit of all three children and the trustee is permitted to allocate the trust resources in accordance with each child's needs. Here, the child with greater needs will have the necessary resources.

Sprinkle trusts for children typically provide that the trust will be divided into separate shares when the youngest child reaches some specified age. The most common ages for division are age 25, when the children should begin to be established in life; age 22, when they have typically completed their undergraduate education; or age 21, the traditional beginning of adulthood. You can select any appropriate age or other triggering event. After the trust is divided into separate shares, each child will get the income/principal from his or her respective trust only.

A "make-up" provision is often included whereby distributions to children prior to the division into separate shares are taken into account at the time of division. Distributions prior to the time of division are considered "advancements" to be deducted from that child's share at the time of division. Frequently, the make-up provision is limited to prior distributions to a child for extraordinary things such as travel, purchase of an automobile, or similar nonessential distributions, if those types of distributions are permitted.

Sprinkle trusts may be used for beneficiaries other than children, for example, in the case of a trust established for parents and/or siblings or in the case of a trust established for charitable purposes. Here again, the inclination, philosophy, experience, and ability of your chosen trustee and successor trustees will be relevant. A sprinkle trust without clear objective standards may be unacceptable to a corporate trustee and difficult to administer for any trustee.

Generation-Skipping Trust (GST)

A generation-skipping trust is usually designed to benefit your children, nieces or nephews, or some other lower generation beneficiaries without being included in their estates for taxation and other purposes.

> **Example:** You leave property in trust for your daughter; the trust provides that she will receive income and/or principal in accordance with certain guidelines set forth in the trust. The trust does not specify a particular age or ages when the principal will be distributed outright from the trust to your daughter. Rather, the trust is intended to remain in effect throughout her lifetime with income and/or principal being distributed for her benefit as prescribed in the trust agreement.

By not requiring principal to be distributed at a certain age or ages, the trust may provide one or more of the following benefits:

- Property held in trust for the benefit of your child (or other beneficiary) may be insulated from the reach of his or her creditors (see "Spendthrift Trust" below in this chapter).
- Assets held in a trust for the benefit of your child (or other beneficiary) will be less susceptible to loss in the event of his or her divorce.
- Within a certain limitation, assets left for your child in a generation-skipping trust will not be included in your child's estate and will not be taxed again at your child's death before the assets pass on to grandchildren. As wealth is passed down through the generations of your family, the use of a generation-skipping trust may substantially reduce transfer taxes and, therefore, preserve more of your family's wealth.

Example: In a very simplistic illustration, assume your parents accumulated an estate valued at $4.0 million at the time of their deaths. Assume further a 50% tax bracket and that your parents' estate pays $2.0 million in tax. The remaining $2.0 million is inherited by you. Further assume that you survive your parents by 30 years and at the time of your death the $2.0 million inherited from your parents is still held by you. If the $2.0 million of assets were left outright to you by your parents, then those assets will again be taxed at your death. Again assuming a 50% tax, the tax will be $1.0 million and $1.0 million will remain for your children. Because of the multiple taxation that occurs at each generation, the $4.0 million accumulated by your parents during their lifetimes will pass $3.0 million to the IRS in taxes and only $1.0 million will remain for the benefit of the grandchildren.

Your parents' estate	$4.0 million
Your parents' estate tax	<2.0>
You receive	$2.0
Your estate tax	<1.0>
Your children receive	$1.0

Obviously, it would be helpful to avoid the second tax on the estate of the deceased child. Within a certain limitation, a properly designed generation-skipping trust will avoid the second generation tax.

The generation-skipping tax limitation is $1.0 million per person (indexed for inflation starting in 1998). You and your spouse may each leave $1.0 million in a trust for the benefit of your children or other lower generation beneficiaries. That $2.0 million will eventually pass to grandchildren or other named beneficiaries free of a second estate tax upon the death of the child. The exemption applies to the $2.0 million placed in trust by you and your spouse, plus it also applies to all appreciation or growth on the $2.0 million occurring during your children's lifetimes surviving you.

Example: You and your spouse leave $2.0 million in trust for your children. Your children may be their own trustees and the trust may provide that they receive all income and have liberal access to principal (or more restrictive access in accordance with your wishes). Assume further that your children survive you by 30 years and that during that period the $2.0 million left in trust for your children appreciates to $6.0 million. The entire $6.0 million will pass on to your grandchildren or other named beneficiaries free of estate tax. If your children are in the 50% estate tax bracket, $3.0 million will be saved for the benefit of your grandchildren or the other named beneficiaries. A properly designed generation-skipping trust may provide one of the greatest tax benefits possible for grandchildren or other lower generation beneficiaries.

In addition to substantially reducing transfer taxes for the benefit of grandchildren and other beneficiaries, the generation-skipping trust will also provide a large measure of security for the trust assets. As a general rule, a properly designed generation-skipping trust with appropriate spendthrift provisions will be difficult or impossible to penetrate by a creditor of your child or other beneficiary. Similarly, it may be difficult or impossible for your child's spouse to receive an interest in the trust in the event of your child's divorce or death.

Because of the substantial tax savings and added security associated with the generation-skipping trust, it is becoming one of the more commonly used estate planning techniques.

You may at first think it inappropriate to leave property in trust for your children in those cases where your children are mature, responsible, and perfectly capable of managing substantial wealth. However, if that is the case, then simply appoint your child as the trustee or co-trustee of his or her trust fund. In that event, the child may have the best of all worlds:

- The assets will be better protected from the reach of creditors or ex-spouses;
- Substantial transfer taxes will be avoided for the benefit of grandchildren; and
- Your child, as trustee, will have full control over the investment and use of trust assets if that is your desire.

In most cases, a generation-skipping trust is not a separate trust. Rather, it is simply a provision or design feature added to your existing living trust, insurance trust, or other estate planning trust. The design feature is that provision which permits trust property to remain in trust throughout the child's lifetime yet permits the child the degree of control over trust assets and access to the trust income or principal that is appropriate under the circumstances.

Q: I expect to inherit a significant amount in investments and other property from my parents. I am concerned that my inheritance would be lost if I am sued as a result of an automobile accident, a business investment, or some other misfortune. How can my inheritance be protected?

A: You should ask your parents to leave your inheritance to you in trust. Even though your parents may appoint you as your own trustee and may grant to you virtually unlimited control over your inheritance, a properly designed trust will provide a very significant level of protection from lawsuits and other creditor problems. It will also protect your inheritance should you suffer the misfortune of a divorce.

Q: I should be able to leave significant assets to my son at the time of my death. However, he already has a sizable estate and the property I leave him will only worsen his own estate tax problem. May I leave the property in such a manner that it will be available for my son's use if needed, but will not be included in his estate at the time of his death?

A: Up to $1.0 million ($2.0 million from you and your spouse) can be left in trust for the benefit of your son and yet be excluded from his estate at the time of his death. That amount is indexed for inflation starting in 1998.

Q: Can I establish a generation-skipping trust that will benefit additional generations beyond my grandchildren?

A: Generation-skipping trusts are often established to benefit multiple generations. However, the law of most states limits the duration of a trust to the lifetimes of grandchildren or great-grandchildren. See "Dynasty Trust," below.

Q: Are there any possible techniques that can be used to increase the $1.0 million generation-skipping limitation?

A: Family limited partnerships, GRITs, and life insurance are some of the methods that may be used to multiply or leverage the GST exemption. See chapter 7, "Advanced Planning Techniques."

Dynasty Trust

Dynasty trusts have been used by wealthy families for centuries to provide a legacy of wealth for future generations. A dynasty trust permits substantial property to pass from generation to generation without being decimated by estate taxes. The savings for future generations can be several millions of dollars. The dynasty trust will also better protect family wealth from divorces, lawsuits, and other similar misfortunes. Today, dynasty trusts are not limited to the very rich.

A dynasty trust is simply a generation-skipping trust that is designed to skip multiple generations.

Example: Assume you establish a trust providing that after you and your spouse are deceased, all of your property will be held in trust for the benefit of your children. They will receive income and principal as needed. As each child passes away, his or her share will be held for his or her children (your grandchildren). The grandchildren will receive income and principal as needed and when they pass away, remaining property will be held for the benefit of your great-grandchildren and they will receive income and principal as needed.

The above example describes a basic dynasty trust. It can end after great-grandchildren or can pass on to benefit many additional generations.

Q: Are there any limitations on the amount of property that can be left in a dynasty trust?

A: The Generation-Skipping Tax was specifically enacted to limit dynasty trusts. However, it provides a fairly generous $1.0 million exemption from the tax (indexed for inflation). Therefore, you and your spouse can each leave $1.0 million in a dynasty trust and it will avoid estate taxes at each generation. Assuming the property appreciates at a reasonable rate, many millions of dollars of estate tax will be saved over the next few generations.

Example: Assume that after you are deceased and all taxes are paid your children will receive $1.0 million. Assume that your children and each successive generation survives 30 years after their parents are deceased. Assume that your legacy grows at a consistent 6.0% after-tax rate. The first column shows the results if your legacy is left outright, and the second column shows the effect of a dynasty trust.

	Inheritance Outright	Dynasty Trust
Children receive	$ 1,000,000	$ 1,000,000
30 years' growth	4,740,000	4,740,000
Total	$ 5,740,000	$5,740,000

	Inheritance Outright	Dynasty Trust
Estate Tax (55%)	<3,157,000>	<-0->
Grandchildren receive	$2,583,000	$ 5,740,000
30 years' growth	12,252,000	27,228,000
Total	$ 14,835,000	$ 32,968,000
Estate Tax (55%)	<8,159,000>	<-0->
Great-grandchildren receive	$ 6,676,000	$ 32,968,000
30 years' growth	31,718,000	156,383,000
Total	$ 38,394,000	$189,351,000
Estate Tax (55%)	<21,117,000>	<-0->
Great-great-grandchildren receive	$ 17,277,000	$189,351,000

The above example shows that the dynasty trust can result in your grandchildren receiving $5.7 million, rather than $2.6 million without the trust. The example shows that with the dynasty trust your great-grandchildren will receive almost $33.0 million. At that time, $33.0 million may not be a great deal of money. However, it will certainly be a great deal more than the $6.7 million that they would receive without the dynasty trust. Similarly, regardless of the rate of inflation between now and then, your great-great-grandchildren will certainly be much better off receiving $189 million with the dynasty trust than the $17 million without the trust.

Nearly every state has adopted a complicated and arcane law known as the rule against perpetuities. The rule varies from state to state but generally prohibits the establishment of trusts that will last for more than two or three generations, depending on the particular state. In most such states, it may be necessary to design a trust so that assets will finally be distributed to grandchildren or great-grandchildren rather than held for later generations. However, South Dakota, Delaware, Idaho, and Wisconsin have no rule against perpetuities. As a result, trusts there may be established to benefit several generations. Idaho and Wisconsin are less desirable in this respect because they impose a tax on trust income. Delaware also has some limitations not found in South Dakota. As a result, in the last few years many residents of other states have been establishing dynasty trusts in South Dakota in order to take advantage of its liberal rules.

Q: How is a dynasty trust established?

A: A dynasty trust may be established and funded during your lifetime or it may be included in your will to be established and funded at the time of your death.

Q: In order to receive the tax benefits, must the dynasty trust be restrictive?

A: Because of the long term nature of dynasty trusts, they are typically written in a flexible and liberal manner. Each generation is often granted the right to remove all income and principal as needed. The members of each generation often become their own trustees after attaining a specified age. Also, each generation may be granted a power of appointment to designate the recipient of the remainder interest.

Q: Must I live in South Dakota in order to establish a dynasty trust?

A: No, it is not even necessary to visit South Dakota. However, it is generally necessary to have a South Dakota trustee or co-trustee. It is also necessary that the trust document contain special provisions that are acceptable under South Dakota law.

Q: Are there any methods to further enhance the benefits of a dynasty trust?

A: The benefits of a dynasty trust are often multiplied through the use of insurance or through the use of a Family Limited Partnership or other leveraging technique. See chapter 17, "Advanced Planning Techniques."

Trust for Surviving Spouse

There are a great many choices when creating a trust for your surviving spouse. Some of the same factors described above regarding trusts for children are also applicable when establishing a trust for your spouse.

As in the case of trusts for children, the design of a trust for your spouse may involve conflicting concerns and goals. You may wish to be the least restrictive and to provide your surviving spouse the greatest degree of control and autonomy concerning your estate. But at the same time, you may wish to provide a large measure of protection for the trust assets for the benefit of your surviving spouse and for your children or other ultimate beneficiaries.

The first consideration is the degree of access to trust income for your surviving spouse. In the case of a "marital deduction" trust, the tax rules require that all income be distributed. Therefore, access to income is not an issue. However, the first $625,000 (increasing to $1.0 million after 2005) of assets are often left in a credit bypass trust for the benefit of the surviving spouse. In that case, you have a great number of choices. Frequently, the credit bypass trust will simply require that all income be distributed currently. That may be appropriate where the trust estate is modest and the income will clearly be needed. It may also be appropriate if you simply wish to afford the maximum control to your surviving spouse.

Often, the credit bypass trust will permit distributions of income not only to the surviving spouse, but also to children or other descendants. In that case, the trustee may direct trust income where needed within the family or the trustee may direct trust income to maximize tax planning for the benefit of the entire family unit. If the trust is properly designed, distributions of income to children will be taxed to them, distributions to the surviving spouse will be taxed to him or her, and income retained by the trust will be taxed to the trust at its respective income tax bracket. That arrangement will permit the greatest income tax planning flexibility. Of course, the trustee may be empowered to distribute income to other family members or other beneficiaries as you deem appropriate. However, if there is a class of permissible beneficiaries, then there must be clear and objective distribution standards, or the trust will be difficult to administer and perhaps may be unacceptable to a corporate trustee.

As shown above, your spouse's rights to trust income must be considered in light of various factors, including the appropriate tax rules and the amount of flexibility desired. The appropriate degree of access to principal may also require some consideration. You may wish to provide the greatest degree of control and the most liberal access to principal for your spouse. On the other hand, you may wish to provide some restrictions that will serve a useful purpose in protecting and conserving the trust assets. The size of the trust fund, the confidence level you have in your spouse's ability to manage and preserve your family's resources, the needs of your children or other ultimate beneficiaries, and their relationship to you and your spouse are some of the considerations.

Example: You and your spouse have been married for many years and accumulated all of your wealth during the marriage. You and your spouse have had three children together and neither of you has a child from another marriage. Your children are mature, healthy, and self-sufficient. In that case, you may want to grant the maximum flexibility and self-determination to your surviving spouse and may want to grant the most liberal access to principal. In the case of the marital deduction trust, there is no limit on the degree of access to principal; in fact, the surviving spouse may be granted authority to remove all trust assets at any time. In the case of the credit bypass trust, the tax rules often require that principal be distributed for the spouse's health, education, maintenance, and support needs only. That is especially true if the surviving spouse is to be the trustee of the credit bypass trust. Even in the case of the credit bypass trust, however, liberal access to principal may be granted if desired.

Example: Your spouse is not inclined to conserve and protect his or her limited resources. If there is a reasonable possibility that trust assets could be squandered, then it may be appropriate to prescribe more restrictive standards. It may also be appropriate to have someone other than the spouse serve as the trustee or as co-trustee with your spouse in some situations.

Example: The trust might provide for the distribution of principal for health, maintenance, and support, but only in the event that all other resources available to the surviving spouse are insufficient for those purposes.

Example: You married a second time later in life. You have children only from your first marriage. It is important to you to leave an inheritance for those children, but you wish to provide a secure retirement for your spouse in the event of your death. In that case, depending on the size of your estate, it may be appropriate to leave all or a portion of your property in trust with income only to your spouse and with the remaining principal to pass ultimately to your children or other descendants or beneficiaries. In that manner, you will be assured that trust principal will pass intact to your children after your surviving spouse has enjoyed the income interest for life. Of course, you may also grant to your wife some level of access to principal, but that may result in less passing ultimately to your children.

It may or may not be appropriate to grant your surviving spouse a power of appointment so that he or she can designate who will ultimately receive trust assets after you and your spouse are both deceased. See "Powers of Appointment" at the end of this chapter.

> **Example:** You do not have children or other beneficiaries that are important to you and you do not have a need to provide an inheritance for any particular beneficiary. In that event, you may want to allow your surviving spouse to determine who shall ultimately receive remaining trust assets.

> **Example:** It may be important to you to assure that after you and your spouse are both deceased, remaining assets will pass only to your children or certain other beneficiaries. In that case, you may wish to specify that upon your spouse's death, the remaining trust assets will pass to particular named beneficiaries and not grant a power of appointment to your spouse.

You may wish to grant a limited power of appointment to your spouse to sprinkle assets among your children, descendants, or other named beneficiaries in accordance with their needs and appropriate tax planning. You may wish your surviving spouse to have the ability to determine which of your children or other beneficiaries will ultimately receive your estate or you may not want your spouse to have that authority, either because you do not have confidence in his or her ability to exercise that authority or because you want to avoid the possibility that your surviving spouse will be subjected to pressure from your children or other beneficiaries. If, for example, your children know that upon your surviving spouse's death, all assets will pass equally to all of the children, then there will be no incentive to pressure or otherwise seek to obtain a larger share. On the other hand, it will also take from your surviving spouse a "carrot" or "stick" that could be used to control or motivate the children if that is needed or desired.

Another consideration is choosing the trustee of a trust established for your surviving spouse. Most often, the surviving spouse himself or herself will be the sole trustee. That may not be appropriate if the surviving spouse is inexperienced with financial matters or not responsible with significant resources, or if there is a concern that trust resources may be prematurely depleted to the surviving spouse's detriment or to the detriment of children or other ultimate beneficiaries. In some cases it may be appropriate for the surviving spouse to serve as co-trustee with one or more individuals or with a corporate trustee. That may be desirable if additional investment or managerial experience is needed, or if you do not have complete confidence in your surviving spouse's ability to limit distributions to an appropriate level in light of anticipated needs and the level of trust resources.

Credit Bypass Trust

A credit bypass trust is designed to preserve the estate tax exemption of the first spouse to die. For 1998 the exemption amount is $625,000. That amount is scheduled to increase in steps until it becomes a $1.0 million exemption for 2006 and after. A husband and wife are each entitled to an exemption. Therefore, the estate of a married couple dying in 1998 should not pay tax on the first $1,250,000 of their combined estate. But unless a credit bypass trust or some other technique is utilized, the exemption of the first spouse to die will be lost. From 2006 on, the $1.0 million exemption of the first spouse to die will be lost without a credit bypass trust.

A credit bypass trust is established to provide income and/or principal for the benefit of your surviving spouse, but is designed so that upon your surviving spouse's death, the trust assets will not be included in his or her estate for tax purposes. It is generally funded with assets equal in value to your remaining lifetime exemption (that is, $625,000 for 1998).

Example: You and your spouse have combined assets worth $1,250,000. Assume you do not establish a credit bypass trust. Rather, all of your share of the property is left outright to your spouse at the time of your death. As a result, your $625,000 exemption is lost. Later, when your spouse is deceased, only your spouse's exemption will be available and substantial tax will be owed:

Surviving spouse's estate	$1,250,000
Spouse's exemption	<625,000>
Taxable estate	$ 625,000
Approximate estate tax owed	$ 246,000

Example: As an alternative to the above, you establish a credit bypass trust and arrange your property holdings so that upon your death $625,000 of property is held by the credit bypass trust. If you wish, your surviving spouse can be the trustee, or someone else may serve as trustee or co-trustee. You may permit your surviving spouse to have liberal access to income and principal or more restrictive access. However, even though your surviving spouse may have significant access to income and principal of the trust, if it is properly designed, assets in the trust will not be included in your surviving spouse's estate. As a result the estate tax bill will be considerably less.

Surviving spouse's estate	$625,000
Spouse's exemption	<625,000>
Taxable estate	$ -0-
Approximate estate tax owed	$ -0-

The credit bypass trust is the only effective method of assuring that one spouse's $625,000 exemption will not be wasted while still permitting the surviving spouse virtually unlimited access to all of the couple's assets if desired.

Example: Assume you die after 2005 and that you and your spouse have a combined estate of $2.0 million. Without a credit bypass trust your estate will pay an additional $435,000. With a properly designed credit bypass trust the tax will be reduced to zero.

For individuals who die after 2005 and who are in the 55% bracket, an immediate tax savings of $550,000 will result. However, the credit bypass trust will also avoid tax on all of the appreciation in value of the trust assets from the time of the first spouse's death until the second spouse is deceased.

Example: Assume you pass away after 2005, leaving $1.0 million in a bypass trust for your wife. Assume that fund is invested in stocks that appreciate at 10% per year. If your wife lives 10 years beyond you the fund will have appreciated to approximately $2.6 million and if her estate is in the 55% tax bracket, the total savings for your children or other beneficiaries will be over $1.4 million.

A credit bypass trust may be established in your will (a testamentary trust), or it may be established during your lifetime as part of your living trust. A credit bypass trust contained in a living trust provides the added advantage of avoiding probate proceedings in the event of death or incapacity. Of course, those benefits will be realized only if your assets are properly transferred to the living trust. See chapter 4.

Credit bypass trusts are frequently designed as sprinkle trusts so that the trustee may distribute income or principal to the surviving spouse and/or children or other descendants. That arrangement will permit the trustee to allocate trust resources among the specified family members in accordance with their needs. It may also permit substantial income tax planning flexibility. For example, income may be distributed to children who are taxed in a lower bracket. Also, if income is distributed to the surviving spouse only and is retained by the surviving spouse until death, it will then be subject to estate tax. That tax would have been avoided had the income been distributed directly from the trust to the children as earned each year.

As mentioned above, a credit bypass trust must be designed so that it will not be included in the surviving spouse's estate. Fortunately, if carefully designed, the trust can accomplish that goal while still permitting the surviving spouse nearly unrestricted access to the trust income and principal.

Marital Deduction or QTIP Trust

A marital deduction trust is designed to benefit your surviving spouse and also qualify for the marital deduction for purposes of computing your taxable estate. See "Marital Deduction" in chapter 7.

Property left to your surviving spouse may be deducted from your gross estate. In effect, such property will not be taxed at your death. Rather, it will be included in your spouse's estate and will be taxed at his or her death.

Unlike the credit bypass trust which is designed to be excluded from your surviving spouse's estate, the marital deduction trust is designed specifically to be included in your surviving spouse's estate. If it is not included in your surviving spouse's estate, then it will not qualify for the marital deduction in your estate and will be taxable at your death. As a result, up to 55% of your estate could be lost at the first death which, of course, may cause a substantial hardship for the surviving spouse.

There are two basic rules that must be followed in designing a marital deduction trust:

- **All income must be distributed currently to the surviving spouse for the duration of his or her life.**
- **No one other than the surviving spouse may receive income or principal during the surviving spouse's lifetime.**

The credit bypass trust may permit distributions of income or principal to the spouse or to any other individuals. A marital deduction trust, however, must distribute all income to the spouse and to no other person. Also, unlike the credit bypass trust, principal may not be distributed to children or any person other than the surviving spouse. There is a great variety of choices as to the surviving spouse's permitted access to principal. The terms of the trust may vary from no principal access to very liberal principal access. Distribution of principal is permitted only to the surviving spouse during his or her lifetime. Therefore, sprinkle provisions permitting distributions to children or other family members may not be included in a marital deduction trust.

A QTIP trust is a type of marital deduction trust. It is designed around the Qualified Terminable Interest Property rules which came into effect in 1982. The QTIP rules permit you to leave property in trust for your surviving spouse in a manner that will qualify for the marital deduction while still permitting you to designate the ultimate beneficiaries of the principal after your surviving spouse is deceased. Prior to 1982, it was difficult to create a marital deduction trust without permitting your surviving spouse the right to decide the ultimate beneficiaries. A QTIP trust is frequently used where you wish to assure that after your death and your spouse's death the remaining trust assets will pass to your children or other designated beneficiaries. The QTIP rules will permit you to leave property in trust and yet specify the ultimate beneficiaries. That may be especially important if you have children from a prior marriage and it is not certain that your surviving spouse will be inclined to leave remaining property to them. A QTIP trust will permit you to benefit your surviving spouse and still decide who will ultimately receive the remaining property after your surviving spouse's death.

"A-B" Trust

An "A-B" trust is simply a trust, living or testamentary, that contains both a credit bypass trust and a marital deduction trust. It is the most common trust arrangement used by married couples.

> **Example:** Your trust may provide that upon your death assets equal to the exemption amount ($625,000 in 1998, increasing to $1.0 million in 2006) will be allocated to trust "A" (the credit bypass trust), and all assets in excess of that amount will be allocated to trust "B" (the marital deduction trust). The "A" trust will be designed to benefit your surviving spouse and/or descendants without being included in your surviving spouse's estate. The "B" trust will be designed to qualify for the marital deduction so that it will not be taxed until the second death.

"A-B-C" Trust

An "A-B-C" trust is simply an "A-B" trust as described above with a third trust included. The "C" trust is typically a marital deduction trust funded with the balance of your generation-skipping tax exemption. It permits your personal representative to allocate your $1.0 million generation-skipping tax exemption partly to the bypass trust (the "A" trust) and to allocate the remainder of your generation-skipping tax exemption to the "C" trust. The term "A-B-C trust" is also used to refer to a type of joint trust containing a credit bypass trust, a marital deduction trust, and a third trust which holds the surviving spouse's one-half interest in the trust assets.

Spendthrift Trust

A spendthrift trust is simply any one of the other types of trusts with an additional provision designed to protect the trust assets from the reach of the beneficiary's creditors. A trust containing proper spendthrift language will generally not be attachable by the beneficiary's creditors. Similarly, the beneficiary will not be able to successfully pledge the trust property as collateral for a loan. As a result, the trust assets are much better protected for the beneficiary.

A spendthrift provision should be added to virtually all trusts so that the trust assets will be better protected in the event the beneficiary should suffer the misfortune of a serious creditor problem or divorce.

Q: Can I establish a trust for my own benefit and then transfer my assets to the trust so that they will be unreachable by my creditors?

A: It is generally not possible to exempt your own assets from the reach of a creditor by transferring them to a trust (except, possibly, a foreign situs trust; see chapter 15). If someone else establishes a trust for your benefit and transfers property to it, your creditors generally will not be able to reach that property if the trust contains proper spendthrift language. However, if you establish the trust and transfer your property to it the property will remain reachable by your creditors. If you establish a trust for someone else's benefit and transfer property to that trust, their creditors will not be able to reach that property as a general rule if it contains proper spendthrift language, since your beneficiary did not establish the trust for his or her own benefit.

Insurance Trust

An insurance trust is an irrevocable trust designed to exclude life insurance proceeds from your taxable estate. If you own a life insurance policy insuring your life, or if you have even a limited interest in a policy insuring your life, then the life insurance proceeds will be fully includable in your estate for tax purposes at the time of your death. An important planning strategy for many estates is to transfer life insurance policies out of the insured's estate. The most common technique is to transfer policies to a properly designed life insurance trust.

A life insurance trust may be established for the benefit of your surviving spouse, your children, your grandchildren or other descendants, or for a combination of family members or any other beneficiary you choose.

Life insurance trusts are frequently designed as follows:

During your lifetime, your spouse or children may withdraw income or principal as needed for their support. That provision is typically included so that your family will have access to the insurance policy and its cash value in the event new circumstances make removal of the policy or its cash value important. It is a "safety hatch" to permit continued access to the policy by your family.

After your death, the insurance proceeds will be held in trust for the benefit of your spouse and/or children. Almost any degree of access to income or principal may be provided for your surviving spouse, from very restrictive access to very liberal access. However, as in the case of a credit bypass trust, care must be taken to assure the trust is designed to be excluded from your surviving spouse's estate.

After the death of your surviving spouse, remaining trust assets will be divided into shares for your children. The trust for children may be distributed outright to the children or may be held in trust for a number of years or throughout the children's lifetimes. See "Trusts for Children" earlier in this chapter.

Your spouse may serve as trustee during your lifetime if you desire. Similarly, your spouse may serve as trustee during his or her lifetime after your death. In no event should you serve as your own trustee.

Your surviving spouse may be granted the right to select the ultimate beneficiaries to receive the principal upon his or her death (a power of appointment), or the ultimate beneficiaries may be specified by you in the trust document.

In the case of joint and survivor insurance (see chapter 8), the two insured persons often create a joint life insurance trust. Typically a joint trust designed to hold a survivorship policy will be established only for the individuals' children or other beneficiaries. Under the tax rules, neither the husband nor the wife can be a beneficiary of the trust; however, neither needs to be a beneficiary since the trust generally will not have significant assets until both are deceased. The tax rules also prohibit either spouse from being a trustee.

If you transfer an existing life insurance policy to a life insurance trust or otherwise transfer it out of your estate, the insurance proceeds will still be taxable if you die within three years of the transfer. Therefore, in the case of newly acquired insurance, it is important that the policy be initially issued in the name of the trust. If, instead, the policy is issued in your name and you then transfer it to the trust, the three-year rule will apply.

Q: Who may serve as the trustee of a life insurance trust?

A: The insured generally cannot serve as trustee. However, nearly anyone else can serve. If it is intended that the life insurance proceeds will also be excluded from the beneficiary's estate, then special care must be taken if the beneficiary will serve as his or her own trustee. The surviving spouse may serve as trustee of a life insurance trust established for his or her benefit. Similarly, if desired, children may serve as trustees of life insurance trusts established for their benefit. Of course, in some situations a corporate trustee may be most appropriate. See "Selecting a Trustee" in chapter 3.

Q: How will I pay insurance premiums on a policy after it has been transferred to my life insurance trust?

A: The preferred method is for the trustee to establish a small bank account in his or her name as trustee. Then, each year, if you wish, you may contribute additional funds to the trust which the trustee will then deposit in the trust's bank account. The trustee can then write a check on the trust's account payable to the insurance company for the amount of the premium (see p. 80).

Q: Will my contributions to the trust be taxable?

A: Contributions to the trust will be considered as gifts to the underlying beneficiaries. For example, assume you contribute $30,000 this year to a life insurance trust established for the benefit of your wife and two children. In that case, you will be considered as having made a gift of $10,000 to each of them. Most life insurance trusts are designed so that the annual contributions to the trust will qualify for the $10,000 annual exclusion from the gift tax. (See "Insurance Trusts" in chapter 4.)

Q: Will my life insurance trust be required to file an annual income tax return?

A: Generally, no income tax return is required during the insured's lifetime. A trust income tax return is required only if the trust has some taxable income or at least $600 of gross income. Since the earnings within a life insurance policy are generally not counted for this purpose, most life insurance trusts have no taxable income and, therefore, need not file a tax return. However, a life insurance trust that is also funded with income-producing assets may be required to file a return. Similarly, after the insured is deceased and the insurance proceeds are invested and earning income, an annual tax return may be required.

Q: Can I establish a life insurance trust for the benefit of my son and yet for tax purposes have the proceeds excluded from his estate as well as from my estate?

A: It is not difficult to design the trust so that trust income and/or principal will be readily available for your son's needs and yet will not be taxable in his estate when he passes away. However, unless additional steps are taken, the trust assets may be subject to the generation-skipping tax upon your son's death. (See "Generation-Skipping Tax" in chapter 7.)

Educational Trust

As the name implies, an educational trust is one that is established and funded to assist with the education of a particular beneficiary or class of beneficiaries. It may be established to assist with the education of a single child, all of your children, one or more grandchildren, or anyone you wish to benefit. Educational trusts may be designed to assist the attainment of a baccalaureate degree, a higher degree, or any other form of education. The expenses of a preparatory school education or trade school or technical school may also be covered if appropriate.

Educational trusts may be established as separate independent trusts or as a subtrust contained within your revocable living trust or some other trust established by you. An educational trust may be established and partially or fully funded during your lifetime, or it may simply be included in your will or living trust to be established and funded at the time of your death.

> **Example:** Assume you previously established a revocable living trust for the benefit of your children and descendants. It provides that after you and your spouse are both deceased, the remaining assets will be held for the benefit of your children who will receive income and principal in accordance with their needs. After the death of a child, the remaining assets in his or her trust fund will be held for the benefit of your grandchildren. Assume you now wish to help assure that your grandchildren will have adequate resources to receive an appropriate education. In that case, you may wish to "carve out" an educational subtrust for the benefit of your grandchildren. There are a number of ways in which it might be structured. One way is to add a provision as follows: After you and your spouse are both deceased, remaining trust assets will be divided into equal shares for the children. However, from each child's share some amount, say $50,000 or $100,000, will be set aside in a separate trust for each grandchild. Those separate subtrusts established for the grandchildren will be dedicated to assisting their achievement of a suitable education.

A variety of provisions may be included in an educational subtrust. If desired, it may be designed as a motivational tool and have its income and/or principal distributions tied to the beneficiary's academic achievement.

> **Example:** Assume you have sufficient assets to permit substantial lifetime gifts, you wish to reduce the size of your taxable estate, and you also wish to assist in providing resources for your children's or grandchildren's educations. In that case, you may wish to establish an irrevocable living trust to receive annual gifts. The purpose of the irrevocable trust may be dedicated primarily to providing educational resources for one or more of your children, grandchildren, or other beneficiaries. In this situation, it would be important to design the trust so that your gifts will qualify for the $10,000 annual exclusion.

An educational trust may be included in your will. Your will may provide that upon your death, a certain percentage of your estate or a certain dollar amount will be segregated into a separate fund or funds to assist with the education of your chosen beneficiaries. Of course, that trust can be funded only with assets passing through your probate estate, as in the case of any testamentary trust. (See "Testamentary Trusts" in chapter 1.)

As summarized above, an educational trust may be an irrevocable trust created during your lifetime to serve as the recipient of annual gifts from you, or it may be created as a testamentary trust, or it may simply be a subtrust within your revocable living trust. The common element is that the educational trusts are primarily (or entirely) dedicated to the providing of educational resources.

You must decide on the disposition of any remaining trust principal or income after your child or other beneficiary has attained the desired level of education. Frequently, educational trusts provide that remaining trust assets will be distributed to the beneficiary at a certain age, such as 30 years. Sometimes remaining assets are distributed upon the earlier of attaining a certain age or achieving a baccalaureate degree or other level of education.

In those cases where the educational trust for a grandchild was carved out of your child's share of your estate, it may be appropriate to return any unneeded resources of the educational trust to the trust established primarily for your child.

In some cases, assets remaining after the beneficiary's education is complete may be transferred to the trust of a different beneficiary whose education is not complete.

Example: Your educational trust might provide that three separate subtrusts should be established for the education of your three grandchildren. When any one of the three completes his or her education, then any remaining assets in that grandchild's trust fund will be added to the trust funds of the other two grandchildren to better help assure they will have the full needed resources. This approach would be most appropriate where only a modest amount will be available to fund the educational trusts.

Example: An alternative to the preceding example would be to establish a sprinkle trust for the three grandchildren's education. In that event the entire educational fund would be left in a single trust and the trustee would be authorized to use it for any one or more of the grandchildren in any proportion in accordance with their respective needs. Finally, when the youngest child attains a baccalaureate degree or reaches a specified age, then remaining assets would be distributed outright to the grandchildren.

Lifetime Gift Trust

In some situations, a consistent annual gifting program may be one of the best estate tax planning techniques. If you have sufficient resources to permit substantial lifetime gifts, then significant estate taxes may be avoided through a program of annual gifting. (See "Lifetime Exemption" in chapter 7.)

The annual gifts may be made outright to your children, grandchildren, or other beneficiaries. However, your family may be better served if the annual gifts are made to a trust for the benefit of your beneficiary, rather than outright to the beneficiary. For example, some situations where a gift to your child in trust might be preferable to an outright gift are as follows:

- Your child is not of sufficient age or maturity to receive substantial amounts outright.
- There is a concern that after substantial gifts have been made your child could suffer the misfortune of a divorce or serious creditor problem and the gifted property would be diverted to an ex-spouse or creditor.
- You intend to make gifts annually of interests in a closely held business and you wish to retain control over the gifted interests or you wish to assure that all gifted business interests will remain in the family.
- Your child will likely have substantial assets at the time of his or her death and you wish to assure that the assets gifted to your child during your lifetime will not be taxed at the time of your child's death.

Where it is not appropriate or desirable to make outright gifts to your beneficiary, a lifetime gift trust may be established to receive, hold, and administer the gifted cash or other assets. There are a great number of different provisions that may be included in a lifetime gift trust. The beneficiary may be accorded very generous and liberal access to income and/or principal, or distributions can be limited to maintaining a certain standard of living or any other particular purpose.

In general, under the tax rules, the person making the gifts cannot serve as the trustee. But a husband can make annual gifts to a trust and his wife can serve as trustee or vice versa.

Q: I wish to make annual gifts to a trust for the benefit of my child. Can I use a revocable trust for that purpose?

A: A revocable trust is generally not appropriate for this purpose. Assets transferred to a revocable trust will be taxable to your estate at the time of your death.

Q: Will my lifetime gift trust be required to file an annual income tax return?

A: If the trust's gross income for the year is more than $600, or if it has any taxable income, then a federal income tax return must be filed. You may be able to avoid filing a return if trust principal is invested in tax-exempt bonds or some asset, such as vacant land, that will yield only long-term appreciation and no current taxable income.

Q: Can more than one person make gifts to a lifetime gift trust?

A: Yes, any number of individuals may make gifts to the same trust. However, the trustee generally should not make gifts to the trust as the gifts will usually be included in his or her estate. Also, the beneficiary generally should not make gifts to the trust.

Q: I wish to make lifetime gifts in trust for my three children. Should I establish a separate trust for each of them or can one combined trust be used?

A: Either approach may be appropriate. In the majority of cases, you will be better served by establishing individual trusts for each child because that will permit greater tax and financial planning flexibility. A combined trust may be more appropriate in some situations, such as where "sprinkling" powers are important. (See "Sprinkle Trust" above.)

In most cases, it will be important to design the trust so that gifts to the trust will qualify for the $10,000 annual exclusion from gift tax. There are different techniques that may be used to qualify trust contributions for the $10,000 annual exclusion. Each technique has its own particular advantages and disadvantages, and care must be taken to select the technique most appropriate to a given situation.

Q: Rather than establishing a trust, may I simply transfer cash or other assets to a custodian account under my state's Uniform Gifts to Minors Act or Uniform Transfers to Minors Act?

A: Gifts may be made to an UGMA or UTMA account and the gifted property will usually be excluded from your estate if you are not the custodian. However, a major disadvantage of a UGMA or UTMA account is that the child must receive all assets outright upon attaining age 18 or age 21. Gifts to a trust may be retained and protected for a much longer time.

Trust for a Disabled Beneficiary

A trust established for a disabled child or other beneficiary may be a testamentary trust or a living trust. It may be revocable or irrevocable and it may contain one or more of the other provisions or features discussed in this chapter. Trusts for disabled beneficiaries often utilize a bank or other third-party trustee. They are often designed to remain in effect throughout the beneficiary's lifetime. They usually contain spendthrift provisions and in some cases they may be created only to provide specialized benefits.

Trust for an Elderly Parent

In many cases it may be appropriate to establish a trust for the benefit of one or more of your parents or grandparents. That would be especially appropriate where they are financially dependent on you. You may add a provision to your living trust that will require that a certain percentage or dollar amount of your estate be set aside for the benefit of your parents in the event of your death. Typically, your children or other named beneficiaries would receive the remainder after your parents' deaths.

Charitable Trust

As the name implies, a charitable trust is established to wholly or partially benefit one or more named charitable organizations. Occasionally, trusts are established with the sole purpose of benefitting a charitable organization. Such trusts may be established as part of your will, or they may be a subtrust to be carved out of your revocable living trust at the time of your death, or they may be a separate irrevocable trust established and/or funded during your lifetime.

For estate planning and tax planning purposes, individuals frequently establish "split interest" trusts which benefit both named individuals and charitable organizations. The use of those charitable trusts may substantially reduce estate tax and/or income tax while also providing a generous benefit to one or more named charitable organizations.

Split interest charitable trusts generally are either charitable remainder trusts or charitable lead trusts. Those are discussed in more detail in chapter 17. The tax rules relating to charitable trusts are highly technical and exacting. Very unfavorable tax results may occur if they are not carefully designed.

Qualified Personal Residence Trust (QPRT)

A Qualified Personal Residence Trust, or QPRT, is a tax-motivated trust designed to permit you to transfer your home to your children or other beneficiaries at a reduced gift tax value. Depending on your age and the interest rates prevailing at the time of the transfer, you may be able to make a gift of the home and yet pay gift tax on only a small portion of its true value. QPRTs are discussed in greater detail in chapter 17.

Qualified Domestic Trust (QDT)

If you leave property to your surviving spouse it will not be taxed until his or her subsequent death because of the marital deduction. You are permitted to deduct from your gross estate property left to your surviving spouse. Therefore, property left to your spouse is not taxable at the time of your death. (See "Marital Deduction" in chapter 7.) However, as a general rule, a marital deduction is permitted only if your surviving spouse is a U.S. citizen. If your surviving spouse is not a U.S. citizen, then the tax will be owed immediately upon your death and will not be deferred until your spouse's death. The one exception to that rule is that if property is left for your surviving spouse's benefit in a qualified domestic trust, then it will qualify for the marital deduction even if your spouse is not a U.S. citizen. Qualified Domestic Trusts are discussed in more detail in chapter 14.

Medicaid Trust

A Medicaid trust is designed to provide benefits for your spouse, child, or other beneficiary without causing the trust assets or income to disqualify the beneficiary from qualifying for Medicaid or other similar governmental benefits. The ability to create such trusts is now highly limited.

S Corporation Trust

An S corporation is a corporation that has elected to be taxed much like a partnership is taxed. Namely, earnings are not taxed at the corporate level, but are allocated to the shareholders and are taxed on their individual tax returns only.

As a general rule, an S corporation may have only individuals as shareholders and a transfer of S corporation stock to an entity such as a trust will cause a termination of the S corporation status. However, there are several exceptions to the general rule that make it possible to design a trust that will qualify as an S corporation shareholder. Where you intend to transfer S corporation stock to a trust or where such a transfer may occur in the future, it will be important to assure that the trust will qualify as a permissible S corporation shareholder. An ordinary revocable living trust will generally qualify as an S corporation shareholder. Certain irrevocable trusts can also be made to qualify as S corporation shareholders.

Blind Trust

One of the basic duties of a trustee is to provide trust accountings or other financial reports on the trust's activities to the beneficiary. However, in some situations, such as in the case of an elected official, it may be important to establish a trust that will hold and administer trust assets for the benefit of the beneficiary without permitting the beneficiary to know details of the trust's investments. Such a trust is known as a blind trust.

Rabbi Trust

A rabbi trust may be a useful tool in some situations for income tax or compensation planning. A rabbi trust permits an employer to segregate assets for a particular employee's retirement without the segregated assets being currently taxable to the employee. The name is derived from an early IRS private letter ruling concerning a synagogue that had established such a trust for the benefit of its rabbi.

Intentionally Defective Trust

Trusts may be designed so that the trust assets will be included in your estate for estate tax purposes, or they may be designed so that trust assets will be excluded from your estate for estate tax purposes. Trusts may also be created that will cause trust income to be taxed to the grantor who created the trust, or they may be designed so that trust income will be taxed to a beneficiary of the trust or to the trust itself.

In some cases, it may be appropriate to establish a trust in such a manner that the trust assets will be excluded from your estate for estate tax purposes, but yet the income of the trust will still be included in your estate and be taxable to you for income tax purposes. Such a trust is known as an intentionally defective trust.

> **Example:** You wish to establish a lifetime gift trust so that you can transfer assets out of your estate without incurring gift tax or using any of your $625,000 exemption (increasing to $1.0 million in 2006). Unfortunately, only $10,000 can be gifted to the trust each year for each beneficiary ($20,000 each if your spouse consents). Assume the trust acquires substantial assets and has a significant annual income. If the trust is designed to be a defective trust, then the tax liability for the trust's income will be allocated to you. When you pay the income tax each year, in effect, you will be making an additional tax-free gift to your children. You will be paying their income tax liability for them, which will reduce your estate while maintaining your children's estates, free of transfer tax.

Land Trust

Land trusts are not estate planning tools. They are simply a method used in some states to hold legal title to real estate. Equitable ownership of the real estate can be transferred by simply assigning beneficial interests in the land trust. Legal title will remain in the name of the trustee.

> **Example:** You and three other investors wish to jointly acquire a parcel of real estate. Assume the four of you establish a simple land trust and designate you as the trustee. The new real estate is then acquired by the trust rather than in your four names directly. If in the future you wish to sell your interest in the land, you need only sign a simple assignment of your interest in the land trust. It will not be necessary to prepare a formal deed or, in some states, it will not be necessary to record the assignment document or incur recording costs or other transfer taxes.

Totten Trust

A Totten trust is simply a type of bank account or other financial account that permits withdrawal of the account balance by the beneficiary upon the death of the depositor. Totten trusts are also referred to as ITF ("in trust for") accounts and as POD ("pay on death") accounts.

Example: Assume an account at a bank is established and titled as follows: "Mother Doe, in trust for Daughter Doe." Upon the death of Mother Doe, the account balance will automatically transfer to Daughter Doe.

Q: May I establish a Totten trust at a bank in order to exclude the bank account from my estate for probate and estate tax purposes?

A: A Totten trust will cause the account balance to be transferred automatically to the named beneficiary without passing through probate. However, the Totten trust balance will still be included in your estate for tax purposes. It will also continue to be reachable by any of your creditors.

Powers of Appointment

One of the most useful tools in the design of trusts is the power of appointment. A power of appointment permits the named power holder to designate who will ultimately receive all or a portion of trust assets.

Example: You have established a trust for the benefit of your spouse. The trust provides that all income will be paid to your spouse and principal may be distributed as well. The trust further provides that upon the death of your spouse, remaining trust assets will pass as directed by your spouse's will. Your spouse is said to hold a testamentary power of appointment.

Example: You establish a trust for the benefit of your daughter. It provides that all income will be distributed to your daughter and that she may also withdraw principal if needed. The trust further provides that at any time during her lifetime she can direct the trustee to distribute portions of the principal to any one or more of her children or other descendants. Your daughter is the holder of a lifetime power of appointment.

There are a variety of powers of appointment that can be used in different situations. The use of a particular power of appointment can have significant tax effect depending on the type of power of appointment and to whom it is granted.

As illustrated above, a power of appointment can be testamentary, meaning that it is exercisable only by your will at the time of your death, or it may be an *inter vivos* power of appointment that may be exercised by the power holder during his or her lifetime.

Example: Assume you wish to leave property in trust for your son. You want him to have the income from the property and to have access to principal if needed. Upon his death, you want remaining trust assets to pass to whomever he decides. Here, you may wish to grant to him a testamentary power of appointment. If properly designed, such a power will give your son almost unlimited discretion, yet the trust assets will not be included in his estate for tax purposes.

Example: You wish to leave property in trust for your spouse. You wish your spouse to enjoy the income from the trust and principal if needed. Upon your spouse's death, it is important that all remaining trust assets pass to your children. However, you want your spouse to be able to "sprinkle" remaining trust assets among your children or other descendants so that remaining assets can be allocated in accordance with your family's needs and overall family tax planning. Here, you may wish to grant a limited power of appointment so that your spouse can specify who is to receive remaining trust assets, but the recipient must be selected from the children or other descendants. If you wish your spouse to have the ability to sprinkle assets among your descendants at the time of your spouse's death, then you may wish to grant to your spouse only a limited testamentary power of appointment. If you wish your spouse to also be able to direct distributions of trust assets to your descendants during your spouse's lifetime, then you will want to grant to your spouse a limited *inter vivos* power of appointment. In many cases, both an *inter vivos* and testamentary power will be granted.

Powers of appointment can be highly useful and effective estate and tax planning devices. Each time a trust is created, it will be important to decide who will ultimately receive trust assets. If that decision is better made by someone else or is better made at a future date, then it may be appropriate to grant a power of appointment to the trust beneficiary or to some other trusted individual.

3

Trustees

Duties of a Trustee
Selecting a Trustee
Serving as a Trustee
Banks and Trust Companies
Successor Trustees
Co-Trustees
Trustee Compensation

IN MOST CASES, you or your spouse or some other family member will
be the primary trustee of a trust that you might establish. Most likely
your spouse will be the trustee of a trust established for him or her and
your adult children will be trustees of trusts established for them. It
might be the case, however, that your family members may not be appropriate trustee candidates and third parties, such as close friends,
trusted advisors, or trust companies must be selected. In some cases, the
tax rules will limit who may serve as trustee.

Whether choosing a trustee from your family or from possible third
parties, the selection and appointment of a trustee is one of the most
critical aspects of the estate planning process. There are several factors
to be considered when choosing a trustee and the decision should not be
made lightly.

Similarly, if you are asked to serve as a trustee, that decision also
should not be taken lightly. Serving as a trustee can present many problems. A trustee will often be called upon to make difficult decisions. Service as a trustee may require a substantial commitment of time. It may
also involve the possibility of incurring personal liability.

Duties of a Trustee

A trustee has three basic duties:

- Investing and protecting trust assets;
- Making distributions of income or principal to the beneficiary; and
- Assuring that administrative requirements are satisfied.

In some situations, carrying out the duties of trustee will not be overly demanding or difficult. For example, in those situations where you are your own trustee no difficulty should arise. However, in those situations where one person is serving as trustee for the benefit of another, some degree of conflict or other difficulty may be encountered. The success or failure of the trustee-beneficiary relationship depends primarily on the honesty, maturity, and experience of the trustee and the reasonableness and expectations of the beneficiary when compared to the available trust resources. Other factors, such as the terms of the trust, the composition of trust assets, and the tax structure of the trust, may also be important.

One duty of the trustee is to distribute income or principal of the trust in accordance with the terms of the trust. That distribution function may be relatively simple or it may be very complicated, depending in part on the terms of the trust.

> **Example:** Assume a certain trust provides that all income is to be distributed to the beneficiary currently and no distribution of principal is permitted during the beneficiary's lifetime. Here, no trustee discretion is permitted concerning distributions and the distribution function should be easy to fulfill. Each month or each quarter the trustee will write a check to the beneficiary for the amount of the income earned and there should be no cause for disagreement or other difficulty concerning distributions. There should be no problem concerning distributions of principal since no such distributions are permitted. There should be no conflict concerning distributions of income since all income is required to be distributed. Of course, there may still be disagreements in connection with the trustee's investment function.

Example: The trust provides that income or principal may be distributed as needed for the beneficiary's health, education, maintenance, and support. Here, there is great potential for disagreement. The trustee may feel that the beneficiary continually makes unreasonable demands for excessive distributions in light of the resources of the trust and the real needs of the beneficiary. Conversely, the beneficiary may believe that the trustee is unreasonably conservative. Because this trust involves trustee discretion concerning distributions, the potential exists for significant disputes and other problems.

Example: The trust provides that income or principal may be distributed for health, education, maintenance, and support "after considering other available resources." Now the trustee will have the added duty to inquire into the beneficiary's own income, investments, or other sources of support. Since the trustee may make distributions from this trust only to the extent the other resources available to the beneficiary are insufficient for his or her health, education, maintenance, and support, there is now an additional basis for disagreement and dispute.

The above examples show that the degree of trustee discretion required by the trust will partially determine the ease or difficulty of administering the trust. The choice of a particular trustee candidate and the decision whether to appoint an individual or a trust company should be made in light of the dispository terms of the trust.

Most trusts are designed to benefit more than one beneficiary. There may be two or more beneficiaries who are to receive benefits concurrently. In nearly all cases, there will be a primary beneficiary who currently receives trust income or principal and a secondary beneficiary who is to receive trust principal or income after the death of the current beneficiary or after some other specified event. In either case, the trustee must balance the rights of the beneficiaries while considering the requirements of applicable law and the grantor's intention as expressed by the trust document.

Example: Assume you have established a trust for the benefit of your three children. Trust assets are to be maintained in a single fund. Income or principal will be distributed to any one or more of the children as the trustee deems appropriate for their health, education, maintenance, and support. Here, the trustee will be required to weigh the respective needs of each beneficiary after considering the extent of the trust resources and possibly each beneficiary's individual resources.

Example: Assume you have established a trust for the sole benefit of your only child. Even here there are adverse interests. Some day, when your child passes away, the remaining trust assets will pass to a successor beneficiary (the "remainderman"). The remainderman may believe that distributions made to the initial beneficiary were excessive and have caused the remainderman to receive less than the amount he should have received. If it is determined that distributions to the initial beneficiary were excessive, the trustee may be personally liable to the remainderman.

Example: Your brother has asked you to serve as trustee of a trust established for the benefit of his children. The trust agreement provides that income or principal shall be distributed to the children "in accordance with their needs." In this case, you may want to decline to serve as trustee. Since the term "need" is highly subjective and there is no other language clarifying the grantor's intention, it is very possible that controversy will arise.

The second duty of the trustee is to preserve and invest trust assets. Here again, problems and disputes may arise. The current income beneficiary may insist on high income/low appreciation investments. The remainderman may insist on investments that favor growth at the cost of current income. Relevant law generally provides that trustees must treat all beneficiaries fairly and, therefore, a reasonable balance between current income and capital appreciation is required. However, the language of the particular trust agreement may modify the general rule in favor of one beneficiary or another.

Trustees are held to a very high standard of performance. A trustee may be held personally liable where trust assets decline in value or fail to earn income or appreciation at a suitable rate. For most trustees, it will be imperative to obtain competent investment advice. However, care must be taken in selecting investment advisors as the trustee may be held liable if he or she negligently selects a so-called expert whose advice results in financial losses to the trust.

Trustees are held to such a high standard that they may be personally liable for a loss suffered by the trust even though the trust's overall performance is a huge success. If a poorly performing investment is found to have been negligently selected, you may be personally liable for the loss even though an outstanding rate of return was received on the trust's overall portfolio.

Example: Assume you are the trustee and you invest $1,000 in ABC stock and $2,000 in XYZ stock. Assume a year later those stocks are sold for $10,000 and $1,000 respectively.

	Bought	*Sold*	*Gain/<Loss>*
ABC	$1,000	10,000	9,000
XYZ	2,000	1,000	<1,000>
	$3,000	$11,000	$8,000

Even though you did a great job overall and trust assets increased from $3,000 to $11,000, you might be personally liable for the $1,000 loss on the XYZ investment if it was negligently selected by you.

The third duty of a trustee is to assure that administrative requirements are satisfied. The trustee must assure that proper books and records of trust finances are maintained, the appropriate tax returns are filed on time, and all other legal obligations of the trust are satisfied. The trustee may be personally liable for any loss suffered by the trust or its beneficiaries due to the failure to complete administrative details in a timely manner.

Selecting a Trustee

Most likely you will serve as the sole trustee of your own trust. If you are married, your spouse will often serve as the successor trustee, or the two of you may initially serve as co-trustees. However, it will usually be important to select successor trustees to serve in the event that you are unable to serve or you and your spouse are both unable to serve. In some situations, because of certain tax rules or other factors, it may not be possible for you or your spouse to serve as trustee. Therefore, in most cases it will be necessary for you to select one or more trustees or successor trustees in addition to yourself or your spouse.

It is absolutely essential that you have complete confidence in the trustee's integrity. Trust assets will be titled in the name of the trustee. In most cases the day-to-day activities of the trustee will not be monitored. As a result, it is a simple matter for a trustee to misappropriate trust assets. Such misappropriation would likely be a criminal act. It would also likely result in the trustee being personally liable to the beneficiaries. But as a practical matter, where an individual trustee serves alone, there will be no mechanism in place to prevent malfeasance. It is very important to select a trustee who is not likely to have drug problems or personal financial problems that could possibly affect his or her judgment. It is not unheard of for a trustee who is suffering financial difficulties to rationalize that a "temporary borrowing" from the trust is really not wrong.

Aside from the highest degree of integrity, a trustee must have sufficient financial or business experience to obtain competent investment advice, tax advice, accounting advice, and legal advice. The trustee must be able to intelligently select advisors and judiciously consider their recommendations (which occasionally may conflict). After factoring in his or her own common sense and experience, the trustee must reach intelligent decisions that will preserve and protect the trust assets and will assure that income or principal is distributed to the beneficiaries in accordance with their best interests and the terms of the trust.

When selecting a trustee, you must consider the interpersonal or emotional aspects of your decision.

Example: Assume you have three children, one of whom is a highly experienced and successful investor and entrepreneur. That child may be an ideal candidate to serve as successor trustee in the event that neither you nor your spouse can serve as trustee. But if that child's appointment as successor trustee will be resented by the remaining children, he may not be the ideal candidate.

It is generally best to avoid appointing a trustee who would have a conflict of interest. Unfortunately, family members, who would otherwise be ideal trustee candidates, often have a conflict of interest.

Example: Assume you have children from a prior marriage. Assume you wish to leave property in trust for the lifetime of your present spouse with the remainder passing to your children after your spouse dies. Although your daughter may be an investment and business wizard, she may not be a suitable candidate to serve as trustee due to the conflict of interest. Assuming the trust permits discretionary distributions of principal, then each dollar of principal distributed by your trustee/daughter to her stepmother will be one less dollar available to pass to her and your other children upon the death of your spouse. Obviously, that situation could possibly result in disagreements and disputes. Here it might be preferable to select a different individual trustee or a trust company.

Another factor to consider when selecting a trustee is the amount of time that may be required. Some trust situations may require only limited attention, but others may require a substantial time commitment.

Example: Assume a trust is established for a young adult. Assume all income is required to be distributed currently, but no principal distributions are permitted. In that case, serving as trustee may not require substantial time. Aside from investment decisions and administrative details, the only responsibility will be to distribute all trust income to the beneficiary on a monthly or quarterly basis.

Example: Here, assume the trust is established to benefit a child or an aged parent. Assume discretionary distributions of principal are permitted. Here, substantial time may be required. The trustee may become involved in the day-to-day financial needs of the beneficiary. It may be necessary to pay the beneficiary's bills and to assure that the beneficiary has adequate automobile insurance, casualty insurance, and health insurance. It may be necessary to assure that the beneficiary's tax returns are filed. It may be necessary to hire nurses, companions, or other caregivers. It may be necessary to consult with the beneficiary's guardian, physicians, dentists, psychologists, and other professionals.

If the terms of the trust, the needs of the beneficiary, or the types of trust assets indicate that significant time will be required of the trustee, then you must carefully judge whether the particular trustee candidate will realistically be able to devote that amount of time. You may want your brother to serve as successor trustee because he is highly trained, experienced, and successful in business and financial matters; however, those same desirable qualities may mean that he will not have adequate free time to devote to the administration of the trust.

Serving as a Trustee

A request to serve as trustee should never be taken lightly. It is most important to thoroughly investigate the relevant facts of a particular trust relationship prior to agreeing to serve as trustee. Consider how well you know the beneficiary and whether you and the beneficiary will be compatible for an extended period of time. Consider the beneficiary's financial needs and expectations in light of the trust's resources. Consider the amount of time that may be required. Consider how clearly the grantor's investment and distribution intentions are expressed in the trust agreement. Consider the current trust assets and whether you believe they are suitable investments of the appropriate investment grade and diversity, or whether it may be necessary to liquidate and reinvest trust resources. Consider the degree of conflict that may exist between any concurrent beneficiaries or between the current income beneficiary and the remaindermen.

Only after a thorough review of all the relevant facts and circumstances of a particular trust should you agree to serve as trustee. Once you have begun to serve as trustee, you may find it difficult to extricate yourself from the position. As a practical matter, you will be required to serve until a suitable successor can be appointed. In some situations, particularly where the trust presents unusual problems, a suitable successor trustee may not be readily available.

Banks and Trust Companies

Many banks have a trust department, the principal purpose of which is to serve as trustee, executor, or other fiduciary on behalf of its clients. There are also stand-alone trust companies whose sole business is serving as a trustee or other fiduciary. In recent years most of the large brokerage firms have also established subsidiaries that are licensed to serve as a trustee or other fiduciary. All of those commercial trustees are often referred to as "corporate" trustees.

One of the more frequent decisions encountered when selecting a trustee is whether to use an individual trustee, a corporate trustee, or a combination thereof. Many people who establish a trust wish to appoint a family member, friend, or trusted advisor as an individual trustee rather than appoint a corporate trustee. Nevertheless, there are many situations where the beneficiaries would be better served by a corporate trustee. The use of a corporate trustee is too often rejected without adequate deliberation. In most situations, serious consideration should be given to appointing a corporate trustee or co-trustee.

Corporate trustees offer longevity compared to individual trustees. Unlike individuals, corporate trustees do not die or become incapacitated or senile. Rather, they continue to operate and function year after year. Although a particular trust company or bank may be acquired by another trust company or bank, the successor will continue to function as trustee. All individual trustees will eventually die or reach a point where they are not competent to serve as trustee. Although your brother may be the ideal trustee, when you are aged and infirm and need a successor trustee, most likely so will your brother. Because of the longevity problem, many people name a corporate trustee as a successor to serve in the event that named individuals cannot serve.

Corporate trustees generally have substantially more resources than would an individual trustee. That may mean the corporate trustee is better able to fulfill its obligations, especially in the event of difficulties.

Example: Your uncle has been appointed to serve as trustee of your trust. If he makes poor decisions and substantial trust assets are lost, you will have no practical remedy if your uncle does not have adequate assets to satisfy his liability to you. On the other hand, if a corporate trustee caused an unnecessary loss to the trust, it would have the resources to stand behind its liability.

Unlike most individuals, corporate trustees are experienced in investment and trust matters and have a staff of administrators, investment advisors, and other professionals needed to competently administer trusts and estates. Unlike most individuals, you can determine how successful a given corporate trustee has been with its investment decisions during the last several years, since nearly all corporate trustees will provide summaries of their investment experience upon request.

In some cases an additional advantage to a corporate trustee is the fact that the corporate trustee is objective and disinterested. Oftentimes, beneficiaries are best served by an individual or corporate trustee who can make calm, rational, and dispassionate decisions from an unbiased perspective. If you have no family member, friend, or trusted advisor who can offer that quality, then you may be better served by a corporate trustee.

Q: I have decided to establish a trust for the benefit of my son and I am considering the appointment of a corporate trustee. However, I worry that my son will be controlled or dominated by the corporate trustee throughout the duration of the trust and will be at the mercy of whichever trust officers may be assigned to his particular trust account. Is there a solution for that concern?

A: If a particular corporate trustee is appointed in a situation where it will likely serve for many years and cannot readily be replaced, the beneficiary may, in fact, receive something less than the best possible service. To solve that problem, it is often appropriate to add a provision to the trust that allows the income beneficiary to remove the corporate trustee and replace it with a different corporate trustee of suitable substance. When the trust officers assigned to the particular trust realize that their trust company can be fired and replaced at any time, the quality of service will tend to remain high and the fees charged by the corporate trustee will tend to remain reasonable. With that type of provision, the beneficiary will generally not be controlled or dominated by the corporate trustee since the beneficiary may remove and replace the trustee at any time.

Successor Trustees

It is often desirable to appoint one or more successor trustees to serve in the event that the primary trustee fails or ceases to serve. Many times one or two individual successor trustees will be appointed and a corporate trustee will be appointed to serve in the event that none of the individual trustees can serve.

It is often helpful to include a mechanism to select a new trustee in the event that none of the named trustees can serve. It is sometimes appropriate to permit the last serving named trustee to designate one or more successor trustees. In some cases it may be appropriate to permit the beneficiaries to name a successor trustee.

Example: You have established a trust for the benefit of your son. The trust provides that when he reaches age 40 he will become his own trustee. The trust is designed to remain in effect throughout his lifetime and, upon his death, remaining assets will be held for the benefit of his children. Because this trust is designed to remain in effect throughout his life, a time may come, in his later years or otherwise, when he is unable to serve as his own trustee. With that possibility in mind, it may be appropriate to include in the trust document authority for him to designate one or more successors. Similarly, it may be appropriate to authorize his appointment of one or more successor trustees to administer the trust for the benefit of the grandchildren after his death.

Q: What happens if none of the trustees named in the trust document can serve and no mechanism is provided for the appointment of a successor?

A: In that event, it will probably be necessary for the beneficiaries to petition the probate court for the appointment of a successor trustee.

Co-Trustees

In some cases, it may be best to name two or more individuals to serve together as co-trustees. A co-trustee arrangement will provide a check and balance for investment decisions and distribution decisions concerning the trust. A co-trustee arrangement may also help avoid a possible misappropriation of trust assets. If investment accounts owned by the trust are set up to require both trustee signatures before a withdrawal may be made, then a misappropriation would require the knowledge and consent of both co-trustees.

In some situations it may be appropriate to appoint a trustee to serve as co-trustee with the beneficiary.

Example: You want your adult son to serve as the trustee of the trust established for his benefit, but you are not totally comfortable with his business and financial experience and maturity. In that case, it may be appropriate to appoint an individual or corporate trustee to serve as co-trustee with him. The co-trustee could serve for the remainder of your son's lifetime or until he reaches a specified age.

In some cases, the co-trustee may serve for a limited time or until the occurrence of some specified event.

Example: After you and your spouse are both deceased, trust assets will be divided into separate shares for your two daughters. Each daughter who has attained the age of 25 will serve as co-trustee along with a corporate trustee as to her separate trust fund. After the daughter attains the age of 35 years, then she will serve as the sole trustee from that time on. That sort of arrangement will permit the daughter to initially serve as co-trustee and acquire experience and confidence with business and financial matters. Finally, at a later age, when she has presumably acquired experience and maturity, the daughter will become her own trustee.

Example: You wish to leave property in trust for your husband. After his death, the remaining trust assets should pass to your children from a prior marriage. If your husband is the sole trustee of his separate trust fund, he may be inclined to remove the maximum possible amount of principal permitted by the trust so that such removed principal will ultimately pass to his children at his death, rather than to your children in accordance with the terms of the trust. In that situation, it may be helpful to appoint one of your children or some independent individual or corporate trustee to serve as co-trustee with your husband to assure that only reasonably needed distributions are made to him in order to better protect your children as remaindermen.

Trustee Compensation

If a trust company is appointed to serve as trustee, fees will be charged for its services. The amount of trustee fees varies from company to company, but such fees are typically in the range of 1% of the trust principal annually on the first $1.0 million of trust assets with a lesser percentage on amounts in excess of $1.0 million. In some cases, an initiation fee may be charged upon establishment of the trust account or a final distribution fee may be charged upon termination of the trust arrangement. The fee schedule of each corporate trustee candidate should be reviewed.

Q: My spouse and I are establishing revocable trusts. We are considering appointing a trust company as successor trustee in the event that neither of us can serve. Will the trust company charge fees from the inception of the trust?

A: Corporate trustees do not charge trustee fees until they actually serve as trustee. Therefore, there should be no trustee fee while you or your spouse are able to serve as your own trustees. When the time comes that neither of you is able to serve, and the trust company assumes the role of trustee, it will begin to charge fees.

Individual trustees may or may not be compensated for their services. Family members or friends who are serving as trustee typically do not receive compensation except in those situations where the particular trust arrangement involves an inordinate amount of time. If you appoint your attorney, accountant, or other professional advisor to serve as trustee, he or she will typically charge customary hourly rates for the time actually involved, but some other arrangement may also be established.

4

Funding of Trusts

Funding Mechanics
Insurance Trusts
Tax Effects

THE "FUNDING" OF A TRUST simply refers to the transfer of assets to the trust. The funding of a trust is generally not difficult, but although it is one of the most important details in the estate planning process, it is often overlooked.

Failure to fund a trust properly may create myriad problems and undesirable results. Improper or incomplete trust funding can result in the following predicaments:

- Unnecessary probate proceedings in the event of death or incapacity;
- Substantially increased estate taxes; and
- The possibility that property will pass to unintended beneficiaries.

Example: Assume you have established a revocable trust in order to avoid probate at the time of your death, but you continue to hold real estate, investments, and other assets titled in your name individually. Upon your death, all of the assets titled in your name must pass through probate. Even though you may have a "pour-over" will, which leaves all property to your revocable trust, such property nonetheless must pass through probate, with the usual delays and costs that probate proceedings usually produce. Had the assets been properly retitled in the name of your trust, no probate proceedings would have been necessary.

Example: Assume it is after 2005 and you and your spouse have total combined assets of at least $2.0 million. You have each established a revocable trust to assure that both of your $1.0 million lifetime exemptions will be preserved. However, all of your assets continue to be owned by you and your spouse jointly with rights of survivorship. If you are the first to die, all of your property will pass automatically to your spouse because of the joint ownership. No property will pass to your revocable trust and your lifetime exemption will be wasted. The result is that the estate tax bill will be increased by at least $435,000 and perhaps as much as $550,000, depending on your particular tax bracket. If your spouse survives you by several years, the additional estate tax cost of failing to fund the trust could be in excess of $1.0 million.

Example: Assume you predecease your spouse in 2006 or after, when the exemption will be $1.0 million. Assume all assets were jointly owned so that all pass to your surviving spouse and none is transferred to your bypass trust. Because that $1.0 million passed to your spouse, instead of to the trust, it will be taxed in your spouse's estate along with all future appreciation. If your spouse then lived for several years after your death and the $1.0 million grew to be $2.0 million at the time of your spouse's death, an additional $1.1 million of tax would be owed if your spouse is in the 55% tax bracket.

Example: Assume you have a sizable estate that will be partially taxed in the 55% bracket. You have a $2.0 million life insurance policy and you establish a life insurance trust so that the policy proceeds will not be subject to estate tax. At the time of your death the policy continues to be owned by you individually. Because ownership of the policy was not properly transferred to the trust, the insurance proceeds will be included in your estate and your tax bill will be increased by $1.1 million.

The above examples illustrate that failure to fund your trust can have serious consequences. Assuring that assets have been properly transferred to the appropriate trust is a vital step in the estate planning process. Additionally, it is an important part of the periodic estate plan review to list all of the assets owned by each trust, estimate their approximate values, and assure that each trust is properly funded.

Funding Mechanics

The funding of a trust simply involves the retitling of assets that you intend to be owned by the trust. Assets to be owned by the trust should be retitled in the name of the trustee. Even if you are your own trustee, it will be necessary to retitle assets into your name as trustee.

Example: John Doe has established a revocable trust and wishes to transfer all of his assets to the trust to avoid probate in the event of his death or incapacity. To properly fund the trust, all of his assets should be retitled as follows:

"John Doe, Trustee of the John Doe Revocable Trust dated July 4, 1995." Bank accounts should be titled as indicated above, as should certificates of deposit (CDs), brokerage accounts, mutual funds, partnership interests, real estate, and all other assets.

Most assets have a certificate or some other document indicating the owner of the asset. For example, stocks, bonds, CDs, real estate, investment funds, and most other assets have an ownership document identifying the owner. Stock and bond certificates should be returned to the transfer agent for reissuance in the name of the trustee. Banks and brokerage firms should be asked to establish new accounts in the name of the trustee. In the case of real estate, a deed should be prepared transferring the property from you to the trustee.

Some assets may not have a certificate of title or other document showing the identity of the owner. For example, furniture, household effects, and other tangible property generally do not have an ownership document. Similarly, gold, silver and other precious metals, jewelry, artwork, and other tangible assets may not have an ownership document. Some securities, such as bearer bonds, are not issued in any particular name. In the case of such assets, it is generally satisfactory to prepare and execute a bill of sale, an assignment, or some other appropriate document that identifies the property and states that it is being transferred to the trustee.

In the case of co-trustees, it is generally best to title assets in the names of all of the currently acting trustees.

Example: John Doe has created a revocable trust and has appointed himself and his wife, Mary Doe, as co-trustees. Assets to be transferred to that trust should be titled as follows:

"John Doe and Mary Doe, Co-Trustees of the John Doe Revocable Trust dated February 26, 1996."

Q: I have established a revocable trust to avoid probate proceedings. I am not concerned about estate taxes. I want my life insurance proceeds payable to my trust so they will pass to my beneficiaries consistently with the rest of my assets. Should I simply change the beneficiary of the policy to the trust?

A: Naming the trust as beneficiary of the insurance will result in insurance proceeds passing to the trust for administration and those insurance proceeds will avoid probate in the event of your death. It is also generally preferable to change the ownership of your policy to your revocable trust as well. In that event, should you become incapacitated, the successor trustee will have control over the policy and access to any cash values without the necessity of establishing a guardianship.

The title to trust assets can be abbreviated in various ways. That may be important where a particular financial institution's computer system will not accommodate long names.

Example: Assume you established a revocable trust and named yourself and your wife as co-trustees. Assets to be transferred to the trust could be titled as follows:

"John Doe and Mary Doe, Co-Trustees of the John Doe Revocable Trust, Agreement dated March 15, 1999."

The above ownership designation could be abbreviated as follows:

"John Doe and Mary Doe, Co-Trustees U/T/D March 15, 1999."

The "U/T/D" stands for "under trust dated." If you and your wife are also co-trustees of a trust established by her on that same date it would be important to distinguish between the two trusts. In that event the title of assets in your trust could be stated as follows:

"John Doe and Mary Doe, Co-Trustees U/T/D March 15, 1999, F/B/O John Doe."

The "F/B/O" stands for "for the benefit of" and that distinguishes your trust from your wife's trust, which is labelled "F/B/O Mary Doe."

Insurance Trusts

If you own an insurance policy on your life, the proceeds will be considered part of your gross estate and will be fully subject to estate tax at the time of your death. The primary method to avoid estate tax on insurance policies is to transfer them to a specially designed irrevocable trust. Insurance trusts are discussed in chapters 2, 8, and 17.

The mere establishment of an insurance trust will not serve to avoid tax on the insurance proceeds. It is necessary to transfer ownership of the insurance policy to the trust if the tax is to be avoided. You will also generally want to name the trust as beneficiary of the policy.

> **Example:** You have established an irrevocable life insurance trust naming your wife, Mary Doe, as trustee. The ownership of the policy should be transferred to:
>
> > "Mary Doe, Trustee of the John Doe Irrevocable Trust dated April 1, 2001."
>
> The beneficiary of the policy should be changed to:
>
> > "Trustee or Successor Trustee of the John Doe Irrevocable Trust dated April 1, 2001."
>
> It may also be necessary for the trustee to establish a bank account to facilitate payment of insurance premiums. The bank account should be titled as follows:
>
> > "Mary Doe, Trustee of the John Doe Irrevocable Trust dated April 1, 2001."
>
> In the future, if you wish to contribute cash to the trust to pay the insurance premium, you would write a check for the amount of the premium payable to:
>
> > "Mary Doe, Trustee."
>
> Mary Doe should deposit that check in the trust's bank account and then write a check on that account to the insurance company for the amount of the premium.

Many practitioners recommend that after the premium money is contributed to the irrevocable trust the trustee should retain those funds and not use them to pay the insurance premium for thirty days or such other time as the trust prescribes in connection with the annual withdrawal rights specified in the trust. (See "Life Insurance Trusts" in chapter 8.)

Many practitioners also recommend that the exact amount of the premium not be contributed each year. For a few years some additional amount in excess of the premium should be contributed and then for a year or two, less than the amount of the premium can be contributed. This is intended to help counter a possible claim by the IRS that the insurance should be included in the grantor's estate because the trustee has not acted independently and has been the mere agent of the grantor.

Tax Effects

The transfer of an asset to a trust may or may not be a taxable event. Also, the transfer may affect how income earned by the asset will be taxed in the future.

The transfer of assets to a revocable trust will not be a taxable event and will not affect future taxation of the assets. For federal income tax purposes, a revocable trust is disregarded. A transfer from you to your revocable trust will be a nonevent for federal income tax purposes. Similarly, if the transferred asset earns interest, dividends, rent, capital gains, or other income, it will be reported on your individual income tax return and will be taxed directly to you.

The transfer of assets to an irrevocable trust gives a much different result in most cases. The transfer itself will generally be considered as a gift to the trust beneficiaries. The gift may or may not be currently taxable depending on whether the $10,000 annual exclusions apply and whether any of your $625,000 to $1.0 million lifetime exemption remains (see chapter 7).

Irrevocable trusts are generally separate tax paying entities. Interest, dividends, and other income earned by an irrevocable trust must be reported on a trust income tax return if, for the year, there is any taxable income or any gross income in excess of $600. That income may be taxed to the trust itself, to the beneficiary of the trust, or to the grantor of the trust depending on the terms of the trust and whether the income is distributed or retained.

It should be remembered that the transfer of assets to a trust, revocable or irrevocable, may have other results. The transfer may affect the assessment of county or municipal property taxes. It may affect whether the asset can be reached by a creditor. As to real estate or other property subject to a mortgage, it may have an impact on the mortgage.

Q: I intend to transfer my CDs to my newly established revocable trust. Will that result in an early withdrawal penalty?

A: The vast majority of banks will not impose an early withdrawal penalty in that circumstance. After all, you are not making a withdrawal; rather, the bank will continue to hold your money. But before completing the transfer, confirm with your particular bank that no early withdrawal penalty will be incurred.

Q: How are partnership interests transferred to a trust?

A: In the case of a closely held partnership, it will be necessary to prepare and execute an assignment of the partnership interest to the trustee. The partnership agreement should be reviewed because many partnerships prohibit transfers without the consent of one or more of the other partners. In the case of large, publicly syndicated partnerships, you should request from the general partner the necessary transfer documents. Many publicly syndicated partnerships impose a fee to transfer ownership. Such fees generally are in the range of $200 or $300 per transaction.

Q: I intend to transfer real estate to a newly established trust. Must I obtain the consent of the mortgage holder?

A: Most mortgages contain a "due on sale" clause which permits the mortgage holder to call the mortgage in the event of a transfer of the property. The transfer of real estate to a revocable trust for estate planning purposes will generally not violate the due on sale clause; however, the safest course would be to first request the consent of the mortgage holder.

Q: I intend to transfer bonds, stocks, and other income producing assets to my revocable trust. How will that affect my income tax situation?

A: In general, there should be no tax effect. Most revocable trusts are disregarded for income tax purposes. Interest, dividends, or other income earned by the revocable trust will simply be reported on your individual income tax return as though the revocable trust did not exist.

Q: I have established a revocable trust to avoid probate court proceedings in the event of my death or incapacity. Is it necessary to transfer all of my assets to the trust?

A: Ideally, every asset should be transferred to the trust. If any significant asset is omitted, then some probate proceedings may be required. Most states have now adopted simplified and inexpensive probate proceedings for small estates. Therefore, if simplified probate procedures are available in your state, it may not be significant if some assets of small value are omitted from the trust. Also, many states have a provision permitting the retitling of an automobile after the owner's death without the necessity of probate proceedings. In such states, it may not be essential to retitle automobiles in the name of the trust.

Q: How should my IRA be transferred to my revocable trust?

A: The ownership of an IRA cannot be transferred. It should continue to be listed in your name individually. The beneficiary of your IRA can be changed to your revocable trust, although that may produce undesirable income tax consequences in some cases. (See "Minimum Distribution Rules" in chapter 9.)

5

Probate Administration

Decedents' Estates
Guardianship of the Property
Guardianship of the Person

IN MOST STATES, the probate court handles cases involving settling the affairs of deceased persons ("decedents' estates") or incapacitated persons ("guardianships"). Decedents' estates and guardianships have many similarities, as you will notice in the discussion that follows.

Probate proceedings can be time consuming, frustrating, and expensive. Therefore, one aspect of estate planning may involve arranging your financial affairs so that probate proceedings will not be necessary in the event of your death or incapacity.

Decedents' Estates

If you die with significant property titled in your name individually, it will be necessary for your heirs to commence probate proceedings to settle your affairs. The administration of decedents' estates is often referred to as "probate." The cost of probate varies greatly, but it will often cost between 3% and 5% of the value of the estate and may cost several times that amount.

A very simple probate case will often take six to nine months to complete. In some states it may take much longer. If a federal estate tax return is required, that will usually add nine months to a year to the probate process.

Because of the considerable time delay and potential cost, many individuals arrange their estates so as to avoid probate proceedings. Maintaining privacy is an additional reason to avoid probate. In most states, probate records are fully open to public inspection. Therefore, the financial affairs of the deceased person and his family will become public knowledge if his estate must be probated. In recent years, a few states have passed laws restricting public access to probate records. Even in those states, however, much information may still be readily available.

Probate is the procedure whereby the decedent's assets are retitled in the name of the person or persons who are rightfully entitled to them. Without the probate process, intended beneficiaries could not gain access to the decedent's assets.

> **Example:** Your uncle recently passed away. His will leaves everything to you. He owned a home, a securities portfolio, and a bank account. Even though he may have left a will leaving everything to you, you will not be able to take title to the home or take possession of the investments or bank account without the probate process. Unless your uncle's estate is probated, you will not be able to sell or mortgage the home, you will not be able to collect the interest or dividends from the investments, nor make withdrawals from the bank account. Even though the will leaves everything to you, the assets will not become legally yours until the probate process is complete or nearly complete.

Q: If I have a very small estate, will probate still be required?

A: Although many states have streamlined probate procedures for very small estates, some form of probate is generally required if you pass away owning any significant property individually in your own name.

Probate is the process by which property passes from the decedent to his creditors or heirs in accordance with state law and the terms of the deceased person's will, if any. The probate process is intended to provide an orderly system for the transfer of ownership from the decedent, while protecting the interests of creditors, federal and state tax authorities, and heirs or beneficiaries.

The probate process is commenced by filing a petition to inform the court of the basic facts:

- The name of the decedent, his or her residency, date of death, age, etc.;
- What he or she owned and its approximate value;
- Names and addresses of interested parties;
- Name and address of intended executor or personal representative.

Early in the probate process an executor or personal representative (or administrator) will be appointed by the court. Frequently, the judge will require the posting of a bond to help assure the executor's faithful performance of his or her duties.

After the executor is appointed and the bond is posted, letters of administration are granted. The letters of administration empower the executor to transact business on behalf of the estate. They authorize him to take possession of estate assets, pay taxes, pay creditors, and distribute remaining assets to the persons rightfully entitled to them.

Early in the process, notice of the estate is published in a local newspaper. Depending on the state, creditors have a set number of days after the publication of notice in which to file their claims. If they do not file within that period, their claims may be barred. However, in addition to publishing notice, the rules also require the executor to diligently search for possible creditors of the decedent and to give them individual written notice of the proceedings.

If you serve as an executor and if you fail to diligently search for creditors, you may become personally liable to them. Therefore, you must carefully look through the decedent's bank statements, correspondence, tax returns, and other records to assure there are no unknown creditors.

If estate assets are distributed to heirs, the executor will be liable to creditors who did not get paid if they did not receive the required notice. In many states, creditors cannot file a claim after 90 days from the first publication of notice. However, if a particular creditor could have been discovered through diligent inquiry, then that creditor's right to file his claim will extend long beyond the 90-day or other prescribed period and the executor will continue to be liable.

If the diligent inquiry, publication, and notice procedures are not properly followed, the executor may remain personally liable for many years. In some states that liability period may continue for two years or more after the decedent's date of death. Failure to assure that federal and state taxes have been properly paid in full may also result in the executor being held personally liable.

The executor also has the duty to file necessary tax returns. Some of the tax returns which may be required are:

- The decedent's final federal income tax return;
- The estate's federal income tax returns;
- The decedent's state income tax return;
- The estate's state income tax return;
- Any gift tax returns the decedent failed to file;
- The decedent's federal estate tax return;
- The state's estate tax return (these may be required in more than one state);
- Intangibles tax returns;
- Income tax returns, federal and state, for any trusts relating to the decedent.

The probate estate may finally be closed when the following have been accomplished:

- The creditors' claim period has lapsed and the executor has diligently attempted to discover possible creditors and all such possible creditors have received notice of the proceedings and have been allowed the prescribed time to file a claim.
- The executor has discovered all of the decedent's assets and has filed an inventory of those assets with the court.
- The IRS and the state tax authorities have issued their certificates showing that all transfer taxes have been paid.
- The heirs have signed appropriate documents acknowledging receipt of their shares of the estate and consenting to the discharge of the executor.
- The executor has filed with the court a detailed accounting showing the assets collected, income earned, debts and costs paid, distributions made or to be made to beneficiaries, and all other transactions concerning the estate. In some cases, the requirement of a final accounting may be waived by the beneficiaries.

After the above steps have been completed, the judge will close the probate proceedings. The executor will be discharged and his bond, if any, will be released. The entire process will generally take between six and nine months and if an estate tax return is required, an additional nine months to a year will be required. Those time frames assume that the estate is not involved in litigation. Suits filed by creditors and disputes among heirs or heir hopefuls disputing the validity of the will may add years to the process, as will disputes with the IRS or with state tax authorities.

The job of executor is not without difficulties. If the estate involves significant assets, the executor may have to devote considerable time and energy to fulfilling his or her duties. That is particularly true if the estate is involved with the liquidation of a business, or is involved with litigation or tax disputes. Serving as an executor may also involve considerable exposure to personal liability. In most cases, it is extremely important that the executor adhere strictly to all of the various laws and rules.

An executor is entitled to compensation for his or her services. Such compensation is generally a function of the amount of time required and the difficulties encountered. In some states the executor's compensation is prescribed by statute as a certain percentage of the estate assets.

Frequently, the executor is also one of the major beneficiaries of the estate or the only beneficiary. In that situation, it may be helpful to pay no executor's fee or to pay a substantial executor's fee depending on an analysis of the tax situation. If the estate is not subject to transfer taxes, it will generally be advantageous not to receive an executor's fee if you are the sole beneficiary. If a portion of the estate flows to you as an executor's fee, that will constitute ordinary income and must be taxed on your individual income tax return. If that fee had, instead, flowed to you as an additional bequest, then it would generally be received by you income tax–free.

If the estate is subject to estate tax, and if you are the sole or a major beneficiary, then the analysis involves a comparison of the estate tax rate and your income tax bracket. For example, if you are in the 35% income tax bracket and the estate is subject to a 55% estate tax, it would be appropriate to pay substantial executor compensation. Although the compensation will be taxable to you at your 35% income tax bracket, it will be deductible by the estate and will, therefore, reduce the estate tax by 55% of the amount of the executor's compensation. The net saving to you would be 20% of the executor's compensation. Of course, the total amount distributed as executor's compensation must be reasonable.

There are two basic types of decedents' estates: those in which the decedent had a will, and those in which the decedent died without a valid will. If the decedent had a will, then the probate case is referred to as a "testate" case. If the decedent had no valid will, then it is known as an "intestate" case.

Q: If I have a will does that mean that my beneficiaries will receive the property I left them without the necessity of probate?

A: No. A will does not avoid probate. In fact, a will operates only through probate.

Q: Are probate proceedings required in each state where the decedent owned property or only in his state of residence?

A: Unless steps are taken to avoid probate, it is generally required in the state of residence, and also in each additional state where the decedent owned real estate. Those additional probate proceedings are known as ancillary probate.

Q: We often hear of the disadvantages and problems of probate. Are there any advantages?

A: In some states, the probate process may serve to reduce the period during which your creditors can file a claim against your estate. However, for most estates that is not a significant benefit.

Guardianship of the Property

If a person is incapacitated as a result of illness, an accident, or old age, or if the person is a minor, it may be necessary to establish a guardianship to administer his or her property. The incapacitated person is known as the "ward" and the person charged with administering the ward's estate is known as the "guardian."

As discussed above, the probate of a decedent's estate may involve sub-stantial time and money. A guardianship is generally even worse and in some cases may be disastrous to you and your family's financial security.

One of the problems with a guardianship is that it may last for years or even decades. The guardianship will last until the ward's competency is restored, until his or her death, or until all of the guardianship assets have been depleted.

In most cases it is expensive to establish a guardianship. In addition, the annual expenses of maintaining the guardianship will generally con-tinue throughout the remainder of the disabled person's life.

> **Example:** Assume that because of illness or accident you are not capable of managing your financial affairs. If there are investment assets or other as-sets titled in your name, it will most likely be necessary for your spouse, your children, or some other interested person to petition the probate court to have you declared legally incompetent and to have a guardian appointed to oversee your financial affairs. Without the appointment of a guardian, your family may not have access to investments or other property titled in your name.

Most estate planning is undertaken to benefit other persons—your surviving spouse, surviving children, or other beneficiaries. Planning to avoid a guardianship is one aspect of estate planning that can benefit you during your lifetime as well your family or other beneficiaries. Be-cause of the time delays, frustrations, and costs involved in probate, many individuals plan their estates to avoid the necessity of a guardian-ship in the event of incapacity.

As explained above, the principal method of avoiding the probate of your estate when you die is through the use of a living trust. Fortunately, a properly designed living trust will also serve to avoid guardianship proceedings in the event of your incapacity.

> **Example:** Assume you have transferred all of your real estate, investments, and all other property owned by you to your living trust. If you are now in-capacitated, the successor trustee, who was named by you in the trust doc-ument, will immediately be able to manage your financial affairs for your benefit and the benefit of your family without the necessity of probate court interference. The successor trustee will be able to make investment deci-

sions and apply trust income or principal to your needs or the needs of your family as directed by the terms of the trust agreement. Because of the trust, it will not be necessary to petition the court or to have you declared incompetent or to have a guardian appointed or to incur any of the costs and delays of guardianship proceedings. Rather, your selected trustee will be able to immediately assume responsibility for your financial affairs.

If you are incapacitated and a guardianship is necessary, the process usually will be commenced by a family member or other interested party filing a petition with the probate court setting forth the facts of your case. You will then be examined by psychiatrists and other health care specialists who will report to the court on your condition. The judge will usually appoint a lawyer to represent your interests, but you are entitled to have an attorney of your choosing.

The initial guardianship process usually takes several weeks, but may be accelerated if the circumstances warrant. A hearing will be held and the judge will decide whether or not you are incapacitated. If he concludes that you are incapacitated, he will appoint someone, usually a close family member, to be the guardian of your property. Often the judge will require the posting of a bond.

The duties of the guardian are similar to the duties of an executor. The guardian is required to take possession of the ward's property, file an inventory of assets setting forth their approximate value, and pay any legitimate creditors or claims. The guardian is then required to hold remaining assets for the benefit of the interested party, in this case the ward rather than heirs. Like an executor, the guardian will be personally liable for any loss suffered by the ward as a result of the guardian's negligence. Guardians are held to a high standard of care in connection with investment decisions and other financial issues.

Guardianship resources generally may be invested only in conservative, publicly traded securities and certain other assets. In some cases, the guardian will be required to liquidate investment real estate or interests in closely held businesses. That may result in substantial losses to your estate. The imposition of a guardianship is always a great misfortune. In the case of an estate comprised largely of real estate or closely held business interests, it may be disastrous.

Once the guardianship is established, in many states the judge will decide how your assets will be invested. If he believes your real estate, closely held business interests, or other investments are not prudent investments, he may require their liquidation. Forced liquidations are usually not accomplished on the most favorable terms.

The judge will generally continue to oversee your financial affairs for the remainder of your lifetime. If your competency is restored, remaining guardianship assets will be returned to your possession. If the guardianship is ended by your death, then the guardian will distribute remaining guardianship property to your executor, who will proceed to administer a decedent's estate as described above. Ultimately, remaining assets will be distributed to your legal heirs if you died intestate or to your named beneficiaries if you died with a will.

Each year during the term of the guardianship the guardian must file an accounting with the court. The accounting will set forth any income received by the ward during the year and will list the ward's expenses that were paid during the year. The accounting will then list the remaining assets on hand. The cost of preparing and filing the annual accounting will be incurred each year for the duration of the guardianship.

Q: I understand that a guardian will be appointed if I should become incapacitated. How can I assure that the court will appoint a guardian of my choosing?

A: Some states permit the filing of a document with the probate court in which you name the guardian you wish to have appointed in the event of your incapacity. However, for that to be effective, you must assure that it is filed in each county where you reside or might reside at the time of your incapacity. Also, if all of your assets have been transferred to a revocable living trust, then in the event of your incapacity, your estate will be administered by the successor trustee named in your trust document. As a result, the establishment of a guardianship may not be necessary.

Guardianship of the Person

Most guardianships involve the appointment of a guardian of the incapacitated person's property only. If the ward is not capable of making decisions concerning his or her physical well-being, it may also be necessary to appoint a guardian of the person to make decisions on health care, residency, and similar matters pertaining to the ward's physical needs.

The process is similar to the establishment of a guardianship of the property. A family member or other interested party will file a petition setting forth the relevant facts and requesting that the ward be declared incompetent and that a guardian of his or her person be appointed. The alleged incapacitated person will be examined by medical and other specialists who will report to the court. Other witnesses may be called and the judge will reach a decision concerning the incapacitated person's need of a guardian of his or her person.

The appointed guardian of the ward's person will then have authority to make decisions concerning the ward's health care, living arrangements, and other physical considerations. During the term of the guardianship, routine decisions concerning the ward's well-being may generally be decided by the guardian without leave of court. Anything unusual such as a change in the ward's program of medical treatment or place of treatment or a change of residence to a different county or state may need prior court approval.

A guardian of the person must annually file additional reports with the court concerning the ward's health condition, living arrangements, and related matters.

A guardianship of the person will end if the ward's capacity is restored, in which event his or her legal rights will be restored. In the usual case, however, the guardianship will end upon the death of the ward. In that event, the final act of the guardian of the person will be to give formal notice to the court of the ward's death. Remember, however, that if you are also guardian of the property, you may have several additional duties to fulfill after the death of the ward, including transferring remaining assets to the executor of the ward's estate.

6

Property Ownership and Beneficiary Designations

Individual Ownership
Tenants in Common
Joint Ownership with Rights of Survivorship
Tenants by the Entirety
Community Property
Indirect Ownership
Beneficiary Designations
Joint Ownership and Inadvertent Gifts

THERE ARE SEVERAL different ways that real estate, investments, or other property may be owned or titled. The manner in which property is owned or titled will affect how and to whom it will pass at death. It may also affect the amount of taxes to be paid and whether court proceedings will be required in a particular situation.

Most assets such as real estate, bank accounts, securities, and other investments have a deed, certificate, or some other document showing how the asset is owned and by whom. In addition to an ownership designation, some assets such as life insurance, IRAs, and similar items also have a beneficiary designation permitting the owner to designate a beneficiary who will receive the asset upon the death of the owner.

You may own property individually, as tenants in common, jointly with rights of survivorship, or any one of several other ways. You may own property directly, meaning it is titled directly in your name, or you may own it indirectly through your ownership of an entity such as a corporation, partnership, or trust.

Individual Ownership

If you own an asset individually, it is titled solely in your name. Upon your death an individually owned asset will pass in accordance with your will or, if you have no will, then in accordance with the intestacy laws of your state (see chapter 1). Whether or not you have a will, probate proceedings will generally be required at the time of your death with respect to individually owned assets. Similarly, individually owned assets may be subject to guardianship proceedings in the event of your incapacity (see chapter 5).

As discussed below, some assets, such as life insurance and IRAs, have a beneficiary designation. At your death, those assets will pass to the named beneficiary regardless of the terms of your will or the intestacy laws.

Tenants in Common

If you own an asset with another person as tenants in common, then upon your death your one-half interest will pass in accordance with your will or the intestacy laws. Although you have a co-owner, your one-half interest is treated like individually owned property. As a tenant in common you are generally free to sell or mortgage your one-half interest in the asset and upon your death it passes along with your individually owned property.

Q: I own a parcel of real estate and some CDs and other investments with my brother as tenants in common. If I die before my brother, will those assets pass to him?

A: Upon your death, your interest in those assets will pass in accordance with your will or the intestacy laws. They will not automatically pass to your brother.

Joint Ownership with Rights of Survivorship

If you own an asset with another person jointly with rights of survivorship ("survivorship property"), then upon your death, the asset will pass automatically to the surviving joint tenant. Because survivorship property automatically passes to your surviving joint tenant, the terms of your will or your state's intestacy laws will not be relevant as to that asset in most cases.

Even though a bank account or other investment account is titled jointly with rights of survivorship, in some circumstances it may still pass in accordance with your will or the intestacy laws. A survivorship account may not pass to the surviving owner if it can be proven that survivorship was not intended by the account owners.

> **Example:** Assume that you are the first deceased and that you owned a bank account titled jointly with your sister. Your executor can prove that all of the funds in the account belonged to you and that your sister's name was added to the account as a mere convenience so that she would have access to the funds for your needs in the event of your incapacity. Under those conditions, under the laws of many states, the account would be treated as individually owned property passing in accordance with your will or the intestacy laws even though the account appears, on its face, to be jointly owned. "Convenience accounts" are an exception to the general rule that jointly owned property automatically passes to the survivor.

Q: I own several bank accounts, brokerage accounts, mutual funds, and other investment accounts jointly with my husband and I own some investment accounts jointly with my daughter. I have been reviewing the signature cards, certificates, account forms, and other ownership documents, but find it difficult to distinguish the various forms of ownership.

A: The manner in which jointly owned investment accounts were intended to be owned is often ambiguous and often leads to disputes and unintended results. It is most important that the intended manner of ownership be clearly described.

If you intend to own a joint account or other asset as tenants in common, then the signature card, account form, or other ownership document should clearly spell that out. It should read: "John Doe and Mary

Doe, as tenants in common." Alternatively, a regularly accepted abbreviation may be used: "John Doe and Mary Doe, TIC."

If you intend joint ownership with rights of survivorship, then that should be spelled out: "John Doe and Mary Doe, joint tenants with rights of survivorship." Alternatively, the generally accepted abbreviation could be used: "John Doe and Mary Doe, JTWROS."

If a tenancy by the entirety is intended, then it should be spelled out: "John Doe and Mary Doe, tenants by the entirety"; or its abbreviation should be used: "John Doe and Mary Doe, TBE."

In some states there is a presumption that accounts titled with an "or" between the names (John Doe or Mary Doe) are survivorship accounts. Some states also have a presumption that accounts titled with an "and" (John Doe and Mary Doe) are tenancy in common accounts and not survivorship accounts. It is uncertain and risky to rely on any such presumptions. For each of your jointly owned assets you should make an informed decision as to the appropriate manner of ownership and then assure that the intended manner is clearly spelled out on the signature card, certificate, account form, or other ownership document. When establishing an account with a financial institution, insist that the intended manner of ownership be clearly set forth on the account form or other ownership document. If the manner of ownership has been abbreviated in some unusual way or is otherwise not clearly spelled out, then insist that the ownership document be corrected. You should read any fine print contained on ownership forms because it frequently clarifies (or confuses) the manner in which the account will be treated as owned.

Q: My spouse and I own all of our assets together with rights of survivorship. Will that serve to avoid probate proceedings in the event of death?

A: The ownership of all assets with rights of survivorship will usually serve to avoid probate proceedings on the first death, but probate will not be avoided upon the second death. Also, if the combined estate is more than the lifetime exemption, substantial additional taxes may be incurred as a result of that form of ownership. (See "Credit Bypass Trust" in chapter 2.) Furthermore, that form of ownership may not avoid the imposition of a guardianship in the event that either of the joint owners should become incapacitated. Therefore, you should carefully analyze whether the ownership of all assets jointly with rights of survivorship best serves your goals.

Tenants by the Entirety

An additional form of ownership is known as tenancy by the entirety. Only a husband and wife may own an asset as tenants by the entirety. Tenancy by the entirety is similar to joint tenancy with rights of survivorship in that upon the first death, the entire asset automatically passes to the surviving joint owner.

The principal difference between tenancy by the entirety and joint tenancy with rights of survivorship is that, in general, a creditor of the husband or a creditor of the wife cannot attach entireties property. In other words, tenancy by the entirety property is not subject to the claims of creditors of either one of the owners; however, a creditor of both the husband and the wife may attach entireties property.

Some states do not recognize that form of ownership and other states limit it to real estate only. However, in some states, such as Florida, virtually any asset may be owned by a husband and wife as tenants by the entirety.

In the case of real estate, a deed to a husband and wife is presumed to create a tenancy by the entireties in some states unless the deed states to the contrary. In some states, the rule for all other property is the opposite: namely, personal property owned by a husband and wife is presumed not to be held as tenants by the entirety unless the ownership document specifically provides that it is owned as tenants by the entirety. In most cases, it is preferable not to rely on any possible legal presumption, but rather to clearly designate "tenants by the entirety" or "TBE" on the signature card, certificate, account form, deed, or other ownership document.

Community Property

Those states that were originally founded by the Spanish—Arizona, California, Nevada, New Mexico, Texas, Idaho, and Washington—plus the state of Louisiana, have a special form of ownership between a husband and wife known as community property. In recent years, Wisconsin has also adopted community property rules.

The rules vary somewhat among the community property states, but in general, the rules relating to community property are as follows:

- Each spouse retains as his or her separate property those assets that were acquired before the marriage or are received during marriage as a gift or bequest. Generally, appreciation in value of separate property, and interest, dividends, and other earnings from separate property, are also considered to be that spouse's separate property.
- All other property acquired during the marriage is generally considered to be community property. Therefore, investments or other assets acquired by either spouse from his or her earnings during the marriage will constitute community property.
- Upon the death of one spouse, his or her share of the community property will pass as directed by his or her will or the intestacy rules. The remaining one-half of community property will continue to be owned by the surviving spouse.

Community property will generally retain its character even if the married couple relocates to a non–community property state. Therefore, in all states, it may be important to determine if a married couple acquired assets while residents of a community property state in order to determine how the assets will pass in the event of either party's death.

Q: I live in Florida, a separate property state, but have acquired real estate in Texas, a community state. Which state law will apply?

A: Generally, the law of the state where the property is located will apply. Therefore, it is likely that your Texas real estate is community property.

Indirect Ownership

Many assets may be owned indirectly through a separate entity. You may believe that you own a particular asset, when, in fact, you technically own a much different asset. Although the distinction may at times seem unimportant, the difference between direct and indirect ownership may have a significant effect on the resulting tax liability, to whom the asset may pass at death, and other factors.

Example: You reside in New York state, but own a parcel of real estate in Connecticut. If you own the real estate directly in your individual name, then upon your death, Connecticut will likely impose its inheritance tax. Also, at your death, the property will pass in accordance with Connecticut law and ancillary probate will be required in Connecticut.

On the other hand, assume that you created a corporation and transferred the Connecticut real estate to the corporation. Here, you technically do not own the real estate. You simply own the stock in a corporation that owns the real estate. Now, Connecticut likely will not be able to impose its inheritance tax since you do not own real estate located in Connecticut. Rather, you own intangible personal property (the stock), which is typically taxable only by the state of your domicile at the time of your death. Also, ancillary probate proceedings will not be required in Connecticut. Since your stock in the corporation is intangible personal property, it will be subject to probate only in your state of domicile.

Other examples of indirect ownership involve partnerships or trusts. Rather than owning a particular asset directly, it may be transferred to a partnership in which you are a partner or it may be transferred to a trust of which you are a beneficiary.

Q: My wife and I reside in Florida, but own a home in New York. When we pass away, will probate proceedings be required in New York and will New York impose its inheritance tax on the value of that property?

A: When you and your wife are both deceased, probate proceedings will be required before the New York home can pass to your intended beneficiaries. Also, New York will impose its inheritance tax. Both problems may be solved if you and your wife establish a partnership to own the New York home. Then, at your death, your partnership interest will be included in your Florida probate and ancillary probate in New York will not be necessary. Also, you may avoid the New York inheritance tax.

Q: My wife and I reside in Florida, but own real estate in Michigan. Can we avoid ancillary probate in Michigan and also avoid the Michigan inheritance tax by transferring that property to one of our revocable trusts?

A: Transferring the property to your revocable trust will avoid the necessity of ancillary probate in Michigan. However, it will not affect Michigan's right to impose its inheritance tax. In order to avoid the tax you will need to first transfer the Michigan property to a corporation or partnership. Your stock in the corporation or your interest in the partnership can then be transferred to your revocable trust so that probate proceedings will also be avoided in connection with that asset.

Beneficiary Designations

Many assets provide for the direct designation of a beneficiary. For example, life insurance will be payable to the named beneficiary in the contract regardless of the terms of your will. Similarly, the named beneficiary of your IRA or other retirement plan will receive the remaining balance upon your death regardless of the beneficiaries named in your will. Annuities and deferred compensation arrangements are examples of other assets that generally provide for a beneficiary designation.

For assets that permit the direct designation of a beneficiary, selection of a beneficiary will not only determine who ultimately receives the asset but will also affect how the asset is received and how it will be taxed. An inappropriate beneficiary designation may seriously affect the results of a particular estate.

Example: You have created a revocable trust that includes a credit bypass trust for the benefit of your spouse (chapter 2). Most of your estate is composed of life insurance. Your spouse is the named beneficiary of the insurance policy. In that case, upon your death, insurance proceeds will be paid directly to your spouse. They will not pass to the trust established for her benefit. As a result, significant additional estate taxes may ultimately be paid. Additionally, the insurance proceeds will not be held and administered in accordance with your intention as expressed in the trust agreement. In this case, your trust should have been designated as the beneficiary of the insurance rather than your spouse directly.

Joint Ownership and Inadvertent Gifts

Care must be taken when transferring an asset into joint ownership with another. The creation of the joint ownership may constitute a taxable gift. In general, a taxable gift will occur upon the creation of joint ownership if both signatures are required in order to transfer or liquidate the asset.

> **Example:** Assume that you add your son's name to your bank account. That generally will not be a current taxable gift if either of you may individually make withdrawals from the account. In that case, the IRS will not consider the gift as complete until your son withdraws cash from the account. However, if the consent of both you and your son is required for a withdrawal, then you have probably made a taxable gift.

7

Transfer Taxes

Federal Transfer Taxes
Lifetime Exemption
Annual Exclusions
Marital Deduction
Generation-Skipping Tax
Qualified Family Owned Business Interests
State Transfer Taxes
Estate Inclusion

MOST PEOPLE ARE not familiar with the transfer tax system. Unlike income taxes you pay each year, transfer taxes are paid only at the time of your death or after substantial lifetime gifts have been made. As you will see, the transfer taxes can be substantial and may significantly deplete an estate unless steps are taken to reduce their impact. The estate planner often devotes considerable effort to analyzing and alleviating the client's anticipated transfer tax liability.

Federal Transfer Taxes

Federal tax law imposes a substantial tax on the transfer of assets by gift during your lifetime or by bequest upon your death.

Under current rules, there is no estate or gift tax on a certain threshold amount of transfers during your lifetime or at death. The exemption amount of $625,000 for 1998 is scheduled to increase to $1.0 million in 2006 as follows:

	Exemption
1998	$625,000
1999	$650,000
2000 and 2001	$675,000
2002 and 2003	$700,000
2004	$850,000
2005	$950,000
2006 and after	$1.0 million

After the threshold amount is exceeded, the tax is substantial. There is a graduated tax schedule, which starts at 37% and increases incrementally to the 55% level. Estates of between $10 million and approximately $21 million are taxed at a 60% marginal rate. The table below summarizes the gift and estate tax rates at various levels for 1998 and 2006.

Gift and Estate Tax Rates

For taxable gifts and estates above	Rate	
	1998	2006
$ 625,000	37%	-0-%
750,000	39	-0-
1,000,000	41	41
1,250,000	43	43
1,500,000	45	45
2,000,000	49	49
2,500,000	53	53
3,000,000	55	55

The tax rates are applied to the total of your taxable gifts made during your lifetime and the value of all assets in your estate at the time of your death. If the total of those amounts exceeds the exemption amount, the excess is taxed at the above rates.

The following table applies those rate brackets to estates of various sizes and shows the total tax owed. For example, in the case of a $3.0 million estate, $1,098,000 of federal tax will be owed in 1998 ($945,000 in 2006 or after) unless steps are taken to reduce the tax.

Sample Estates

Taxable gifts and estate	Total Tax	
	1998	2006
$ 625,000	$-0-	$-0-
800,000	75,000	-0-
1,000,000	153,000	-0-
1,500,000	363,000	210,000
2,000,000	588,000	435,000
2,500,000	933,000	680,000
3,000,000	1,098,000	945,000
4,000,000	1,648,000	1,495,000
5,000,000	2,198,000	2,045,000
10,000,000	4,948,000	4,795,000

Estate and gift taxes are imposed on the true market value of assets transferred. At the time of your death, the value of all of your assets and property must be reported to the IRS if the combined value exceeds a certain threshold amount described below. The value of marketable securities is determined by reference to market prices as of the day of your death (in most cases). All real estate must be appraised. The value of closely held business interests must be determined by valuation experts.

Similarly, in the case of a lifetime gift, the value of the transferred asset must be reported to the IRS if it exceeds an annual threshold amount described below. Again, real estate must be appraised, closely held business interests valued, and the value of marketable securities determined by reference to market quotes on the date of the gift.

Although the details of the transfer tax law are highly complicated, the basic transfer tax system can be summarized in three simple rules:

- Lifetime exemption—The exemption for 1998 is $625,000 and that amount is gradually increasing until it reaches $1.0 million for 2006 and after. Gifts up to the amount of the lifetime exemption can be made during your lifetime or at death without incurring a tax.
- Annual exclusion—The first $10,000 of gifts to each person each year is not taxed and does not deplete any of your lifetime exemption. The amount of the annual exclusion is indexed for inflation starting in 1999.

- Marital deduction—Most transfers to your spouse during your lifetime or at death are free of transfer tax.

Lifetime Exemption

There is currently a credit against the gift and estate tax that converts to the equivalent of a $625,000 exemption for 1998. That amount is scheduled to gradually increase until it becomes a $1.0 million exemption for 2006 and after. Gifts during your lifetime or at your death that do not exceed the exemption amount in the aggregate will not be taxed. The credit is referred to as the Unified Credit because it unifies the gift tax and estate tax and provides a single credit applicable to both.

The unified credit may be used during your lifetime or at death, or partly during your lifetime and partly at death. However, the total of all taxable gifts made during your lifetime and at death that exceed the exemption amount will be taxed. For the following three examples assume it is 2006 or after.

Example: If you make no taxable gifts during your lifetime, then upon death, the first $1.0 million of assets will not be taxed.

Example: If you made $1.0 million of taxable gifts during your lifetime, then no credit would remain and all assets owned by you at the time of your death would be subject to the estate tax.

Example: If you made $400,000 of taxable gifts during your lifetime, then the first $600,000 of assets in your estate at the time of your death would not be subject to tax. However, all assets in excess of $600,000 would be fully subject to the tax.

Every U.S. citizen or resident is entitled to an exemption. A husband and a wife are each entitled to an exemption. Therefore, for example, in 2006 and after a married couple should not pay tax on the first $2.0 million of assets. However, in the usual case, one exemption will be lost unless active steps are taken to preserve both lifetime exemptions.

Example: Assume it is 2006 or after and you and your spouse have combined assets of $2.0 million. You have a will leaving all property to your spouse if living. Some property is owned jointly with your spouse with rights of survivorship.

Upon your death, survivorship property will pass to your spouse by operation of law and any property in your name individually will pass to your spouse pursuant to your will. Therefore, after you are deceased, your spouse will own outright the entire $2.0 million.

Upon your spouse's death, the tax will be computed as follows:

Gross Estate	$ 2,000,000
less exemption	< 1,000,000>
Assets subject to tax	$ 1,000,000
Total tax owed	$ 435,000

The above example shows that even though husband and wife had a combined estate of $2.0 million, the total tax imposed before property can pass to their children or other beneficiaries is $435,000. In effect, the $1.0 million exemption of the first spouse to die was lost. The cost to your children of losing one $1.0 million exemption will be $550,000 if you are in the highest bracket.

The loss of one lifetime exemption is generally prevented through the use of a unified credit bypass trust.

Example: Assume it is 2006 or after and that $1.0 million of assets are titled in your name and $1.0 million are titled in your spouse's name for a combined estate of $2.0 million as in the prior example. At your death, your $1.0 million of assets are placed in a trust for the benefit of your surviving spouse. If the trust is properly drafted and funded, your spouse may have virtually unrestricted access to the trust assets if you wish, but they will not be included in your spouse's estate at the time of his or her death. In that case, the $435,000 tax as computed above will be eliminated. The total savings would be $550,000 for those in the highest bracket.

The estate tax rules are written in such a manner that the exemption of the first deceased spouse will be lost in the usual case. The unified credit bypass trust easily solves that problem and is a basic foundation of most estate plans involving estates in excess of the lifetime exemption threshold.

There are other techniques to avoid loss of the lifetime exemption.

But the unified credit bypass trust is generally the only practical solution that avoids loss of the exemption while permitting the surviving spouse to have full enjoyment of the couple's total combined estate.

For those individuals who can afford to make substantial lifetime gifts, use of the exemption during their lifetime, rather than at death, can be highly advantageous for their beneficiaries.

Example: Assume it is 2006 or after and you make a $1.0 million gift to your daughter, which she invests at a 10% rate of growth. After ten years, that amount will have increased by $1,593,742. Had the gift not been made, then that additional amount would have been included in your estate at the time of your death and your estate tax bill would have increased by $876,558 at a 55% tax rate. If you survived twenty years after the gift, then the savings to your daughter would be $3,150,125.

Gift of Lifetime Exemption

Year	End of Year Value of Gift	Cumulative Growth @ 10%	Federal Estate Tax on Growth @ 55%
1	$1,100,000	$ 100,000	$ 55,000
2	1,210,000	210,000	115,500
3	1,331,000	331,000	182,050
4	1,464,100	464,100	255,255
5	1,610,510	610,510	335,780
6	1,771,561	771,561	424,359
7	1,948,717	948,717	521,794
8	2,143,589	1,143,589	628,974
9	2,357,948	1,357,948	746,871
10	2,593,742	1,593,742	876,558
(Years 11–19 omitted)			
20	6,727,500	5,727,500	3,150,125

Obviously, a gifting program of the magnitude described above is appropriate only if you have substantial assets that exceed your possible future needs. If your estate is adequate to permit lifetime gifts, very significant amounts of estate tax can be avoided.

Individuals with very large estates generally wish to use their exemptions during their lifetimes so that future appreciation on the gifted assets will avoid tax as illustrated above. A number of techniques have been developed to leverage or multiply the amount of the exemption. If an asset can be valued for gift tax purposes at 50% of its true value, then an amount equal to twice the amount of the exemption can be transferred free of tax. Some of the leveraging techniques are described in chapter 17. Obviously, the sooner your exemption is used, the better, since the gifted asset will have more years to accumulate tax-free appreciation.

Q: I wish to transfer substantial assets out of my estate during my lifetime in order to make use of my lifetime exemption. However, I do not wish my children and other beneficiaries to receive the property until later or perhaps not until after my death. Is that possible to accomplish?

A: Yes. Gifts can be made to an irrevocable trust established for the benefit of your children or other beneficiaries. The trust will allow you to control the timing of the ultimate transfer of the gifted property to your children or other beneficiaries.

Annual Exclusions

The gift tax rules provide a $10,000 exemption for each person you make a gift to each year. Therefore, you can give any number of people $10,000 annually without incurring a gift tax or depleting your lifetime exemption. Gifts to any one person during any calendar year that exceed $10,000 will reduce your lifetime exemption. After the lifetime exemption is fully depleted, such gifts will result in a current gift tax liability. The annual exclusion amount is indexed for inflation starting in 1999.

Example: Assume you have three children and seven grandchildren. Assume during this calendar year you give each of your ten descendants $10,000 of cash or other assets. In that case, none of your lifetime exemption will be used and no gift tax will be owed because no single individual received more than $10,000 from you during the year.

Example: Assume during this calendar year you give $20,000 to each of your ten descendants. That will result in the use of $100,000 of your lifetime exemption, computed as follows:

Total gifts ($20,000 x 10)	$ 200,000
less annual exclusions ($10,000 x 10)	<100,000>
Taxable gifts	$100,000

Lifetime exemption (after 2005)	$1,000,000
Exemption used	<100,000>
Remaining exemption	$900,000

The remaining $900,000 of lifetime exemption may be used to offset taxable gifts in future years, or, if any exemption remains at the time of your death, it will be used to offset taxable bequests at that time.

Example: Assume it is 2006 or after and you have not previously used any of your lifetime exemption, but this year you transfer $1,100,000 of bonds to your daughter. The gift tax result will be as follows:

Total gift	$1,100,000
less annual exclusion	<10,000>
Taxable gift	$1,090,000
Unused lifetime exemption	<1,000,000>
Gift subject to tax	$ 90,000
Tax rate	x 41%
Tax owed	$ 36,900

The gift tax of $36,900 will be owed currently. In addition, you will have used your entire lifetime exemption and none will remain for use by your estate at the time of your death.

The annual exclusion is an important tool for many estate plans. A husband and wife can each transfer $10,000 to each of their descendants annually without needing to file a gift tax return or using any of their lifetime exemptions. Therefore, a husband and wife with five descendants could transfer $100,000 tax free annually ($50,000 each).

An additional advantage of lifetime gifts is that all future income and appreciation in value on the transferred asset escapes transfer tax. Over several years that can produce a very significant benefit.

Example: Assume you and your spouse each transfer $10,000 to your son annually. Assume that the gifted cash is invested by your son at 10%. Assume you are in the 55% estate tax bracket and that the gifts are made annually for ten years. After ten years your son will have an investment fund of $350,623. Had the gifts not been made, then at your death, the $350,623 would still be included in your estate and the additional estate tax on that amount would be $192,843. The savings to your son resulting from the gifts is that $192,843 amount. If the annual gifts are made to your son for twenty years, then under those assumptions the total estate tax savings would be $693,026.

Annual Exclusion Gifts

Year	Annual Exclusion Gift	Cumulative Growth @ 10%	Federal Estate Tax @ 55%
1	$20,000	$ 22,000	$ 12,100
2	20,000	46,200	25,410
3	20,000	72,820	40,051
4	20,000	102,102	56,156
5	20,000	134,312	73,872
6	20,000	169,743	93,359
7	20,000	208,718	114,795
8	20,000	251,590	138,374
9	20,000	298,748	164,312
10	20,000	350,623	192,843
(Years 11–19 omitted)			
20	20,000	1,260,048	693,026

Gifts as described above may be made outright to children or other beneficiaries. Frequently, however, individuals wish to make gifts for the benefit of children so that the gifted assets will be transferred out of their estate free of tax, but do not wish the child to have immediate access to the gifted asset. If that is your wish, it is often helpful to create an irrevocable trust for the benefit of your child or other donee. Gifts can then be transferred out of your estate, but will become available for your child or other beneficiary only at a later date or as needed in accordance with the terms of the trust.

Example: You wish to make regular annual gifts for the benefit of your son. Rather than making the gifts outright to him, you make them to an irrevocable trust established for his benefit. Your spouse or another individual chosen by you will serve as trustee and will decide when, and for what purpose, distributions will be made for your son's benefit.

Q: I would like to make gifts in trust for the benefit of my grandchildren. Can I make those gifts to a revocable trust?

A: A revocable trust would generally not be useful for that purpose. The transferred asset would still be included in your estate for tax purposes. All future appreciation in value would also remain in your estate.

An important planning consideration is the leveraging or amplification of the annual exclusions. There are several techniques that may be helpful. One method is to transfer business or investment property to a family partnership or corporation and then make gifts of partnership units or corporate stock. As explained in chapter 17, it is often possible to substantially discount the true value of the partnership units or stocks being transferred. If those closely held securities can be discounted by 50%, then in effect a husband and wife can each transfer $20,000 ($40,000 total) to each child or other donee each year without depleting their lifetime exemptions or incurring any gift tax.

Another common technique to leverage or amplify the benefit of the annual exclusions is through the use of life insurance. As discussed in chapter 8, it is often desirable to place life insurance in an irrevocable trust designed for that purpose. If done correctly, the insurance proceeds will be free of estate tax. If the annual premiums on the insurance policy are paid by way of annual exclusion gifts, and if the insurance proceeds are successfully exempted from the tax, the result may be a huge leveraging or multiplying of the benefit of the annual exclusions.

> **Example:** Assume that based on your age and the condition of your health you are able to purchase a $1.0 million insurance policy at a premium cost of $20,000 annually for 12 years. The policy is acquired by an insurance trust, which you established for the benefit of your two children. You pay the $240,000 over the next 12 years and you later pass away.
>
> Because your two children were beneficiaries of the trust, the tax rules permitted you to gift $20,000 annually to the trust. You did that for 12 years, or $240,000 in total. At the time of your death, your children received $1.0 million free of estate tax. The leveraging of the annual exclusions in this example is more than four to one. Had you died in the first year of the policy, the leveraging would have been fifty to one.

Marital Deduction

Since 1982 there has been an unlimited marital deduction. That means that almost any property transferred from you to your spouse during your lifetime or at death will not be subject to gift or estate tax. The gift tax rules and estate tax rules each provide that gifts to your spouse may be deducted for tax purposes. Therefore, in effect, most transfers to your spouse during your lifetime or at death will avoid transfer taxation.

Virtually all outright transfers to your spouse qualify for the marital deduction whether transferred during your lifetime or at death. However, transfers into trust for the benefit of your spouse may or may not qualify for the marital deduction depending on the terms of the trust. Great care must be used to assure that a trust designed to benefit your spouse will qualify for the marital deduction if that is desired. There are several types of trusts that may qualify for the marital deduction.

In the last few years, the most commonly used marital deduction trust is the Qualified Terminable Interest Property (QTIP) trust. A QTIP trust has the following characteristics:

- All income must be distributed to your spouse.
- The trust may provide for liberal distributions of principal to your spouse, for more restrictive access to principal, or for no principal distributions at all.
- No other individual may receive income or principal from the trust during your spouse's lifetime.

The advantage of a QTIP trust is that it permits you to leave property in trust for the benefit of your spouse and yet be assured that upon your surviving spouse's death remaining assets will pass to your children or other beneficiaries intended by you.

Example: You leave property in trust for your husband. The trust provides that he will receive all income earned by the trust and principal as needed for his health, maintenance, and support. Upon his death, any remaining assets will pass equally to your children. The foregoing describes a QTIP trust that will not be taxed at the time of your death. Your husband will receive income and principal as needed, yet upon his death, all remaining assets must be distributed to your children. The value of the QTIP trust at the time of your husband's death will be taxed in his estate.

Q: Can I leave property in a trust for the benefit of my surviving wife, but only for as long as she does not remarry?

A: If the income from the trust is subject to termination upon her re-marriage (or any other event) then the trust will not qualify for the marital deduction.

Prior to the availability of the unlimited marital deduction many estates incurred substantial tax upon the first spouse's death. In 1981, Congress revised the rules so that married couples may arrange their estates in a manner that will defer all transfer taxes until the second death. However, if deferral of tax is intended, care must be taken to assure that spousal gifts during lifetime or at death are made in a manner that will qualify for the marital deduction.

Q: Why is it important that gifts to my spouse qualify for the marital deduction?

A: A gift to your spouse that did not qualify for the marital deduction would be a taxable gift if it exceeded $10,000 during the year. The taxable gift would count against your lifetime exemption and after that was fully depleted it would result in a current gift tax. Also, the asset could be included in your spouse's estate so that it would result in a second estate tax at the time of his or her death.

If your spouse is not a U.S. citizen, then transfers to him or her will not qualify for the marital deduction unless they are transferred to a special trust designed for that purpose. That issue is discussed in chapter 14.

Generation-Skipping Tax

If you transfer assets by gift or bequest to a grandchild or other "lower generation" person, the generation-skipping tax (GST) may be imposed in addition to the gift tax or estate tax. There is a $1.0 million lifetime exemption from the generation-skipping tax. However, after the exemption amount is exhausted, all future generation-skipping transfers are taxed at a flat 55%. That tax is in addition to the gift tax or estate tax. The $1.0 million generation-skipping exemption is indexed for inflation starting in 1999.

A gift to your grandchild may be subject to both the gift tax and the generation-skipping tax. As if that were not bad enough, a special rule also requires you to pay gift tax or estate tax on the amount of the generation-skipping tax. As a result, the total tax on a gift to your grand-child can significantly exceed the amount of the gift.

Example: Assume that you previously made $1.0 million of taxable gifts to grandchildren so that your estate and gift tax exemption has been fully depleted and your $1.0 million GST exemption has been fully depleted. Assume you are in the 55% gift tax or estate tax bracket. If you now give an additional $100,000 taxable gift or bequest to your grandson, the tax will be $140,250, computed as follows:

Generation-skipping tax (55%)	$ 55,000
Gift tax (55% of $155,000)	85,250
Total tax on gift	$140,250

Because the generation-skipping tax is so onerous, much of the estate planning effort for some estates is devoted to minimizing the effect of the generation-skipping tax. The principal techniques involve various methods of leveraging the $1.0 million lifetime exemption or the $10,000 annual exclusions (which are more difficult to obtain for the generation-skipping tax than for the regular gift tax).

Example: Assume at the time of your death you leave $1.0 million in trust for your daughter. She will receive income from the trust and principal as needed for her support and maintenance. At her death the remainder will pass to her children. The entire trust can be sheltered with your $1.0 million GST exemption. Therefore, no GS tax would apply when your daughter passes away. That would be true even if the $1.0 million of trust assets had appreciated. Regardless of the size of the trust at the time of your daughter's death, the entire remaining principal will pass to grandchildren or other beneficiaries free of generation-skipping tax.

A generation-skipping trust is simply a trust that provides income or principal for your child or other beneficiary as you specify in the trust document, but without being included in his or her estate. If correctly designed it will not be included in your child's estate and will pass on to the next generation free of additional gift or estate tax. It will also be free of generation-skipping tax if it has been sheltered by an allocation of your $1.0 million GST exemption.

Q: My wife and I want to take advantage of each of our $1.0 million generation-skipping exemptions. Do we need to establish separate generation-skipping trusts?

A: GS trusts may be separate trusts established for the purpose of making lifetime gifts to children and their descendants. However, in many cases the GS trust is simply a provision of your existing revocable trust. Your individual situation must be analyzed to determine whether you will be best served by a separate GS trust or whether you should simply amend your existing revocable trust to include GS provisions.

Q: Is it possible to take advantage of the $1.0 million generation-skipping tax exemption without depriving my children of the use of the property?

A: Yes. Most GS trusts are designed to provide income and principal to children, but without being included in their estates for tax purposes.

Q: If I make a gift to someone other than my grandchild or great-grandchild, say a grandnephew, will the generation-skipping tax apply?

A: Nephews are treated like your children, so the generation-skipping tax would not apply on a gift to a nephew. Grandnephews are treated like grandchildren and a gift to them will be subject to the generation-skipping tax. If you make a gift to someone who is related to you through a common grandparent then it is necessary to count the number of generations between you and the donee. If the donee is two or more generations below you, the generation-skipping tax will apply. If you are not related to the donee through a common grandparent, then the generation-skipping tax will apply if the donee is more than 37-½ years younger than you.

Q: I understand that if I make a gift or bequest to my grandchild the generation-skipping tax may apply in addition to the gift tax or the estate tax. If I make a gift or bequest to my great-grandchild will the GS tax apply twice, since two generations are being skipped?

A: The GS tax applies only once per skip regardless of the number of generations involved. For that reason, it is possible to establish dynasty trusts, which are designed to skip many generations.

Q: I understand that I may establish a GS trust that will distribute income and principal to my children during their lifetimes and will then pass to my grandchildren free of estate tax when my children pass away. Can the trust be designed to also skip my grandchildren's estates and pass to great-grandchildren free of tax when my grandchildren pass away?

A: Yes. GS trusts may be established to skip multiple generations. Although each generation will enjoy the benefit of the trust, it will not be taxed as each generation passes away. However, the law of most states prohibits the establishment of trusts that will last more than two or three generations. See "Dynasty Trust" in chapter 2.

Qualified Family Owned Business Interests

The 1997 Tax Act provided some limited relief for family owned businesses. Under the new rule, a portion of the value of a closely held business may be exempt from taxation. A closely held business interest may qualify if it constitutes more than 50% of your estate. Generally, your family must own at least 50% of the business, although if you own at least 30% of the business it still may qualify if most of the remainder of the business is owned by one or two other families.

The amount of a family owned business that may be excluded from taxation is equal to $1.3 million, less the lifetime exemption. Therefore, for someone who died in 1998 when the lifetime exemption stood at $625,000, up to $675,000 of a family owned business could be excluded from taxation. However, by 2006, when the lifetime exemption will be $1.0 million, only an additional $300,000 of a closely held business will be excludable.

State Transfer Taxes

The transfer taxes described above in this chapter are imposed by the federal government and are administered by the IRS. However, in addition to the federal transfer taxes, many states have their own inheritance taxes. The inheritance tax rules vary greatly from state to state. In those states which impose an inheritance tax, the tax generally varies between 5% and 10%, and in many states the rate depends on how closely you are related to the beneficiary. Although state inheritance taxes are not large when compared to the federal estate tax, the state inheritance tax bill is often significant enough to justify some planning effort.

In general, only your state of residence may impose an inheritance tax. Because most assets can be taxed by only your state of residence, many individuals prefer to be considered a resident of a state, such as Florida, that does not impose an inheritance tax. If it is possible to be considered a resident by more than one state, steps may be taken to establish residency in the state of choice. Residency is discussed in detail in chapter 11.

The major exception to the general rule is that real estate owned by you may be taxed by the state where it is located even if you are not a resident of that state. The principal method of avoiding a "foreign" state's inheritance tax is to convert the real estate to intangible property by contributing it to a corporation or partnership.

Example: Assume you are a resident of Florida, which does not impose an inheritance tax, but you own a $500,000 rental property in New York that will be subject to inheritance tax there. If you contribute the property to a corporation, then at the time of your death you will not own real estate in New York, but, instead, will own corporate stock, which is an intangible asset that is not taxable by the foreign state.

Q: I am a resident of Florida, but I own real estate in New York and in Michigan. Both parcels of real estate have been transferred to my revocable trust so that probate proceedings will not be required in New York or Michigan. Will my estate also avoid New York and Michigan inheritance taxes?

A: Whether an asset is subject to state inheritance tax is generally unrelated to whether it will also require probate proceedings. Although a transfer of the New York and Michigan properties to your revocable trust will likely avoid probate proceedings in those states, the value of the real estate will still be subject to inheritance tax in the state where it is located unless additional steps to avoid the state inheritance tax are taken.

Estate Inclusion

If an asset is included in your estate, then it is subject to estate tax at the time of your death or gift tax if you should make a transfer of the asset as a gift during your lifetime. Virtually every asset that you own, have an interest in, or have control over will be included in your estate.

Q: Can I transfer assets to an irrevocable trust for my children, but retain the right to receive the income from the trust during the remainder of my lifetime?

A: If you retain a right to the income from the trust, then it will be included in your estate for tax purposes.

Q: I intend to transfer assets to an irrevocable trust for the benefit of my children and grandchildren. I would like to serve as trustee of the trust and be authorized to "sprinkle" income and principal among my descendants. Will the assets transferred to the trust be included in my estate at the time of my death?

A: In most cases assets will be included in your estate even though you transferred them to an irrevocable trust if you serve as trustee of the trust. Therefore, you will generally need to choose some other individual or a trust company to serve as trustee.

When an asset is owned by two individuals jointly, upon the death of either, the question arises as to what portion of the asset is included in his or her estate for tax purposes. There are two rules: one rule for joint owners who are married to each other and a second rule for all other joint owners.

In the case of an asset owned jointly by a husband and wife, one-half of the value of the asset will be included in the estate of the first deceased regardless of which spouse purchased the property.

If you own an asset jointly with someone other than your spouse, then upon your death your estate will include a portion of the value of the property corresponding to your proportionate contribution to the purchase of the asset.

Example: If you contributed $2,500 and your brother contributed $7,500 for the joint purchase of an asset, then 25% of its value will be included in your estate at the time of your death regardless of the value of the asset at that time.

It is important to maintain records concerning joint purchases because the IRS presumes that 100% of an asset is included in the estate of the first deceased, unless the surviving owner can prove his or her proportionate contribution to the purchase of the asset. For example, even though your brother may have contributed 100% of the purchase price, the asset you own jointly with him will be included 100% in your estate unless your brother can prove that he purchased the asset. Of course, as to property owned jointly by a husband and wife, one-half will be included in each estate regardless of which spouse purchased the asset.

8

Life Insurance

Types of Insurance
Income Replacement
Estate Liquidity
Joint and Survivor Policies
Buy/Sell Funding
Wealth Replacement
Investment Vehicle
Taxation
Life Insurance Trusts
Split-Dollar Arrangements

LIFE INSURANCE IS the most useful and flexible of all assets for estate planning purposes. In many situations, life insurance is the only practical solution to achieve a particular estate planning goal.

Traditionally, life insurance was used only to replace lost income. The principal breadwinner's life would be insured during his or her working years while the family was dependent on his or her earnings. Today there is a great variety of specialized policies that have been designed to solve a number of specific problems. Now policies are often used for purposes unrelated to income replacement. They may be used to pay estate taxes or to otherwise provide estate liquidity, to fund the sale/purchase of a business interest, as a wealth replacement source, as an investment vehicle, as protection for a business against the loss of a key employee, and for various other purposes.

Types of Insurance

The approximately 2,000 insurance companies in the United States have devised an ingenious variety of policies. Most of them fall within one of the following categories:

Term—This is the simplest type of policy. It does not acquire cash value. Rather, you pay a premium each year for that year's coverage. At the end of the year no value remains. If you die during the year, then the proceeds will be paid to the beneficiary you named in the contract. A number of options are available when purchasing a term policy. The most common option is the right to renew. In its simplest form, a renewable term policy will guarantee you the right to renew for a specified number of years, but the cost will increase each year. Alternatively, you may select a renewable term policy with level premiums for a specified number of years. Naturally, a guaranteed renewable term policy will cost more than a policy without that feature and a level premium policy will cost more in the earlier years than a policy without that feature.

Whole Life—This is the most common type of permanent insurance. Whole life policies are designed to remain in effect throughout your lifetime. Whole life policies were originally designed to require annual level premium payments through age 100 or your death if earlier. Traditional whole life policies also provide a level death benefit, paying the same amount whether you die in the first year of the contract or in a later year. The biggest difference between term and whole life insurance is that a whole life policy will develop a cash value. There are numerous variations on the basic whole life policy. For example, Limited Payment Whole Life is designed to require premium payments for a fixed number of years rather than for your entire life. After a stated number of premium years, the limited payment whole life policy will be paid up and no additional premiums will be required. A Single Premium Whole Life Policy requires only one large initial premium payment and is immediately paid up. Modified Life and Graded Premium Life are whole life policies that are designed to have smaller premiums in the first few years. Of course, premiums larger than usual will be required in later years to compensate for the lower premiums in the earlier years. Interest-Sensitive Whole Life Policies have premiums that increase or decrease depending on the company's investment returns and expenses. Indexed Whole Life Policies have a death benefit that increases in accordance with the consumer price index or some other recognized inflation index. Adjustable Life Policies permit you to vary the amount of the premium and/or the amount of the death benefit. If you reduce the amount of the premium, cash values and/or death benefits will also decline. If you elect to increase the death benefit, then any cash value will be more quickly eroded unless premium payments are also increased.

Universal Life—Universal life policies are highly flexible. They permit you to change the premiums or death benefit at any time. The significant advantage of UL is the ability to modify the insurance without obtaining a new policy. Your premium payments are added to a separate account along with insurance company earnings credited to your account. The insurance company's expenses and costs of providing insurance are withdrawn from your account. If you increase your annual premiums then your cash value account will increase at a faster rate. If you increase the desired death benefit, then your account growth will slow or your cash value account may begin to decline. Under UL contracts you may actually discontinue premiums if there is sufficient cash value to carry your contract. UL policies also permit you to borrow out your cash values or simply withdraw a portion of them. Also, of course, you can always surrender your policy for the remaining cash value, less a surrender charge in some cases.

Variable Life—Variable life policies are highly investment oriented. In fact, agents selling variable life policies are required to have a securities sales license. Your cash value account will be allocated within a family of investment funds as you direct. Most VL policies will offer equity, bond, and money market accounts. Many VL policies offer twelve or more separate funds. The performance of your VL contract will depend on the aggregate performance of the various funds in which you have elected to invest your cash value. A traditional VL policy has a fixed premium and fixed death benefit that you cannot elect to adjust. Therefore, as compared to universal life contracts, variable life insurance has less flexibility.

Variable Universal Life—As insurance companies created ever more flexible policies the next logical step was to combine universal life with variable life to create the variable universal life contract. VUL contracts have the same flexibility as universal life contracts. You can increase or decrease the death benefit within underwriting parameters and you can vary the frequency and amount of premiums. In addition, you can allocate your cash value account among a family of investment funds. Like variable life, VUL should be considered only as a long-term investment.

Although VL and VUL policies are highly investment oriented, they still receive the favorable tax treatment afforded a regular insurance policy (assuming the policy is not a Modified Endowment Contract (MEC) as discussed below). Of course, a disadvantage of variable contracts is the possibility of a loss of your cash value depending on the performance of the investment funds selected by you.

Income Replacement

The traditional purpose of life insurance was to replace the "breadwinner's" income in the event of his or her death. When most people think of insurance they primarily think of that type of policy.

Example: Assume that your earnings are the sole source, or a significant source, of your family's income. Your family's standard of living would significantly decline in the event of your death. Under that classic scenario, most people would consider it foolhardy not to have sufficient life insurance, if possible, so that your lost earnings would be replaced by investment income on the insurance proceeds.

After an appropriate policy and death benefit level are selected, estate planning for this type of insurance typically involves two considerations: making sure the insurance proceeds are best protected for the benefit of your beneficiaries, and assuring that the insurance proceeds will not be taxed.

Analyze whether all or a portion of the insurance proceeds will be subject to estate tax. If the proceeds will be taxed, then establish an insurance trust or implement some other mechanism to avoid the tax.

The insurance proceeds, plus your other assets, will likely constitute a sizable amount. If that amount may be payable to children in the event of your death, then it may be important to establish a trust so that the insurance proceeds and investments purchased with the proceeds are better protected and conserved for the benefit of the children (see chapter 2).

Even where the insurance may be payable to your spouse, adult children, or some other responsible adult, it may be appropriate to create a trust to hold the insurance proceeds so they are better protected from divorces, lawsuits, other creditor problems, and taxes.

Estate Liquidity

In the estate planning field, the most common use of insurance is to provide estate liquidity. One of the greatest threats for some estates is the loss that can be incurred due to insufficient liquidity. The estate tax is due nine months after the date of death. Business debts, costs of administration, and other liabilities may be due even sooner. Without sufficient liquidity some estates may be forced to liquidate assets at substantially less than their true value. One aspect of estate planning is to estimate the estate's liquidity needs and create a plan to assure that the necessary liquidity will be available.

Substantial losses are frequently incurred where real estate, closely held businesses, and similar assets must be sold in order to pay taxes and other estate costs. It often takes one or two years or even longer to locate a buyer for those types of assets and to negotiate and conclude a sale at their true value. If an estate has a liquidity crisis, potential buyers are often aware of it. As a result, the sales price will be further deflated. The forced sale of an illiquid asset will often result in a "fire sale" price.

Example: Assume the bulk of your estate consists of a closely held business and some commercial real estate appraised at $4.0 million. Assume those assets must be sold quickly and receive only 75% of their true value.

If you assume a 50% estate tax rate, your heirs could possibly receive only 25% of the true value of your estate:

Appraised value	$4.0 million
Tax rate	50%
Estate tax	$2.0
Sale proceeds (75%)	$3.0
Estate tax	<2.0>
Net to heirs	$1.0

Insurance is often relied upon to provide needed liquidity. Insurance is obviously suited to that need because it produces substantial cash at precisely the time it is needed. Even more importantly, insurance proceeds can usually be made nontaxable through the use of an insurance trust or other mechanism. As a result, insurance may be a much more efficient source of liquidity than any other asset.

Joint and Survivor Policies

An increasingly popular form of insurance is known as a joint and survivor (J&S) policy or a second-to-die policy. A J&S policy insures two lives and does not pay the insurance proceeds until both of the insured are deceased.

J&S policies are considerably less expensive than single life policies. Because the insurance company does not pay until the second death, it has additional time in which to invest cash values. Consequently, policy earnings are greater and the cost of the insurance is less.

J&S policies were designed by the insurance companies specifically to pay estate taxes. In most cases, a married couple will plan their estate so that no tax is owed until both are deceased. At that time, the second-to-die policy proceeds will be available for that purpose.

Like single life policies, the proceeds of a J&S policy will be subject to estate tax at the second spouse's death unless the policy has been transferred to a life insurance trust or some other steps have been taken to avoid the estate tax. In most cases, an investment in a second-to-die policy will be economically viable only if it is structured so as to avoid tax on the insurance proceeds.

Q: I previously established a life insurance trust to hold a policy insuring my life individually. If my spouse and I now purchase a J&S policy, can we include it in the same insurance trust?

A: Generally, it will not be possible to include a single life policy and a J&S policy in the same life insurance trust. In most cases, it will be necessary to establish a separate trust for the new J&S policy.

Buy/Sell Funding

An important aspect of many estates is planning for the orderly succession of a business. Such planning often involves a buy/sell agreement between the business owner and the potential future owner, whether that is the owner's child, a key employee, or the owner's partner or co-shareholder. (See chapter 18, "Business Succession Planning.") In many cases, the potential purchaser of the business will not have sufficient resources to complete the purchase. Insurance is often used to solve that problem.

Example: You and your partner have operated a business successfully for many years. If you were to die, you would want your one-half of the business to pass to your partner and you would want the value of your one-half of the business to pass to your family so that value could be invested for their needs. A common approach would be to have a buy/sell agreement which requires the surviving partner to purchase the deceased partner's share of the business at a specified price. Each partner will own a policy insuring the life of the other partner. In that manner you can be assured that sufficient liquid assets will be available at your death to complete the purchase of your interest in the business.

Wealth Replacement

An additional purpose of insurance is to replace assets that will be shifted away from your family as a result of other planning. The need for wealth replacement can arise in a variety of situations.

Example: Assume you have established a charitable remainder trust (see chapter 17). You and your spouse will receive income for the remainder of your lives and you have obtained a sizable charitable deduction and avoided a potentially large capital gain tax on the property you transferred to the charitable remainder trust. The one drawback to this arrangement is that after you and your spouse are both deceased, remaining trust assets will pass to charity, rather than to your children as you wish. Here, it may be appropriate to establish a wealth replacement trust so that tax-free insurance proceeds will pass to your children in place of the assets you transferred to the charitable remainder trust.

Example: Assume you have a sizable retirement plan which provides only two forms of payout: (1) an annuity for the remainder of your life, or (2) a smaller annuity that will pay for the remainder of your life and your spouse's life. In some situations you and your spouse will be better served if you elect to take the larger annuity payable only for the remainder of your life. In that case you may want to acquire a policy insuring your life so that if you die first, resources will be available for your spouse to replace the lost annuity income.

Investment Vehicle

Over the last several years, many insurance contracts have become very competitive with other investment choices. Insurance policies now exist that permit you to allocate your cash value investment in the contract among various funds including stock funds, bond funds, money market accounts, and other investment funds. Many such policies have performed well.

The income tax rules provide an additional advantage to investing through an insurance contract. The earnings inside the policy will generally accrue on a tax-deferred basis. In addition, except for modified endowment contracts (described below), the earnings may ultimately be withdrawn from the policy on a tax-favored or even tax-free basis. The tax-favored status of insurance policies, combined with the competitive investment performance achieved by some insurance companies in recent years, has resulted in a vast flow of dollars to insurance policies by individuals primarily seeking investment results rather than traditional death protection.

Modified Endowment Contracts (MECs) are insurance policies that are highly investment oriented rather than death benefit oriented. They are contracts with a high cash value in relation to the death benefit and are acquired for a single premium or funded over a short period of years. MECs are denied some of the favorable tax treatment afforded most other insurance policies. When planning to acquire a high cash value policy, it will be important to determine whether the policy will be considered a MEC.

Taxation

In most cases, life insurance death benefits are free of income tax; however, if you own a policy insuring your own life, the death benefits will be fully subject to estate tax. Therefore, the primary planning strategy for life insurance policies is to assure that neither you nor your spouse has an ownership interest in the policy or its future proceeds. The primary technique to accomplish that goal is to establish a life insurance trust.

With the exception of MECs, it may be possible to withdraw the earnings within the insurance policy tax-free. If the policy is cashed out and canceled, you will be taxed on the excess of the cash you receive over the aggregate of the premiums you paid in prior years. In effect, the "profit" earned by the policy will be taxed to you at ordinary income rates. However, many policies provide that cash values may be borrowed from the policy at a minimal interest rate. If that is the case, you may with proper handling have access to the cash values without incurring an income tax. Upon your death, your beneficiaries will receive the death benefits provided by the insurance contract, less any outstanding cash value loans. The net amount received by them will also be free of income tax.

Life insurance policies are tax-favored in that your investment in the contract may be withdrawn tax-free before the earnings in the contract are withdrawn. In addition, the earnings may be borrowed from the contract so that income tax is avoided on the earnings as well. Neither of those benefits is available if the insurance policy is considered a MEC as described above. In the case of a MEC, all withdrawals are considered first to come from income, if any, and then from your investment, and all borrowings are considered as a distribution of earnings if any earnings exist in the policy.

Life Insurance Trusts

Although life insurance proceeds are generally free of income tax, they are fully subject to estate tax unless steps are taken to avoid the tax. The most practical method of avoiding the tax is usually to transfer the insurance policy to a special irrevocable trust established for that purpose.

Upon your death, the trust will hold the insurance proceeds for the benefit of your named beneficiaries. If you intend to first benefit your spouse, then the insurance trust will contain a spousal trust for his or her benefit. Your surviving spouse may be the trustee if you wish and may have liberal or more restrictive access to income and principal as you direct. (See "Trust for Surviving Spouse" in chapter 2.) Of course, the spousal trust would be a bypass trust so that it would not be included in his or her estate.

Similarly, after your surviving spouse is deceased, the trust may be held for the benefit of your children or other named beneficiaries. The children or other beneficiaries will have liberal or more restrictive access to income and principal as you direct. (See "Trusts for Children" in chapter 2.)

Insurance is often obtained to provide estate liquidity at the time of death. It is particularly useful and important where the estate is comprised in large part of real estate, closely held business interests, or other illiquid assets. Life insurance may be designed to provide the liquidity needed to pay transfer taxes and other estate obligations without necessitating the forced liquidation of estate assets. If your estate will be subject to a 50% estate tax rate, then the benefit of your insurance will be doubled if it is properly transferred to a life insurance trust.

If you transfer an existing life insurance policy to a life insurance trust or otherwise transfer it out of your estate, it will still be taxed if you die within three years of the transfer. However, if you transfer cash to your life insurance trust and the trustee purchases a new policy on your life from the insurance company, you will not have made a transfer of the policy and the three-year rule will not apply.

Assume you have transferred a life insurance policy to a life insurance trust established for the benefit of your spouse and children. As premiums become due on the policy, it will generally be necessary for you to transfer additional cash to the trust to be used to pay the premiums. In most cases, you will want your gifts to the trust to qualify under the $10,000 annual exclusion rules. You want your future gifts of premium dollars to qualify so that you will not be required to file a gift tax return and deplete your lifetime exemption each time you make a contribution to the trust.

Generally, gifts you make to the trust will not qualify under the $10,000 annual exclusion rule unless the trust beneficiaries have an opportunity to demand a withdrawal of that year's contribution. Typically, their withdrawal right is limited to a 30-day period after they receive notice of the contribution to the trust. A beneficiary who does not elect to withdraw his or her pro rata share during that time period will not be able to withdraw his or her share in the future. A limited right to withdraw the beneficiary's pro rata share of each year's contribution is referred to as a "Crummey" withdrawal provision, named after a 1968 Tax Court case.

Q: I own a policy insuring my wife's life. She owns a policy on my life. Won't that arrangement result in our insurance being excluded from our estates so that we will not need a life insurance trust?

A: The cross-ownership arrangement you describe was occasionally helpful before the marital deduction rules were revised. Since 1982, however, that arrangement generally provides no benefit. Regardless of the order of your deaths, the proceeds of both policies will be taxed before passing on to children or other beneficiaries.

Q: I have purchased a life insurance policy to pay for estate taxes and other costs at the time of my death. The policy is owned by an insurance trust so that it will not be subject to estate tax. Since the insurance proceeds will be the only asset of the trust and since the proceeds will be spent on taxes and other costs, why does the trust need to provide for my spouse or children?

A: It is a common misconception that if an insurance policy owned by an insurance trust is to be fully expended on taxes or other costs, then the terms of the trust are not important. In fact, the insurance trust cannot directly pay estate taxes or costs. If it is permitted to do so, it will be included in your estate and will be subject to estate tax. Rather, the insurance trust will only indirectly pay taxes and costs. Cash in the trust from the insurance will be transferred to your estate or your revocable trust in exchange for other assets. Your estate or revocable trust will then have the cash to pay taxes and costs and your investments and other assets will be held by the insurance trust for the benefit of your surviving spouse, children, or other beneficiaries. Since the insurance trust will own substantial assets, the provisions of the subtrusts for your surviving spouse, children, or other beneficiaries must be carefully considered.

Q: If I establish a life insurance trust to hold policies insuring my life, who may serve as trustee?

A: You, the insured person, generally cannot serve as trustee. However, if the trust is properly drafted, your spouse can serve as trustee, or your child or anyone else you choose.

Q: Since life insurance trusts must be irrevocable, must I give up access to the policy and its cash value after it is transferred to the trust?

A: During your lifetime, your spouse, children, or other named beneficiary may be granted access to trust assets. That provision provides access by your spouse or other named beneficiary to the insurance policy should you want it or its cash value removed from the trust during your lifetime. However, you may not have direct personal access to the policy. If it is important to have personal access to potential cash values, then in some situations a split-dollar arrangement may be appropriate.

Split-Dollar Arrangements

A planning technique that can be very beneficial in some cases is known as a split-dollar arrangement. There are several types of split-dollar arrangements, but the most typical is where you and your corporation "split" the payment of premiums and the ownership of a life insurance policy.

Example: Assume you own the stock of a closely held corporation that operates a business or professional practice. Assume you need a $1.0 million insurance policy for some business or estate planning purpose. Your corporation and you might agree that the policy will be issued in your name as owner, but the corporation will pay the $10,000 annual premiums. Upon your death, the company will receive the return of its aggregate premiums paid over the years and your named beneficiary will receive the remainder of the death benefit. If you died after ten years, then the company would have paid $100,000 in premiums, which it would receive back. Your named beneficiary would receive the remaining $900,000.

The above example illustrates a traditional split-dollar arrangement whereby the corporate employer pays most or all of the annual insurance premiums, but receives those premiums back, typically without interest, upon the death of the employee. The employee's named beneficiary receives the remainder of the death proceeds. The primary advantage of a split-dollar arrangement is that the dollars spent on insurance premiums will be taxed at the rate for the corporation, rather than at your tax bracket. That may be particularly advantageous where the company can be taxed at a much lower bracket than your own. There are other highly specialized uses of split-dollar insurance. One example is to provide relief for corporations subject to the personal holding company tax.

There are several variations to the basic split-dollar arrangement. One such variation is to establish a split-dollar agreement between your corporation and your life insurance trust. If carefully designed, that technique will provide the added advantage of excluding the insurance proceeds from your taxable estate, yet your corporation may retain access to all or a substantial portion of cash values. Such arrangements are frequently used; however, if you own more than 50% of the company stock, special steps must be taken to avoid taxes on the insurance proceeds.

9

Retirement Plans and IRAs

Taxation of Qualified Plans
Income Tax Deferral
Minimum Distribution Rules
The Income Tax/Estate Tax Dilemma
Estate Liquidity
Excise Tax
Terms of Plan
The Roth IRA
Planning Points
Minimum Distribution Tables

QUALIFIED RETIREMENT PLANS and Individual Retirement Accounts or IRAs (referred to collectively as "qualified plans") provide an excellent means of accumulating wealth. Most contributions to qualified plans are made with untaxed dollars and those dollars are permitted to grow and compound at pretax rates. Despite these apparent tax advantages, you need to be aware that after you have accumulated a substantial amount in one or more IRAs or other qualified plans, you will confront a number of difficult tax issues. Without careful planning, more than 80% of your IRA or other qualified plan can be lost to taxes.

Taxation of Qualified Plans

If you should die owning a substantial qualified plan, much of it could be lost to taxes. Upon your death, your qualified plan may be subjected to any or all of the following taxes:

Federal estate tax (up to 55%);

Federal generation-skipping tax (55%);

Federal income tax (currently up to approximately 40%); and

State income and inheritance taxes.

If you own a qualified plan at the time of your death, it will be included in your gross estate and will be subject to estate tax. Of course, the estate tax can be deferred if the qualified plan is properly payable to your surviving spouse or to a special marital deduction trust (chapter 2) for your spouse's benefit. In that event, the estate tax will be deferred until your spouse's death, at which time it will be included in his or her gross estate.

Withdrawals your beneficiary makes from your qualified plan after your death will also be subject to income tax. Therefore, if you die with a large qualified plan and your beneficiaries are required to withdraw from the plan, such withdrawals will be subjected to both estate tax and income tax. Although there is a partial offset against the income tax for the estate tax paid, in some cases the net aggregate tax can exceed 80% of the qualified plan assets.

Income Tax Deferral

Because more than 80% of plan assets can be lost to taxes, it is often important to formulate a plan to mitigate the effect of those taxes to the extent possible. The principal strategy involves attempting to defer the income tax for an extended period. If the income tax can be deferred for many years, then the net after-tax cash available for your family or other beneficiaries may be greatly increased.

Example: Assume you leave a $100,000 IRA to your grandson. Assume the bequest was not properly planned and the IRA dissolves at the time of your death. If your grandson invests the after-tax proceeds of the IRA at 8%, then at his retirement in 60 years he will have approximately $1.3 million, which may not be a substantial amount at that time. However, if the bequest of the IRA had been properly arranged so that your grandson could continue the IRA, he would have approximately $3.1 million at retirement, assuming the same rate of return. In this example, the added deferral produced a $1.8 million benefit on an original $100,000 of principal. When an IRA is left to your child, rather than your grandchild, the benefit will not be as dramatic, but may be very significant.

The above example illustrates the importance of permitting a continuation of the qualified plan for the benefit of your beneficiaries if possible. Here, the planning strategy focuses on preserving the benefits of tax-deferred compounding rather than on reducing estate tax.

Because of the great advantage of tax-deferred investing, during your lifetime you will want to avoid making withdrawals from your qualified plan for as long as possible if you have other resources sufficient for your needs. Similarly, you may want to provide your surviving spouse, children, or other beneficiaries the ability to defer distributions from your qualified plan so that they can maintain the benefit of tax-deferred growth for as long as possible.

There are several factors that can force your beneficiaries to prematurely terminate your qualified plan, causing a substantial current income tax liability and ending the tax-deferred compounding of your qualified plan. The two most common causes of premature termination are the "minimum distribution" rules of the Internal Revenue Code and insufficient estate liquidity, both of which are discussed below.

Estate planning should take into account those factors that could cause an early termination of your qualified plan to the detriment of your beneficiaries. Estate planning should also be concerned with the important qualified plan elections that must be made after you attain age 70, because they too will have an effect on your qualified plan's continued income tax deferral. Those elections are discussed below.

Minimum Distribution Rules

The minimum distribution rules are designed to prevent you or your heirs from maintaining the benefits of your qualified plan for too many years. The minimum distribution rules specify when regular annual distributions must begin and how quickly remaining qualified plan assets must be distributed. The IRS regulations on the subject run to more than 60 pages. Although the rules are highly complicated, it is important to have a basic understanding of the rules if you have one or more sizable IRAs or other qualified plans.

When you reach age 70 ½ you will need to make some important and irrevocable elections concerning your IRA or other qualified plan, and those elections also require an understanding of the minimum distribution rules. The actual deadline is April 1 of the year following the year in which you turn 70 ½. That April 1 date is known as your Required Beginning Date (RBD). In the case of some qualified plans (not IRAs) your RBD can be postponed if you are still employed. Prior to your RBD you will need to decide the manner in which your qualified plan assets will be withdrawn from the plan. You can elect to make withdrawals over your life expectancy or over a set number of years not to exceed your life expectancy. Alternatively, you can elect to make withdrawals over the joint life expectancy of you and the beneficiary of your qualified plan.

Choosing to withdraw your plan over a joint life expectancy, rather than over your single life expectancy, will result in a smaller required minimum distribution. A portion of the IRS actuarial tables used for this purpose is reproduced at the end of this chapter.

Q: I want to minimize my required annual distribution from my qualified plan. Should I elect a payout over a joint life expectancy based on myself and someone who has a very long life expectancy, such as my grandson?

A: Unfortunately, except where the beneficiary is your spouse, the IRS will not permit a joint-life computation where your beneficiary is more than ten years younger than you. If the grandson or other beneficiary is more than ten years younger, the calculation will be made assuming the beneficiary is only ten years younger.

Q: Can I name my husband as beneficiary of my IRA, but compute the payout using the combined life expectancy of my son and myself?

A: No. The person whose life expectancy you wish to combine with your own must be the actual beneficiary of record at the time the election is made on your RBD.

Q: I have two children whom I wish to name as beneficiaries of my IRA. Which of their life expectancies will be used?

A: The rules require the use of the life expectancy of the oldest beneficiary. However, the ten-year rule described above would also come into play. If you wish to name two beneficiaries of your IRA it is often preferable to split your IRA into two separate funds so that a different child can be named as beneficiary of each separate fund.

On or before your Required Beginning Date it will also be necessary to elect the method by which your life expectancy will be calculated each year. The choice in methods will affect lifetime payments to you and payments to your beneficiaries after your death. The election is irrevocable after your RBD. There are two choices:

> **Term certain**—Under this method, your life expectancy (or a joint life expectancy if you so choose) is determined only once. Each year thereafter that life expectancy is reduced by one year regardless of your actual life expectancy.
>
> **Recalculation**—If the recalculation method is elected, then your life expectancy (or the joint life expectancy) will be recalculated each year by reference to the official IRS life expectancy tables.

Example: Assume you are age 71 on your RBD and your husband, the beneficiary of your IRA, is age 68. According to the IRS mortality tables, your combined life expectancy is 21.2 years. Therefore, under the joint life method, 1/21.2 (or 4.7%) of your plan assets must be withdrawn the first year. If you elected term certain, the minimum required distribution would be 1/20.2 the second year, 1/19.2 the third year, and so on until the remaining balance is withdrawn in the twenty-second year. If you elected the recalculation method, it will be necessary to refer to the IRS mortality tables each year. In the second year your ages will be 72/69 and your joint life expectancy will be 20.3 years. Therefore, you will be required to withdraw 1/20.3 (or 4.9%). In the third year your ages will be 73/70 and the mortality tables specify a combined life expectancy of 19.4 years, requiring a withdrawal of 1/19.4 (or 5.2%). If you and your husband survive 22 years, and you have elected the term certain method, the remaining balance of the qualified plan must be distributed. Under the recalculation method, your combined actuarial life expectancy at ages 93/90 will be 6.5 years; therefore, in the twenty-second year you will be required to withdraw 1/6.5 (or 15.4%). Under the recalculation method, some small portion of your qualified plan may be retained in the plan throughout your lifetime.

The recalculation method will always produce an equal or smaller required minimum distribution than the term certain method during your lifetime. That is because each year that passes does not equate to a full year reduction in your life expectancy.

Example: The following table shows the percentages that must be withdrawn each year from your IRA under the recalculation method and the term-certain method, assuming you and your spouse are the same age.

Ages	Recalculation Method	Term Certain Method
71/71	5.1%	5.1%
72/72	5.3	5.3
73/73	5.5	5.6
74/74	5.8	6.0
75/75	6.1	6.3
80/80	7.8	9.3
85/85	10.4	17.2
90/90	14.1	100.0

The recalculation method will permit longer tax deferral because the minimum distribution percentages will be less; however, the recalculation method can be a disaster for your beneficiaries. That is because upon your death you will have a zero life expectancy and all plan assets may then be required to be distributed.

Example: Assume that you elected to withdraw your qualified plan over the joint life expectancy of you and your wife and that at your RBD you elected to recalculate. Assume that you are now age 75 and your wife is age 74. As shown on the table below, 5.9% of your qualified plan must be withdrawn this year. Next year, at ages 76 and 75, 6.2% must be withdrawn. However, assume that your wife dies before next year. Since you elected to recalculate, and she now has a zero life expectancy, it will be necessary to go to the single-life table. For a single life at age 76, 8.4% must be withdrawn, rather than the 6.2% that would be withdrawn if your wife were living.

Example: Assume the facts of the prior example, except that you pass away at age 76. Since you elected to recalculate, and since both you and your wife are deceased, your children or other secondary beneficiaries must now withdraw the entire qualified plan balance. Had you elected the term certain method, rather than the recalculation method, your children or other secondary beneficiaries could continue to withdraw at the rate that you would have used had you and your wife survived.

Q: I intend to name my daughter as the beneficiary of my IRA. Can she and I elect to annually recalculate our joint life expectancies?

A: If you designate someone other than your spouse as your beneficiary, you cannot elect the recalculation method for his or her life expectancy. (And as a reminder, for any beneficiary other than your spouse, your term certain calculation of joint life expectancy is based on the assumption that the beneficiary is no more than 10 years younger than you.)

The Income Tax/Estate Tax Dilemma

Depending on the total size of your estate and the relative values of your qualified plan and other assets, you may have to choose between minimizing estate taxes and deferring income taxes on the qualified plan.

Example: Assume it is 2006 or after and you and your wife have assets totalling $2.0 million, $1.0 million of which is in your IRA. In order to be assured that you will receive both $1.0 million exemptions, it will be necessary to transfer all assets other than your IRA to your wife so that she will have $1.0 million to fully fund her credit bypass trust (chapter 2). In order to provide the greatest flexibility and opportunity to defer income tax, you may wish to name your wife as the direct beneficiary of your IRA. But if you were the first deceased, your qualified plan in that case would pass directly to your wife and your $1.0 million exemption would be wasted. As an alternative, you may name your bypass trust as the beneficiary of your IRA. In that event, your $1.0 million exemption will be fully utilized. However, your wife will have less flexibility as to the deferral of tax on your IRA and may, in some circumstances, be required to distribute all IRA assets within a year after your death.

The above scenario illustrates the classic dilemma. There may be a trade-off between maximizing estate tax benefits and minimizing the impact of income taxes. The problem arises in those cases where the IRA is substantial and there are not sufficient other assets to fully fund both lifetime exemptions. A common solution to the above would be to name your wife as the primary beneficiary of your IRA and your trust as the contingent beneficiary. That will effectively postpone the decision until the time of your death. By then, the rules may have been amended to correct the problem or you may have withdrawn a substantial portion of your IRA so the problem is less severe. An alternative solution is to use a specially designed trust that will satisfy the estate tax rules without running afoul of the income tax rules. The minimum distribution rules authorize the use of a trust as a qualified beneficiary of a retirement plan as long as certain technical requirements are met.

Estate Liquidity

Even if the disposition of your qualified plan has been fully analyzed and structured in order to maximize tax deferral and the benefits of tax-deferred compounding, your plan still may fail if your estate does not have sufficient liquidity aside from the qualified plan. Upon your death, substantial estate taxes and other liabilities may be owed. If your beneficiaries must withdraw qualified plan assets in order to pay taxes and other liabilities, then substantial income taxes will be incurred in addition to the estate tax. The substantial income tax may require your beneficiaries to withdraw even more from your IRA, which will result in an even greater income tax liability. The worst cases are those in which the qualified plan is subject to estate tax at the time of your death and your plan assets must be withdrawn to pay that estate tax. In those cases, in excess of 80% of the qualified plan may be lost to taxes.

Where a qualified plan is a substantial portion of the total estate, it is generally critical to assure there will be adequate estate liquidity aside from the qualified plan. If there are not sufficient other liquid assets, it may be important to fund anticipated liquidity needs with life insurance. If you are married, a policy insuring your life only may be appropriate if a sufficient liquidity shortfall is expected on your death. A joint and survivor policy may be appropriate if the liquidity need is not expected to occur until the second death. In most cases, such policy or policies should be owned by a properly designed insurance trust (see chapter 2).

Excise Tax

In 1986 Congress added a 15% excise tax on large qualified plans. The 15% tax applied to that portion of your qualified plan which exceeded a threshold amount. The threshold amount depended on your age and the official IRS interest rate at the time of your death. Under those rules, the combination of the estate tax, income tax, and excise tax would sometimes result in a loss of more than 88% of the qualified plan. Fortunately for taxpayers and their advisors, the 1997 Tax Act repealed the excise tax on large qualified plans effective the first day of 1997.

Terms of Plan

If it is desirable to permit a long-term deferral of qualified plan withdrawals, then the terms of the plan must permit a long-term payout to the beneficiary. It may be important to review the terms of the particular qualified plan to assure sufficient flexibility. Assuming you have assured sufficient other liquidity in your estate so that your qualified plan will not be needed to pay estate taxes, and you have also assured that the qualified plan is structured so that the tax rules will not require a premature termination, it would be disappointing to find that the terms of your qualified plan itself require a short-term payout, which will destroy the tax deferral. Most IRAs provide great flexibility in this regard. However, many employer sponsored corporate plans are highly inflexible and your particular plan may not permit a long-term payout to your beneficiaries. The distribution provisions of your qualified plan or IRA should be reviewed to assure needed flexibility exists.

The Roth IRA

A new type of IRA became available on January 1, 1998. The Roth IRA differs from the traditional IRA in that contributions are never deductible. Qualifying withdrawals from a Roth IRA, however, are tax-free rather than merely tax-deferred as in the case of a traditional IRA. Withdrawals from a Roth IRA will qualify for tax-free treatment if you have participated in the Roth IRA for at least five years and you are at least 59 ½ years old. Before age 59 ½ the withdrawal will still qualify in certain circumstances: if you use the money to buy a first home ($10,000 limit), if you are disabled, or in the event of your death.

You may contribute up to $2,000 annually ($4,000 for a married couple filing jointly), subject to an income limitation. If you file a joint tax return you may contribute the full $4,000 if your adjusted gross income (AGI) is below $150,000; if your AGI is between $150,000 and $160,000, the maximum contribution is reduced, and if your AGI is above $160,000 no contribution is permitted. For a single taxpayer, the $2,000 maximum contribution begins to be phased out for adjusted gross income of $95,000 and is fully phased out for an AGI of over $110,000. The $4,000 and $2,000 limits are reduced to the extent that you also contribute to a regular IRA.

Investing the maximum amount in a Roth IRA each year for many years may result in a sizable benefit due to the tax-free treatment of asset appreciation within the Roth IRA. From an estate planning standpoint, however, funding a Roth IRA with a roll-over from a traditional IRA may provide a much greater benefit.

If your adjusted gross income is below $100,000 (whether you are single, or married and filing jointly), you are permitted to roll over some or all of the balance in your traditional IRAs. As a result, the Roth IRA may provide a significant opportunity to individuals who have large traditional IRA balances.

You must pay income tax on any amount that you move from a traditional IRA to a Roth IRA. If the roll-over to a Roth IRA occurs in 1998, the income tax owed may be spread over four years; however, the tax on roll-overs in 1999 and after must be paid entirely for the year of the roll-over.

Deciding whether to roll over a sizable IRA balance to a new Roth

IRA involves a complicated analysis. The obvious disadvantage of a roll-over is that the payment of a sizable income tax will be accelerated; however, the tax-free treatment of Roth IRA earnings and asset appreciation may offset the disadvantage of having accelerated the tax on the traditional IRA balance.

In deciding whether to roll over a portion or all of a traditional IRA, you should consider the following:

Anticipated earnings by the Roth IRA—If you invest the Roth IRA assets only in CDs or some other investment with limited earning potential, then it will take many years before the benefit of tax-free growth offsets the detriment of prepaying the tax on the traditional IRA. A sizable roll-over to a Roth IRA will be especially advantageous where the IRA assets will be invested in growth stocks, a closely held business, or some other investment that produces an unusually high return.

Whether the IRA bears the tax—If a sizable IRA is rolled over to a Roth IRA, a large income tax will be owed. The roll-over will be most advantageous if you use non-IRA assets to pay the tax. If you must withdraw from the IRA the cash needed to pay the tax, then only the after-tax amount will remain in the Roth IRA, and it will take several additional years of tax-free compounding to offset the detriment of having accelerated payment of the income tax on your traditional IRA. In most cases, the conversion of a traditional IRA to a Roth IRA will be advantageous only if you have other non-IRA assets with which to pay the tax.

Your relative tax brackets—If you do not expect to withdraw and spend the funds in your Roth IRA until your retirement years and if you will then be in a significantly lower tax bracket, the conversion to a Roth IRA may produce an unfavorable result. Regardless of how long the Roth IRA is held, the conversion of your traditional IRA may be disadvantageous if you are accelerating the payment of tax at a high bracket in exchange for avoiding tax upon withdrawal from your traditional IRA if that tax would have been in a low bracket.

Because several factors may be involved, there is no general rule as to whether the conversion of a traditional IRA to a Roth IRA will be advantageous. Each case must be individually analyzed. The following examples illustrate how the factors described above can significantly affect the outcome of a conversion to a Roth IRA.

Example: Assume you have a traditional IRA balance of $1.0 million. It will earn 15% annually over the next ten years. You are in the 40% tax bracket and will continue to be ten years from now and throughout your retirement. You pay the tax on the roll-over from other assets so that the entire $1.0 million goes into the Roth IRA. At a 15% annual growth rate, your Roth IRA will be $4,045,558 after ten years. And no tax is owed on that amount. If you had not converted, however, you would have retained the $400,000 of other assets used to pay the tax and at a 15% growth rate and a 40% tax bracket that asset would now have been worth $970,934 on an after-tax basis. Your net position as a result of the conversion is $3,074,624 (the Roth IRA balance of $4,045,558, less the $970,934 cost of the tax paid).

If you did not convert to the Roth IRA, then your traditional IRA of $1.0 million would also be worth $4,045,558 after ten years at 15% annual growth. If you withdrew that amount from the IRA you would pay income tax of $1,618,223 at the 40% rate. After paying that tax you would have $2,427,335 remaining. Comparing that to the net after-tax proceeds of the Roth IRA, $3,074,624, shows that the conversion to the Roth IRA results in an additional $647,289 on an after-tax basis.

Example: Assume you have a traditional IRA with a $1.0 million balance. It will earn 6% during the next ten years. You are now in the 40% income tax bracket, but will be in the 15% bracket ten years from now and during your retirement years. Assume that the income tax owed upon roll-over to the Roth IRA will be paid from the IRA and that only the net amount will be placed in the Roth IRA. After paying the income tax at 40%, $600,000 will remain to be invested in the Roth IRA. If that grows at 6% annually, your Roth IRA balance after ten years will be $1,074,509.

Had you not converted to the Roth IRA, the entire $1.0 million would have remained in your IRA and after ten years at a 6% growth it would have appreciated to $1,790,848. If that balance is then withdrawn from the traditional IRA and if you are then in the 15% income tax bracket, the total tax would be $268,627 and the net after-tax balance would be $1,522,221. In comparison to the $1,074,509 after-tax balance in the event of a conversion to a Roth IRA, the traditional IRA has produced an additional $447,712 on an after-tax basis.

Planning Points

If an IRA or other qualified plan constitutes a significant portion of your estate, it will be important to carefully consider its proper handling. The particular elections that are made and the manner in which the qualified plan is integrated into your overall estate plan may have a major impact on the after-tax value of the qualified plan to you and your family. Unfortunately, the rules are complex and may require difficult decisions. The following is a summary of some planning considerations:

- The greatest planning flexibility will be available where your qualified plan is payable directly to your surviving spouse. However, that may not be ideal if you do not have sufficient other assets to fully fund both of your lifetime exemptions.

- It also may not be appropriate in the case of a second marriage or other situation where you need to assure that your children or other beneficiaries will receive remaining assets after the death of your spouse. In that case it may be important to establish a trust to receive qualified plan assets for the benefit of your spouse and other beneficiaries.

- If your qualified plan is made payable to a trust, be sure the trust will not cause a premature termination of the qualified plan at the time of your death. For that purpose, it will generally be necessary to establish a special trust that satisfies the requirements of the minimum distribution rules.

- In general, it is better to have a qualified plan payable to a marital deduction trust rather than to a credit bypass trust (see chapter 2), if you have sufficient other assets to fully fund your credit bypass trust. Assets in the marital deduction trust will be taxed at your surviving spouse's death. By that time, a substantial portion of your qualified plan may have been withdrawn and the income tax already paid. Therefore, significantly less will be left on which to pay estate tax. Qualified plans are "wasting" assets because a substantial portion will be lost to income tax. Wasting assets which will likely decline in value should generally be used to fund the marital deduction trust. However, the possible loss of continued deferral must be carefully considered whenever a substantial qualified plan is made payable to any trust.

- In general, you should elect not to recalculate your life expectancy for purposes of computing annual minimum distributions. That will slightly shorten the deferral during your lifetime, but will help continue the deferral for your heirs.

- If you have charitable inclinations, your IRA or other qualified plan may be the ideal asset to leave to charity. If 80% of the qualified plan would have been lost to taxes, you will be able to make a charitable contribution for twenty cents on the dollar.

Q: My spouse recently passed away leaving a sizable IRA payable to me. I have decided to roll over that IRA to my own IRA. Can I add my spouse's IRA rollover to my existing IRA, or should a new IRA be established for that purpose?

A: A new IRA should be established to receive the rollover from your spouse's IRA. It is important to segregate an inherited IRA rollover from your own IRA accounts.

Q: My father recently passed away and I am the beneficiary of his sizable IRA. Should I roll over his IRA into a new IRA account established by me?

A: No. The spouse of a deceased IRA participant may roll over the IRA assets to a newly established IRA account. However, if a non-spouse beneficiary of an IRA or other qualified plan rolls the plan over to his or her own IRA, it will become immediately taxable. For a non-spouse beneficiary to maintain the tax-deferred status, the IRA must continue in the name of the deceased participant.

Q: I am the beneficiary of my deceased uncle's IRA. I understand that I must withdraw certain minimum amounts each year from his IRA. Will those be subject to the additional 10% excise tax since I am not yet 59 ½ years old?

A: The rule that imposes a 10% penalty on most withdrawals from a qualified plan before age 59 ½ does not apply to withdrawals from an inherited plan regardless of your age.

Q: My mother recently passed away and I was named as the beneficiary of her qualified retirement plan. I understand that I must withdraw minimum amounts annually from the plan. How quickly must such minimum distributions commence?

A: The first annual minimum distribution must be made on or before December 31 of the year following the death of the plan participant. If the entire required minimum distribution is not made by the deadline, the tax benefits of the qualified plan will terminate in five years, rather than the remaining payout period selected by your mother.

Q: I am now age 75. I was previously not aware of the minimum distribution rules and failed to take any distribution since turning age 70 ½. What penalty will the IRS impose?

A: The penalty is 50% of the amount that should have been withdrawn. Also, if you did not elect otherwise when you reached your RBD, you will not be able to take future distributions based on a joint life expectancy. Instead, future payments must be taken over your single life expectancy.

Q: My daughter was the beneficiary of my IRA on my Required Beginning Date and I elected to calculate my minimum annual distributions on a joint life expectancy basis. May I now change the beneficiary of my IRA?

A: You can change the beneficiary at any time; however, with one exception, tax benefits cannot be increased as a result of changing beneficiaries. The one exception is that if you change the beneficiary to your spouse, he or she will still be entitled to the significant tax advantages afforded spouses of qualified plan participants. Namely, your spouse will be able to roll over the remaining plan assets to a new IRA.

Q: My husband is named as beneficiary of my IRA. If I am the first deceased, when must he begin taking minimum annual distributions?

A: Your surviving husband will have several choices. (1) He may roll your IRA to his own newly established IRA and then begin to take minimum distributions in the year following the year that he turns 70 ½. (2) If you die before your Required Beginning Date, he can commence distributions the year following the year that you would have become 70 ½ had you lived, or he can commence distributions in the year following the year that he turns 70 ½. (3) If you die after your RBD your husband must continue on the distribution schedule you selected, unless he rolls your IRA over to a newly established IRA.

Q: May I name my estate as beneficiary of my qualified plan so that it will be distributed in accordance with the terms of my will?

A: Yes, you may name your estate as beneficiary. However, that will cause an immediate termination of the tax deferral at the time of your death and all income tax will be due on the entire value of the qualified plan.

Q: Next April 1 is my Required Beginning Date. My wife is the beneficiary of my IRA and I will elect to receive payments over our joint life expectancy. I understand that the recalculation method will permit a longer deferral during our lifetimes, but will disqualify our children from further deferral after our deaths. I also understand that the term certain method will permit our children continued tax deferral, but will require greater distributions during our lifetimes. Is there any other choice?

A: Some married couples utilize a hybrid approach. The plan participant elects to recalculate and the participant's spouse elects the term certain method. If the participant dies first, the surviving spouse can roll over to a new IRA and take a payout over his or her life expectancy. If the spouse is the first deceased, the participant will remain on the same distribution schedule (because the spouse did not elect to recalculate) and after both are deceased the children, if properly named as beneficiaries, will be entitled to defer over the remaining years of the payout plan selected by the participant. Since men have a shorter life expectancy, the hybrid approach makes particular sense where the qualified plan is owned by the husband who is the same age as the wife or older.

Q: If I die before reaching my RBD, for how long will my IRA beneficiary be permitted to continue the tax deferral?

A: The beneficiary may withdraw the IRA funds over his or her life expectancy. If the beneficiary is your spouse, he or she will also have the option of rolling the IRA balance over to a new IRA and electing distributions from it over his or her life expectancy.

Q: If my IRA is payable to a trust, will the beneficiaries of the trust be able to continue the deferral of my IRA?

A: If the trust is not a qualified trust, then a complete distribution of the IRA will be required within five years of your death if you die before your RBD, or at least as rapidly as you were making withdrawals if you had reached your RBD. In order to be a qualified trust, it must be irrevocable, the beneficiaries must be clearly identifiable, and a copy of the trust must have been delivered to the IRA custodian.

Q: May I make my IRA payable to my credit bypass trust?

A: That is permitted, but is generally not the best choice. Eventually, the IRA proceeds will be reduced by the amount of income tax owed when distributions are made. Therefore, the amount passing estate tax–free to ultimate beneficiaries may be unnecessarily reduced. However, you may not have a choice if you do not have sufficient other assets to fully fund your credit bypass trust.

Q: What if I have more than one retirement plan?

A: In general you must compute the required minimum distribution for each plan and withdraw that amount from the respective plan. A major exception, however, permits multiple IRAs to be aggregated so that the total required minimum distribution for all of your IRAs can be withdrawn from any one or more as you choose.

Minimum Distribution Tables

The following two tables show the percentage that must be withdrawn each year from your IRA or other qualified plan, depending on whether you elect to base withdrawals on single or joint life expectancy. Of course, nearly all IRAs and many corporate retirement plans permit larger distributions if you wish. Conversely if you fail to withdraw the required minimum amount in any given year, a penalty tax equal to 50% of the under-withdrawn amount will be imposed.

Single Life Expectancy

This table shows the percentage that must be distributed to you each year if you have elected to base the withdrawals on your individual life expectancy. It also illustrates that the recalculation method results in a smaller amount being withdrawn during your lifetime as compared to the term certain method.

Age	Recalculation	Term Certain
70	6.2%	6.2%
71	6.5	6.7
72	6.8	7.1
73	7.2	7.7
74	7.6	8.3
75	8.0	9.1
76	8.4	10.0
77	8.9	11.1
78	9.4	12.5
79	10.0	14.3
80	10.5	16.7
81	11.2	20.0
82	11.9	25.0
83	12.7	33.3
84	13.5	50.0
85	14.5	100.0
86	15.4	
87	16.4	
88	17.5	
89	18.9	
90	20.0	
91	21.3	
92	22.3	
93	24.4	
94	25.6	
95	27.0	

Joint Life Expectancy

The following is a portion of the IRS table showing the amount that must be distributed to you each year if the withdrawals are based on a joint life expectancy of you and another person combined. It is based on the recalculation method for both individuals. The term certain method would require a more rapid payout.

AGE	70	71	72	73	74	75	76	77	78	79	80	81	82
60	3.8	3.8	3.9	3.9	4.0	4.0	4.0	4.0	4.0	4.0	4.0	4.0	4.0
61	3.9	4.0	4.0	4.0	4.0	4.1	4.1	4.1	4.1	4.1	4.2	4.2	4.2
62	4.0	4.0	4.1	4.1	4.1	4.2	4.2	4.2	4.2	4.2	4.3	4.3	4.3
63	4.1	4.1	4.2	4.2	4.2	4.3	4.3	4.3	4.4	4.4	4.4	4.4	4.4
64	4.2	4.2	4.3	4.3	4.4	4.4	4.4	4.5	4.5	4.5	4.6	4.6	4.6
65	4.3	4.4	4.4	4.5	4.5	4.5	4.6	4.6	4.7	4.7	4.7	4.8	4.8
66	4.4	4.5	4.5	4.6	4.6	4.7	4.7	4.8	4.8	4.9	4.9	4.9	5.0
67	4.5	4.6	4.6	4.7	4.8	4.8	4.9	4.9	5.0	5.0	5.1	5.1	5.1
68	4.6	4.7	4.8	4.8	4.9	5.0	5.0	5.1	5.2	5.2	5.2	5.3	5.3
69	4.7	4.8	4.9	5.0	5.1	5.1	5.2	5.3	5.3	5.4	5.4	5.5	5.5
70	4.8	4.9	5.0	5.2	5.2	5.3	5.4	5.4	5.5	5.6	5.6	5.7	5.7
71	4.9	5.1	5.1	5.2	5.3	5.4	5.5	5.6	5.7	5.8	5.8	5.9	6.0
72	5.1	5.1	5.3	5.4	5.4	5.6	5.7	5.8	5.9	5.9	6.0	6.1	6.2
73	5.1	5.2	5.4	5.5	5.6	5.7	5.8	5.9	6.0	6.2	6.2	6.3	6.4
74	5.2	5.3	5.4	5.6	5.8	5.9	6.0	6.1	6.2	6.4	6.4	6.6	6.7
75	5.3	5.4	5.6	5.7	5.9	6.1	6.2	6.3	6.4	6.6	6.7	6.8	6.9
76	5.4	5.5	5.7	5.8	6.0	6.2	6.3	6.4	6.6	6.8	6.9	7.0	7.1
77	5.4	5.6	5.8	5.9	6.1	6.3	6.4	6.6	6.8	6.9	7.1	7.2	7.4
78	5.5	5.7	5.9	6.0	6.2	6.4	6.6	6.8	7.0	7.1	7.4	7.5	7.6
79	5.6	5.8	5.9	6.2	6.4	6.6	6.8	6.9	7.1	7.4	7.5	7.8	8.0
80	5.6	5.8	6.0	6.2	6.4	6.7	6.9	7.1	7.4	7.5	7.8	8.0	8.1
81	5.7	5.9	6.1	6.3	6.6	6.8	7.0	7.2	7.5	7.8	8.0	8.2	8.4
82	5.7	6.0	6.2	6.4	6.7	6.9	7.1	7.4	7.6	8.0	8.1	8.4	8.6
83	5.8	6.0	6.2	6.5	6.8	7.0	7.2	7.5	7.8	8.1	8.4	8.6	9.0
84	5.8	6.1	6.3	6.6	6.8	7.1	7.4	7.6	8.0	8.3	8.6	8.9	9.1
85	5.9	6.1	6.4	6.6	6.9	7.2	7.5	7.8	8.1	8.4	8.7	9.0	9.4
86	5.9	6.2	6.4	6.7	7.0	7.2	7.6	7.9	8.2	8.6	8.9	9.2	9.6
87	5.9	6.2	6.4	6.8	7.0	7.4	7.6	8.0	8.4	8.7	9.0	9.4	9.9
88	6.0	6.2	6.5	6.8	7.1	7.4	7.8	8.1	8.4	8.8	9.2	9.6	10.0
89	6.0	6.3	6.5	6.8	7.1	7.5	7.8	8.1	8.6	9.0	9.3	9.8	10.2
90	6.0	6.3	6.6	6.8	7.2	7.5	7.9	8.2	8.6	9.0	9.5	9.9	10.4

83	84	85	86	87	88	89	90	91	92	93	94	95
4.1	4.1	4.1	4.1	4.1	4.1	4.1	4.1	4.1	4.1	4.1	4.1	4.1
4.2	4.2	4.2	4.2	4.2	4.3	4.3	4.3	4.3	4.3	4.3	4.3	4.3
4.3	4.3	4.3	4.3	4.3	4.4	4.4	4.4	4.4	4.4	4.4	4.4	4.4
4.5	4.5	4.5	4.5	4.5	4.5	4.5	4.5	4.5	4.5	4.5	4.6	4.6
4.6	4.6	4.6	4.7	4.7	4.7	4.7	4.7	4.7	4.7	4.7	4.7	4.7
4.8	4.8	4.8	4.9	4.9	4.9	4.9	4.9	4.9	4.9	4.9	4.9	4.9
5.0	5.0	5.0	5.1	5.1	5.1	5.1	5.1	5.1	5.1	5.1	5.1	5.1
5.2	5.2	5.2	5.2	5.3	5.3	5.3	5.3	5.3	5.3	5.3	5.4	5.4
5.4	5.4	5.4	5.4	5.5	5.5	5.5	5.5	5.5	5.6	5.6	5.6	5.6
5.6	5.6	5.6	5.7	5.7	5.7	5.8	5.8	5.8	5.8	5.8	5.8	5.8
5.8	5.8	5.9	5.9	5.9	6.0	6.0	6.0	6.0	6.0	6.1	6.1	6.1
6.0	6.1	6.1	6.2	6.2	6.2	6.3	6.3	6.3	6.3	6.4	6.4	6.4
6.2	6.3	6.4	6.4	6.4	6.5	6.5	6.6	6.6	6.6	6.7	6.7	6.7
6.5	6.6	6.6	6.7	6.8	6.8	6.8	6.8	6.9	6.9	6.9	7.0	7.0
6.8	6.8	6.9	7.0	7.0	7.1	7.1	7.2	7.2	7.2	7.3	7.3	7.4
7.0	7.1	7.2	7.2	7.4	7.4	7.5	7.5	7.6	7.6	7.6	7.7	7.7
7.2	7.4	7.5	7.6	7.6	7.8	7.8	7.9	8.0	8.0	8.0	8.1	8.1
7.5	7.6	7.8	7.9	8.0	8.1	8.1	8.2	8.3	8.4	8.4	8.5	8.5
7.8	8.0	8.1	8.2	8.4	8.4	8.6	8.6	8.7	8.8	8.8	8.9	9.0
8.1	8.3	8.4	8.6	8.7	8.8	9.0	9.0	9.1	9.2	9.3	9.4	9.4
8.4	8.6	8.7	8.9	9.0	9.2	9.3	9.5	9.6	9.7	9.8	9.9	9.9
8.6	8.9	9.0	9.2	9.4	9.6	9.8	9.9	10.1	10.2	10.3	10.4	10.4
9.0	9.1	9.4	9.6	9.9	10.0	10.2	10.4	10.5	10.6	10.7	10.8	10.9
9.2	9.5	9.8	10.0	10.2	10.4	10.6	10.8	10.9	11.2	11.3	11.4	11.6
9.5	9.8	10.1	10.3	10.6	10.8	11.1	11.3	11.4	11.7	11.9	12.0	12.1
9.8	10.1	10.4	10.7	10.9	11.2	11.4	11.7	12.0	12.1	12.5	12.6	12.8
10.0	10.3	10.7	10.9	11.3	11.6	12.0	12.1	12.5	12.8	12.9	13.1	13.3
10.2	10.6	10.9	11.3	11.7	12.0	12.3	12.6	12.9	13.3	13.5	13.8	14.0
10.4	10.8	11.2	11.6	12.0	12.5	12.8	13.1	13.5	13.8	14.0	14.4	14.7
10.6	11.1	11.4	12.0	12.3	12.8	13.3	13.6	14.0	14.4	14.7	15.1	15.3
10.8	11.3	11.7	12.1	12.6	13.1	13.6	14.1	14.4	14.9	15.4	15.6	15.8

10

Premarital and
Postmarital Agreements

Surviving Spouse's Rights
Divorce
Enforceability
Other Concerns
Palimony Agreements

MARITAL AGREEMENTS ARE BECOMING increasingly popular as estate planning tools. Within certain limits, premarital and postmarital agreements permit you and your spouse to decide the terms of the legal arrangement that will apply to your marriage.

A premarital agreement simply refers to an agreement between two individuals before they become husband and wife. A postmarital agreement is a similar agreement executed during the marriage. Those agreements are occasionally referred to as prenuptial and postnuptial agreements.

Upon the death of one spouse, the surviving spouse is entitled to a certain portion of the deceased spouse's property (discussed under "Electing Against a Will" in chapter 1). Similarly, in the event of a divorce, a judge will determine the rights of the parties to alimony and/or marital property. Married couples who, for estate planning or other purposes, wish to clarify their particular arrangement may wish to enter into a premarital or postmarital agreement.

A marital agreement may specify the parties' rights in the event of a divorce. It may also specify the parties' respective rights in the event of the death of either party. Most marital agreements attempt to govern the parties' respective rights in the event of either divorce or death.

Surviving Spouse's Rights

Some of the rights to which a surviving spouse may be entitled under state law are as follows:

- **Elective share**—the right to receive a certain percentage of the deceased spouse's estate. (See "Electing Against a Will" in chapter 2.)
- The right to a family allowance.
- A right to a life estate in the homestead.
- **Dower**—generally a widow's rights to a certain percentage of her deceased husband's real estate.
- **Curtesy**—rights similar to dower, but granted to a husband.
- Under state or federal law a surviving spouse may be entitled to all or a portion of the deceased spouse's qualified retirement plan.

In some situations, the property rights afforded a surviving spouse under state law may not be appropriate. In that case the married couple may wish to establish their own rules which clarify their rights to the property of the first deceased.

Example: Assume that you are about to be married and that you and your fiancée each have children from a prior marriage. Each of you has an independent estate. You and your bride may each wish to assure that the property of the first deceased will pass entirely to his or her own children. In that case, it would be important to execute a premarital agreement whereby the surviving spouse waives his or her marital rights to those items listed above.

Divorce

In the event of a divorce, the judge will decide how the couple's property is to be divided. The judge will also decide whether one of the parties will pay temporary or permanent alimony to the other party. In deciding those issues, the judge will consider relevant facts such as the length of the marriage, each party's relative contribution to their current financial situation, the relative resources and needs of each of the parties, whether either party may be primarily responsible for the failure of the marriage or otherwise may be "at fault," and a number of other considerations. Because of the highly subjective nature of the decision making process, it is impossible to predict how a particular judge will divide property and award alimony in a particular situation. Individuals who wish to reach their own agreement concerning their rights to property or alimony in the event of a divorce may wish to implement a marriage agreement. Within certain limits, a marriage agreement will permit the parties to specify a property division and/or alimony arrangement that is agreeable to them and best suits their particular needs.

Enforceability

Until recently, marital agreements were considered to be against public policy and were generally not enforceable. Most states have now passed legislation legalizing marital agreements and requiring that they be enforced if certain conditions are satisfied. Nevertheless, there can be no absolute assurance that a given marital agreement will be fully enforced in the future by a judge who analyzes and interprets the agreement, possibly many years after it was executed.

Both parties to the agreement and their lawyers should have a common goal of creating a marital agreement that is likely to be respected. The rules concerning marital agreements vary greatly among the states. However, in general, marital agreements will not be enforceable unless the following conditions exist at the time of the execution of the agreement:

- Each party must be represented by independent legal counsel. This should not be a mere formality. Each party's legal counsel should be involved with the drafting process and with negotiating the terms of the agreement.

- Each party should fully disclose all relevant facts concerning his or her financial situation. Even in those situations where full financial disclosure is not technically required, such disclosure will add considerable strength to the agreement. Typically each party's net worth statement is attached to the marital agreement.
- The marital agreement must be entered into with a full understanding of the issues and each party's rights. To assure satisfaction of this requirement, each party should be represented by independent legal counsel. If one party does not wish to be represented, it is generally better to forego creating a marital agreement since it will likely not be enforceable.
- Where one party has considerably more income or wealth than the other party, the agreement must be written to make a fair and reasonable provision for the "weaker" spouse.

Example: Assume you have a net worth of $5.0 million and are about to be married. Assume your fiancee has no significant assets. An agreement could be written stating that in the event of a divorce your spouse will receive nothing. However, years in the future a judge might determine that provision to be unfair and not enforceable. Therefore, a better strategy might be to make some reasonable provision for your spouse in the event of a divorce. That will add considerable strength and reliability to the marriage agreement.

The length of the marriage is one factor to consider when deciding the fairness of a particular arrangement. Therefore, in many cases, a party's rights to property or income will be a function of the years of marriage. Formula clauses are often used to address that consideration. A formula might provide that if the marriage ends in divorce within the first five years, your spouse will receive total assets of $100,000, and an additional $50,000 for each year of marriage after the initial five years. A similar formula provision may be appropriate regarding inheritance in the event of your death, namely, that your spouse will inherit a certain dollar amount or percentage if you die after five years of marriage and that the amount or percentage will increase with additional years of marriage.

Other Concerns

Marital agreements are primarily concerned with the parties' rights to property or alimony in the event of divorce and to inheritance in the event of death. Other issues that may be considered and clarified in a marital agreement are as follows:

- How finances will be handled during the marriage.
- How property acquired during the marriage will be titled.
- How tax returns will be filed and joint tax refunds will be shared.
- The dollar amount or percentage of the couple's living expenses that will be contributed by each party.
- How existing debts and obligations of a party will be shared.

In some circumstances, a marital agreement may be the single most useful tool in accomplishing a married couple's estate plan goals. However, a marital agreement will be enforceable, and therefore useful, only if the facts of the particular case are fully analyzed and adequate time and attention is devoted to assuring that the various requirements and formalities of a valid agreement are satisfied, including the requirement that the agreement be fair and reasonable on an overall basis.

Palimony Agreements

Over the past several years a number of courts have awarded marital type rights to unmarried couples. The courts have concluded that the parties had an implied contract or implied partnership and have imposed property settlements similar to property settlements in the event of divorce.

Because of the trend in palimony cases, many unmarried couples also enter into agreements to establish their respective rights. Palimony agreements typically involve the same concerns as marital agreements.

11

Residency

State Income Taxes
State Inheritance Taxes
Other Issues
Determining Residency
Nonresident Aliens

FOR SOME INDIVIDUALS, the issue of residency is of great importance in formulating and carrying out an estate plan. Residency is important in the determination of taxes, in determining the validity of your will or trust, in interpreting your will or trust, and in determining the respective rights of your beneficiaries.

State Income Taxes

Many states impose a significant income tax, which is in addition to the federal income tax that we all pay.

In general, a state is permitted to tax the entire income of its residents whether such income is earned in or out of the state of residency. For nonresidents, a state is only permitted to tax salaries and other compensation earned in the state or income relating to real estate or a business located within the state. Therefore, being considered a resident of one state versus another may have a significant impact on your state income tax liability.

> **Example:** New York state imposes a significant income tax. Florida has no state income tax on individuals. Assume each year you spend approxi-

mately one-half of your time in New York and the remaining one-half in Florida. Assume your income for the year is as follows:

Salary for consulting work in New York	$ 10,000
Income from New York real estate	5,000
Interest and dividends	100,000
	$115,000

If you are a New York resident, you will pay state income tax on the entire $115,000. If you are a Florida resident, you will pay New York tax only on the $15,000 of New York income and the $100,000 of interest and dividends will not be subject to state income tax.

State Inheritance Taxes

Many states impose substantial inheritance taxes, which are in addition to the federal estate tax. In states that impose an inheritance tax, the rate generally ranges from a low of 5% to a high of 15%. Although those rates are not nearly as oppressive as the federal estate tax, they can still have a significant impact on the estate. Therefore, if you might possibly be considered a resident of either of two states, it may be important to take some action to establish residency in the more favorable state.

The state of your residence can impose its inheritance tax on all of your assets even if they are located in another state or country. However, a state in which you are not a resident can generally apply its inheritance tax only against real estate and some tangible property located within that state.

Example: Assume you own the following assets:

New York home	$ 500,000
Florida home	500,000
Stocks and bonds	2,000,000
	$3,000,000

If you are a resident of New York, that state will impose its inheritance tax on $2.5 million of your assets (all except the Florida home). If you are a resident of Florida (which, in effect, has no inheritance tax), New York will impose its inheritance tax only on your New York home. The other $2.5 million will escape New York inheritance tax.

Other Issues

In addition to the state income and inheritance taxes, your state of residency may also affect a number of other factors concerning your estate. The validity and interpretation of your will or trust will be determined under state law. The rights of your creditors, beneficiaries, and heirs at law also will be primarily determined by state law. There may also be a significant difference in probate costs and timing depending on your state of residency. In addition, a great number of other factors, which may be important in a particular case, are determined by the laws of your state of residency.

Determining Residency

Some people cannot easily or with certainty determine their residency. They may split their residence between two or more states. They may be in the course of moving, but have not made a decisive move from one state to another. A semiretired business person may be spending more and more time in Florida. An elderly parent may reside for brief periods with each of several children in different states.

The relative amount of time spent in each of two states is a factor in determining residency. It may or may not be an important factor, depending on the circumstances of a particular case. The courts and the tax authorities consider all relevant factors, and the amount of time spent in each state is merely one factor to consider.

Example: Assume each year you spend approximately six months in California and approximately six months in Colorado. In your particular case, the amount of time spent in each state is of no significance in determining your residency. Rather, your state of residency will be determined strictly by the other relevant factors.

Example: Assume you spend ten months each year in California and the remaining two months in Colorado. Here, the amount of time in each state is of great significance and is probably the controlling factor. If you continue to spend ten months annually in California it will be very difficult to establish residency in any other state.

If you spend eight or more months each year in a particular state, it is not likely that you will be able to establish residency in any other state. However, in those cases where your time is split between two states, approximately equally or even seven months/five months, you may be able to take steps that will permit you to select your state of residency.

If, for any reason, there is doubt as to your residency, you should discuss the matter with a lawyer who is experienced with residency issues. If you have a significant connection to two states, you will want to identify the most advantageous state and formulate a plan to establish your legal residence accordingly.

Following are some of the steps you can take to help establish residency within a particular state.

- Be sure that your Last Will and Testament states your intended residency.
- Spend as much time as possible in the state of intended residency.
- If possible, avoid owning a home in a state other than the state of intended residency. If you maintain a residence outside of the intended state of residency, it would be preferable to rent or lease rather than own such residence.
- Receive all mail at the place of residency, with forwarding out of state for temporary periods, if necessary.
- Keep personal papers, books of account, family documents, and other important records at the place of residency.
- Keep certificates for stocks, bonds, notes, and other evidence of ownership of intangible personal property in the intended state of residency.
- Maintain bank accounts and savings accounts at the place of residency only. Particularly avoid having accounts in a state that might be mistaken as your state of residency.
- Maintain a safe deposit box only in the intended state of residency.
- Execute a Declaration of Domicile or Certificate of Residency from the intended state of residency.
- Register to vote in the state of residency only. Be sure to cancel registration in the prior state of residency.

- Make sure all your credit cards, stationery, and other papers reflect your address in the state of intended residency.
- Obtain a driver's license in the intended state of residency.
- Have automobiles titled and licensed in the state of residency.
- Notify insurance companies of your address in the intended state of residency.
- Pay personal property taxes at the place of residency, and no other, if possible.
- Pay income and other taxes on basis of residence within the intended state of residency.
- List the state of residence as the residence on federal income tax returns.
- Notify the Social Security Administration of your address in the state of intended residency. For direct deposit of social security checks, use a bank in the state of intended residency.
- Change all of your lodge, religious, and fraternal memberships to the branches located in your true legal residency.
- If the residency is to be changed from one state to another, tell as many people as possible of that intention at the time of moving, as such statements are admissible in evidence.

Q: May I be a resident of more than one state?

A: You can be a resident of only one state at a time. However, that is not to say that two states will not both argue that you are a resident of their particular state for tax purposes.

Nonresident Aliens

The foregoing discusses the importance of your state of residence. If you are not a citizen of the United States, then whether you are a resident of the United States will determine which of your assets will be subject to U.S. estate tax and what portion of your annual income will be subject to U.S. income tax.

The U.S. estate and gift tax rules for nonresident aliens are discussed in chapter 14.

12

Health Care Documents

Living Will
Durable Power of Attorney for Health Care
Do Not Resuscitate Order

OVER THE LAST SEVERAL YEARS legislation has been enacted in every state acknowledging the right of individuals to make decisions regarding their own health and medical treatment, including the right to refuse medical treatment. Most states have created a mechanism that allows you to express your wishes concerning health care and also to appoint another individual to make health care decisions for you in the event of your incapacity. Because of the new legislation, you are now better able to plan for your incapacity by legally documenting your wishes and by naming another person to make decisions and to help assure that your wishes are carried out.

Living Will

A living will is a document setting forth your desires concerning the provision or withholding of health care. Living wills are also referred to as advance declarations, individual instructions, advance directives, and other similar terms.

The most common issue addressed in living wills is the withholding of life-prolonging procedures. In most states you may authorize the withholding of life-prolonging procedures if you suffer from a terminal condition and your death is imminent, or if you are in a permanent vegetative state and your physician and one other physician have determined there can be no recovery. You can direct that, if either of those conditions exists, life-prolonging procedures be withheld if they would serve only to artificially prolong the process of dying. Some states apply slightly different standards or criteria. Some states also require a greater degree of medical certainty. For example, in some states, if you have entered an irreversible permanent vegetative state, your attending physician and two other physicians must document that there can be no chance of recovery.

The requirements for a validly executed living will vary from state to state. Some states require notarization, some require two or more witnesses, and some require witnesses and notarization. It would be important to be sure that you follow the formalities required by your particular state.

Many states have a suggested form for a living will, but most states also permit individualized declarations. A customized or personalized living will may be appropriate in some circumstances; however, in general, the more standard the living will you execute, the more likely that it will be respected and followed without unnecessary delay.

There has been considerable litigation concerning the definition of medical treatment. Some courts held that the administering of food and water does not constitute medical treatment. Therefore, those courts concluded that the laws that permit you to authorize the withholding of medical treatment do not permit the withholding of nutrition and hydration (because they are not a medical treatment). Cases resulted of brain-dead individuals who lingered for months or years because the administering of food and water could not be terminated. That problem has been corrected by some states at this time. However, in some states it is important to specify whether the administration of nutrition and hydration, such as by intravenous tube feedings, naso-gastric tube feedings, or feedings administered through a tube that enters the stomach wall, should also be withheld if either of the above two conditions exists.

It is important to assure that a copy of your living will is included in your physician's medical records. It is also important to give additional copies to family members or close friends who might be concerned with your care.

Although not required, it may be helpful to initial and date your living will periodically to show that the directions contained therein continue to represent your wishes.

A living will may be canceled at any time. However, it is your responsibility to assure that all copies in the possession of physicians, hospitals, or others are destroyed.

Durable Power of Attorney for Health Care

In addition to living wills, most states now permit you to name another individual to make health care decisions for you in the event that you are incapacitated or otherwise unable to make such decisions for yourself. A living will usually applies only to life-prolonging procedures. The durable power of attorney for health care is much broader than a living will and may apply to any medical situation, whether or not you are in a permanent vegetative state or terminal condition. A power of attorney for health care may also be referred to as a designation of health care surrogate.

The person you have designated as your attorney-in-fact or your surrogate may make decisions concerning your health care consistent with the authority you have granted. Most health care powers of attorney grant to your surrogate the authority to make a great many health care decisions. Some of the more common decisions that are often covered in a health care power of attorney are as follows:

- To employ physicians;
- To consent to or refuse particular treatments;
- To decide whether you will be treated in a hospital, nursing home, hospice, or in your own home; and
- To make anatomical gifts.

As in the case of a living will, copies of the durable power of attorney for health care should be given to your physicians and your family members or friends who may be involved with your medical treatment.

Q: If I spend considerable time in more than one state, should I execute living wills and powers of attorney for health care in each state?

A: Many states have rules which honor out-of-state health care documents. However, it would be much preferable to sign documents in the customary form of each state. It is more likely that physicians and others involved with your health care will honor your health care document if it is presented in a form familiar in that state.

Q: May I specify an alternate health care surrogate to serve in the event that my primary health care surrogate is unavailable or unable to serve?

A: You may designate one or more successor surrogates to serve in the event of the unavailability of your primary surrogate. It is sometimes preferable to sign two separate designations of health care surrogate, each naming a different surrogate, rather than naming both in a single document.

Q: Who will make decisions for me if I do not have a durable power of attorney for health care?

A: Many states have enacted statutes permitting some medical decisions to be made by family members in order of kinship. Where there are no such statutes, many doctors and hospitals permit close family members to make important medical decisions. However, in the absence of a valid power of attorney for health care, decisions may be made contrary to your wishes or by someone other than the person you wish to make such decisions. At the minimum, the absence of a power of attorney for health care will likely cause additional confusion and delay.

Do Not Resuscitate Order

A Do Not Resuscitate Order (DNRO) is a medical order signed by a physician indicating that a patient in cardiac or respiratory arrest is not to be resuscitated. It states what limited medical care should be provided.

Emergency medical service (EMS) personnel are generally not permitted to honor a living will. However, pre-hospital DNROs are authorized in many states and EMS personnel are generally required to honor them. Therefore, in some cases it may be important to obtain from your physician a pre-hospital DNRO so that your wishes concerning medical treatment will be followed by EMS personnel.

13

Income Shifting

Basic Techniques
Kiddie Tax
Shifting Income with Trusts

IT IS SOMETIMES desirable to shift income between family members. The shifting of income may be advantageous for two reasons.

First, the shifting of income from a higher tax bracket to a lower tax bracket may result in less total tax being paid by the family unit.

> **Example:** You are in the 40% income tax bracket and your son has little or no income. Because your son will be in the 15% bracket (under current rules), if you could transfer $20,000 of income to him, the total income tax liability for the year would be reduced by approximately $5,000 ($20,000 x 25%).

A second advantage to the shifting of income is the avoidance of gift tax or estate tax. If you retain property in your estate, then all of the future interest, dividends, or other income earned from that asset will be subject to gift tax or estate tax at the time it is transferred to your beneficiary. On the other hand, if you transfer an asset to your beneficiary now, then all future income and appreciation will occur in your beneficiary's estate free of transfer tax.

> **Example:** Assume you make regular annual $10,000 gifts to your daughter. Assume you wish to increase your annual gifting program. Unfortunately, gifts to your daughter each year in excess of the $10,000 limit will reduce your lifetime exemption. Once the exemption is fully depleted, future gifts

in excess of $10,000 annually will result in a current gift tax liability. However, if income which you would otherwise receive could be shifted to your daughter, then a tax-free transfer of wealth from you to her would occur.

Basic Techniques

Several methods have been devised to shift income to other family members. The following are some of those techniques.

Outright gifts—In some cases it may be appropriate to simply transfer substantial assets to your child or other beneficiary. Future interest or dividends earned on the transferred asset will be taxed to the child (see "Kiddie Tax," below) and all interest or dividends earned in future years will not be included in your estate at the time of your death. A disadvantage of an outright gift is that the transferred asset will be controlled by your child or other beneficiary and might be subject to loss in the event of the beneficiary's divorce or serious creditor problem.

Uniform Transfers to Minors Act (UTMA)—You are permitted to deposit cash, securities, or other assets in an account designated as a custodian account for a minor. Nearly any asset may be owned by a custodian for the benefit of the minor. Income earned on an asset transferred to an UTMA account will generally be taxed to the minor (that is, subject to the Kiddie Tax). The advantage of an UTMA account is that it is inexpensive to establish. The primary disadvantage is that the child must receive all of the transferred assets by age 18 or age 21, depending on the state and the particular circumstances. Also, if you make a gift to an UTMA account and you also serve as the custodian, then the transferred asset will be included in your estate for estate tax purposes.

Gifts in trust—Most families are much better served by a properly designed trust to receive and hold assets for the benefit of a child or other beneficiary. Trusts have virtually unlimited flexibility and may be easily tailored to the particular needs of your family situation. As in the case of an UTMA account, however, assets transferred by you to a trust over which you are the trustee will likely be included in your estate at the time of your death.

Family partnerships—The income of a partnership is generally allocated among its partners and is currently taxable to them. Therefore, gifts of partnership interests to your children or other beneficiaries will cause their pro rata share of the partnership's earnings to be taxed to them in future years. Again, it is often advisable to transfer the partnership interests to irrevocable trusts established for the children or other beneficiaries, rather than making an outright gift of the partnership interests directly to them.

S corporations—Similar to a partnership, income earned by an S corporation is allocated among its shareholders and is taxable on their individual tax returns. Therefore, if S corporation stock is gifted to children or to trusts established for their benefit, their pro rata share of the S corporation's annual income will be shifted to the children or the trusts. If S corporation stock is to be transferred to a trust, special care must be taken to assure that the trust will qualify as an S corporation shareholder (see chapter 2). In those cases where the older generation wishes to retain control of the corporation, a special class of nonvoting stock can be created and gifted to the younger generation family members.

Employment agreements—One of the best income shifting techniques, where appropriate, is to hire your child to work in the family business. Depending on the child's age and experience, he or she might be hired in a bookkeeping, custodial, clerical, or other appropriate capacity. In general, the wages paid to the child will be deductible by the business and will be income taxable to the child as long as the compensation is reasonable in light of the services rendered.

Gift-Leaseback—In the typical case, assets such as equipment or real estate used in the parents' business are transferred to an irrevocable trust established for the benefit of the child. The trust then leases that equipment or real estate to the parents' business. The lease payments are deductible by the parents' business and are taxable to the trust or the child. A gift-leaseback transaction will not succeed in shifting income unless a number of formalities are followed. As a minimum, a written, legally valid lease and other appropriate documentation must be in place. The lease must provide for reasonable rent and other arm's length terms.

Other transfer techniques—There are numerous additional ways in which assets, and the future income to be earned by them, may be transferred to other family members. See chapter 17, "Advanced Planning Techniques."

Kiddie Tax

In 1986, Congress severely limited the ability to shift passive income to children under age 14. In general, all unearned income (interest, dividends, rents, etc.) received by a child under age 14 will be taxed at the parents' income tax rate, except for a small annual exemption.

The Kiddie Tax provisions do not apply to compensation paid to your child for his or her services. Therefore, the hiring of your child by your business to perform personal services for the business may result in an income shift to the extent that the compensation paid to the child is reasonable for the services rendered by him or her.

The Kiddie Tax can be reduced or eliminated by investing the child's assets in a form that produces little or no current taxable income. For example, your child or your child's trust could invest in tax-exempt bonds, growth stocks, vacant land expected to appreciate, or series EE government bonds that will mature after the child reaches age 14. If no taxable income is received until after age 14, the Kiddie Tax will have been avoided.

Shifting Income with Trusts

In many cases, it will be important to add language to various trust agreements that will facilitate the shifting of income among family members.

Example: Assume you establish a credit bypass trust for the benefit of your spouse (chapter 2). Assume the trust requires that all income will be distributed to your spouse currently. Since all income must be distributed to your spouse, your spouse will be taxable on all of the trust's income each year regardless of whether he or she needs the income or wishes to withdraw the income. In some cases, it may be better to permit the trust to retain income if desired. To the extent the income is retained and not distributed to your spouse it will then be taxable to the trust. An even better idea might be to permit the trustee to distribute income to your spouse or children or to retain the income. In that case, income distributed to your spouse will be taxable to your spouse, income distributed to a child will be taxable to the child (subject to the Kiddie Tax) and income retained by the trust will be taxed to the trust. That arrangement will provide great flexibility so that income may be shifted in a manner that will result in the least total tax liability for the family.

Example: Assume you establish a life insurance trust for the primary benefit of your spouse. Assume it requires that all income will be distributed to your spouse currently. As in the case of the credit bypass trust, all income will be taxable to your spouse. It might be more advantageous if the life insurance trust is permitted to distribute income to your spouse or children, or to retain the income. Then, as in the case of the credit bypass trust, income may be shifted as appropriate.

14

Nonresident Aliens

Gift Tax
Estate Tax
Residency
Treaties

NONCITIZENS RESIDING IN the United States are generally subject to the U.S. estate and gift taxes in the same manner as a U.S. citizen. However, non-U.S. citizens who are not considered residents of the United States are subject to a considerably different transfer tax scheme.

Gift Tax

Nonresident Aliens (NRAs) are generally taxable only on gifts made of real estate and some tangible personal property located in the United States. NRAs are generally not subject to gift tax on the gift of intangible property, such as stocks or bonds, wherever they might be located. A common strategy in connection with transfers of U.S. real estate is to convert your holding of the real estate into the holding of stock.

> **Example:** You are a citizen and resident of France and you wish to transfer your $500,000 U.S. vacation home to your daughter. If you simply convey the property to your daughter, or to a trust established for her benefit, you will have made a $500,000 gift and the gift tax due will be approximately $152,000. As an alternative, you may wish to transfer the U.S. home to a corporation and then make a gift of the corporate stock to your daughter. Since the stock is an intangible asset, no gift tax will be incurred.

Although nonresident aliens are entitled to the $10,000 annual exclusion, they are not permitted the lifetime exemption ($625,000 for 1998 and increasing to $1.0 million after 2005). Rather, any taxable gift in excess of $10,000 to a single donee in a given year will result in a current gift tax liability.

Regardless of whether you are a U.S. citizen or a U.S. resident, if your spouse is a U.S. citizen there is an unlimited marital deduction so that you may transfer any amount of property to your spouse free of gift tax (see chapter 7). However, if your spouse is not a U.S. citizen, the marital deduction for gift tax purposes is limited to $100,000 per year.

Estate Tax

NRAs are subject to estate tax on the value of all property located in the United States. Several arbitrary rules mandate whether an asset will be considered located in the United States or outside.

> Stocks of corporations formed in the United States are considered located in the United States regardless of where the actual stock certificates are maintained and regardless of where the assets of the corporation are located.
>
> Similarly, corporations formed in foreign countries are deemed to be located outside of the United States regardless of the location of the stock certificates or the assets of the corporation.
>
> A similar rule applies for bonds, notes, and other debt instruments. If the obligor is located in the United States then the debt instrument is a U.S. situs asset. If the obligor is located outside of theUnited States, the debt instrument is a foreign situs asset.
>
> U.S. real estate and some tangible personal property are considered to have a U.S. situs.
>
> A rule designed to encourage deposits in U.S. banks states that most U.S. bank accounts are considered foreign situs.
>
> The proceeds of a policy insuring the life of an NRA are foreign situs assets.

The usual graduated estate tax rates apply to NRAs. However, instead of the $625,000 exemption (increasing to $1.0 million after 2005), NRAs receive only a $60,000 exemption.

A common strategy employed by NRAs to transfer U.S. situs property free of estate tax is to convert the U.S. situs property into a foreign situs asset.

> **Example:** As in the example above, you are a citizen and resident of France with a $500,000 vacation home in the United States. If you were to die while directly owning the real estate, the tax would be approximately $142,800. However, if you were to transfer the U.S. real estate to a corporation created under the laws of a foreign country, then when you died you would not directly own a U.S. situs asset and the $500,000 home would pass to your named beneficiaries free of U.S. estate tax.

Many NRAs have strong U.S. connections, but still wish to avoid the U.S. estate tax. The basic strategies are as follows:

> Avoid owning U.S. situs property such as U.S. real estate and the stock of U.S. corporations and U.S. debt instruments.
>
> If U.S. situs assets must be owned, then convert them to foreign situs assets by transferring them to a foreign corporation.
>
> Heavily mortgage U.S. situs property since only the equity will be taxed.

NRAs are entitled to the marital deduction (see chapter 7), so no tax will be owed on property left to the NRA's spouse until the spouse's death. It is important to note, however, that if your spouse is not a U.S. citizen (whether or not a resident of the United States), property left to your spouse will not qualify for the marital deduction unless the property is left for the benefit of your spouse in a special trust known as a Qualified Domestic Trust (QDT). Congress was concerned that if property left to a non-U.S. citizen qualified for the marital deduction and, therefore, was not taxed at the first death, it might not ever be taxed if the noncitizen surviving spouse was not a resident of the United States at the time of his or her death. The requirement of a QDT was enacted to solve that problem.

A QDT must have one or more U.S. trustees who will be under the jurisdiction of the IRS and, therefore, more likely to assure that the required estate taxes are remitted to the IRS upon the death of the surviving spouse. The QDT rules also require the trustee to withhold estate tax each time principal is distributed to the surviving spouse. A valid QDT must include a number of special provisions as required by IRS regulations.

Residency

The rules for determining whether a non-U.S. citizen is a resident of the United States are similar to the rules described in chapter 11 for determining state residency for purposes of state inheritance and income taxes. All relevant facts and circumstances are considered and an attempt is made to determine your true residency. As explained in chapter 11, the relative number of days each year spent in and out of the jurisdiction may be the most important factor in some cases, but it is by no means the only factor.

Treaties

The U.S. has estate and/or gift tax treaties with the following countries:

Australia	Ireland
Austria	Italy
Canada	Netherlands
Denmark	Norway
Finland	South Africa
France	Sweden
Germany	Switzerland
Greece	United Kingdom

Those treaties are primarily designed to avoid the imposition of double taxation where a citizen or resident of one country transfers property (by gift or bequest) that is located in the other country. The usual tax results of a particular transaction may be significantly changed if one of the treaties is applicable.

Q: Nonresident aliens pay U.S. estate tax only on U.S. situs property. Therefore, can I avoid the U.S. estate tax by renouncing my U.S. citizenship, relocating to a foreign country, and avoiding U.S. situs investments?

A: A special rule will apply the U.S. estate tax to your entire worldwide estate if you die within ten years of your expatriation.

15

Creditor Protection Planning

Exemption Planning
Lifetime Gifts
Family Limited Partnerships
Foreign Situs Trusts
Fraudulent Conveyances

ONE BRANCH OF the estate planning field involves attempting to protect assets from the reach of an actual or possible creditor. That area is known as creditor protection planning or asset protection planning.

Those professional or business persons who are exposed to a significant risk of lawsuits often have a need to arrange their financial affairs to best protect their assets from the reach of a potential lawsuit creditor. Physicians who practice in the high-risk specialties, real estate developers, lawyers practicing in high-risk specialties, architects, and accountants who certify financial statements are just some of the individuals who have a real need to better protect their assets.

There are several different techniques that may provide protection from creditors. Asset protection planning basically involves reviewing a list of your assets to determine which are protected under state or federal law and devising ways to afford protection to those assets that are currently exposed.

Exemption Planning

The law of most states provides that certain assets may not be attached by creditors. Many states are pro-creditor and tend to have only very limited exemptions from attachment. Florida is one of the most pro-debtor states. In Florida the following are generally protected from the reach of creditors:

Homestead—The Florida Constitution prohibits the attachment of your principal residence if you are a resident of Florida. There is no dollar limitation. A home of any value may be protected from attachment. The protection is granted only to your principal residence. Also, for homes located in an incorporated municipality, only one-half acre is protected. As a practical matter, homes located on a larger lot are often fully protected because zoning laws usually prohibit the partitioning of a lot.

Insurance—In Florida the cash value of insurance policies owned by a Florida resident, insuring his or her life, are exempt from attachment by the owner's creditors.

Annuities—The cash value of annuities and the monthly or other periodic payments received by a Florida annuitant are generally exempt from attachment by creditors.

Retirement Plans and IRAs—The law concerning retirement plans and IRAs has gone through great change in the last few years. A U.S. Supreme Court milestone case in 1986 held that retirement plans, but not IRAs, were reachable by the creditors of a plan beneficiary, but the Supreme Court reversed itself in 1990. Now, most pension plans, profit sharing plans, Keogh plans, IRAs, and other similar plans are exempt from the reach of creditors. Although the rules are now clear that most retirement plans are exempt, a creditor may still penetrate the protection and attach retirement plan assets in some unusual situations.

Example: You have a small business or professional practice that adopted a qualified retirement plan several years ago. The last year or two you have not properly maintained your plan so that for purposes of the Internal Revenue Service, it is not currently a qualified retirement plan. It is possible in that circumstance that your creditor can penetrate the plan and attach your interest in the plan, since the protection afforded retirement plans and IRAs is generally limited to those plans that are properly qualified.

Tenancy by the Entirety—Tenancy by the entirety is a form of joint ownership between a husband and wife (see chapter 6). If an asset is owned as tenants by the entirety, then the husband's interest in the asset is not reachable by his individual creditor. Similarly, the wife's individual creditors are not permitted to attach her interest in the property. However, a joint creditor who has a judgment against the husband and the wife is permitted to attach tenancy by the entirety property. The protection afforded tenancy by the entirety ownership may not apply in all situations.

Many states do not recognize tenancy by the entirety and, therefore, do not afford the protection. Some states limit tenancy by the entirety ownership to real estate only. In some states such as Florida, however, nearly any asset may be owned by a husband and wife as tenants by the entirety.

Miscellaneous Exemptions—In addition to the exemptions listed above that may be helpful in a great many circumstances, many states also afford a number of other exemptions that may be useful in a particular situation. Some of those special exemptions are:
- Disability income benefits;
- Federal and state pensions;
- Personal property up to $1,000;
- Unemployment compensation;
- Veterans' benefits; and
- Workers' compensation benefits.

Exemption planning to protect assets is highly technical. Most of the exemptions apply only if very specific conditions are satisfied. A slight change in the fact pattern of a particular case may result in the loss of a particular exemption.

Lifetime Gifts

Transferring assets into the name of a family member or friend is a common, though often unsuccessful, planning strategy.

Example: You have accumulated $3.0 million of assets consisting of your home, marketable securities, an interest in a closely held business, and a piece of commercial property. You now wish to transfer an asset worth $300,000 to an irrevocable trust you have established for the benefit of your children. If the transfer is legitimate, is properly documented, is complete, and if you have retained no control over, or interest in, the gifted asset, then that asset is likely not reachable by your creditors. Assuming the transfer was not motivated by a desire to avoid a particular known creditor then it will likely succeed in the event that a creditor problem should arise. It will likely succeed because the value of the gift to the trust, as a percentage of your entire estate, is reasonable. The transfer also makes sense for legitimate non–creditor protection purposes. The transfer would generally be sensible from a strictly estate tax planning prospective.

Example: You have accumulated the same $3.0 million of assets described above. Here, assume you have transferred 100% of those assets to your spouse and now hold no asset individually in your name. That strategy will likely fail to protect the assets from the reach of a creditor. In most cases, the creditor will have little difficulty in establishing that your spouse actually holds the assets for your future benefit. The creditor will likely convince the judge or jury that there is an unwritten agreement between you and your spouse that, after the creditor problem is resolved, the transferred assets will be transferred back to you or made available for your use. It simply is not believable that you would impoverish yourself by transferring 100% of your assets to your spouse without an understanding that the assets will still be available for your future needs. Therefore, those assets will be reachable by your creditor.

Transferring substantially all assets to your spouse, child, or other family member or friend is one of the most commonly attempted strategies, and it is the strategy which most often fails. It fails because the transfer of 100% of your assets generally would have no legitimate business or tax planning motive other than an attempt to evade creditors. In contrast, the transfer of a reasonable portion of your estate to a family member or to a trust, if it achieves some legitimate tax planning, estate planning, or business planning objective, will likely be respected by the courts and will succeed in protecting the transferred asset.

Making lifetime gifts or transfers to family members or to trusts for their benefit may be a highly effective method of protecting the transferred assets as long as it is used in moderation and as one of several components to an overall asset protection strategy. However, when lifetime transfers are used as a simplistic method to protect your entire net worth, they will generally fail to provide any significant degree of protection.

Family Limited Partnerships

Family limited partnerships are used primarily as a method of efficiently transferring wealth out of your estate while maintaining control over the transferred assets (see chapter 17). In recent years family limited partnerships have also been used increasingly as an asset protection vehicle.

There is a variety of limited partnership structures that can be used. In most cases, however, you will transfer significant assets to a limited partnership in exchange for a limited partnership interest. The general partnership interest often is held by a trusted family member or friend.

Under the Uniform Limited Partnership Act, which has been adopted by all states, a creditor who attaches your limited partnership interest does not, himself, become a substitute limited partner. Rather, his only recourse is to hold your limited partnership interest and wait to receive any distributions that may be made to the limited partners. In most cases, it is only the general partner who can direct that distributions be made to limited partners. If your family member or friend who is the general partner decides not to distribute cash or property to the limited partners, then the creditor holding your partnership interest will receive nothing.

As time passes and your creditor continues to be unable to collect, he should become more motivated to settle his claim against you. Of course, during this "Mexican standoff" you will not be receiving partnership distributions either.

Although two recent cases in California have permitted creditors to penetrate a limited partnership, family limited partnerships can be a highly effective tool if properly designed and used in the correct situation. It will be especially effective in those cases where the use of a family limited partnership is also appropriate and useful for purposes other than asset protection.

Foreign Situs Trusts

In recent years, the establishment of a trust in a selected foreign country has become a popular method of protecting assets. The theory of a foreign situs trust is simple: since the laws of the U.S. and the laws of most countries are fairly balanced between the rights of creditors and debtors, find a country that has adopted highly anticreditor laws. At this time, some of the best places in which to establish a foreign situs trust are the Cook Islands or the Isle of Man. The Bahamas are also occasionally used. Although a discussion of the specifics of their laws is beyond the scope of this book, suffice it to say that assets properly transferred to a Cook Islands trust will be virtually impossible to reach.

Although any asset may be protected through the use of a foreign situs trust, U.S. real estate and illiquid securities may not be fully protected. The foreign situs trust is primarily designed to protect marketable securities and other liquid assets.

Fraudulent Conveyances

If you transfer an asset to another individual with the predominant purpose of hindering or delaying creditors, the transfer will likely be considered a fraudulent conveyance. As such, the creditor may be able to attach the asset in the hands of your transferee. In the course of asset protection planning you must always be mindful of the fraudulent conveyance rules.

In some circumstances, the burden of proof will be on the creditor to prove that your predominant purpose was the hindering or delaying of creditors. In other circumstances, there may be a presumption that you intended to hinder or delay. For example, if the transfer of the asset rendered you insolvent, it will generally be presumed that the transfer was a fraudulent conveyance. A transfer may also be presumed fraudulent when it occurs shortly after you receive notice of a pending claim.

16

Capital Gains and
the Basis of Assets

Lifetime Gifts
Gifts at Death
Planning Illustrations

THE BASIS OF AN ASSET is generally the amount you paid to acquire the asset. The basis of an asset is used to determine gain or loss on sale of the asset.

> **Example:** If you paid $10,000 to acquire a block of stock, then your basis in that stock would be $10,000. If you paid $100,000 to acquire a home, then your basis in the home would be $100,000.

Assets used in a trade or business may be depreciable. In that case, your basis in the asset is generally the amount you paid, less all the depreciation you were allowed on that asset.

In general, it is desirable to have as large a basis as possible in a particular asset. That will serve to reduce any gain you incur when the asset is sold. Basis is deducted from sale price to determine taxable gain. Therefore, the more basis you have in an asset, the smaller the gain when it is sold.

> **Example:** You purchased stock for $10,000. You now sell the stock for $15,000. Your gain is $5,000.
>
> | | |
> |---|---|
> | Sale Price | $15,000 |
> | Less Basis | <10,000> |
> | Gain | $ 5,000 |

Basis issues are an important consideration in estate planning. Where possible you will want to maximize asset basis for your beneficiaries.

Lifetime Gifts

In the case of a lifetime gift of an asset, your basis is said to "carry over" to your donee. He or she will receive the asset with your basis.

> **Example:** You acquire stock for $10,000. If you make a gift of the stock to your daughter during your lifetime, then for purposes of computing her gain on sale, she will have a $10,000 basis. If she were to sell the stock for $15,000, she would have a $5,000 gain.

The general rule is that assets gifted during lifetime receive a carry-over basis. However, a special rule prevents you from transferring potential tax losses. If you transfer an asset whose value is less than your basis, and if the donee later sells the asset at a loss, he or she must compute the loss using the fair market value of the asset at the time of the transfer.

> **Example:** You purchase stock for $10,000 and transfer it to your nephew when its value is $5,000. If your nephew sells the stock for a loss, say for $4,000, then he will use the fair market value basis of $5,000 and would report a $1,000 loss. If he sells the stock for $15,000, then the general rule will apply and he will have your carry-over basis of $10,000 and will report a $5,000 gain.

Gifts at Death

Most assets owned by you at the time of your death will receive a "stepped-up" basis equal to their fair market value at the time of your death. That rule, in effect, forgives capital gains existing at the time of your death.

> **Example:** You purchase stock for $10,000. At the time of your death, the stock is worth $25,000. The beneficiary who receives the stock will have a

$25,000 basis. If he or she later sells the stock, the taxable gain or loss will be computed using a $25,000 basis. Therefore, for example, a sale by your beneficiary shortly after your death for $25,000 will result in no taxable gain.

Most, but not all, assets receive a basis step-up upon the death of the owner. Assets which do not step up in basis include some installment notes receivable and IRAs and other retirement plans.

Q: My wife and I own several assets as community property. I understand that each of us is considered to own one-half of the community property assets (see chapter 6). Upon my death, what portion of our assets will receive a basis step-up?

A: Surprisingly, there is a peculiar rule which permits a full basis step-up for all community property, including the surviving spouse's one-half.

Planning Illustrations

A variety of situations provide planning opportunities that will permit you to take advantage of the basis rules.

Example: It is frequently important to divide assets between a husband and wife or between their revocable trusts so that neither lifetime exemption will be wasted (see chapter 7). If one spouse is significantly older than the other or is in significantly worse health, then, in general, low basis assets should be allocated to that spouse so that upon his or her death the survivor will receive the benefit of a basis step-up.

There is a rule intended to restrict deathbed transfers designed to generate a basis step-up. That rule provides that if the donee of a gift dies within one year of the transfer and the property is left to the original donor, then no basis step-up will occur.

Example: Your spouse is diagnosed with a terminal condition. You transfer low basis assets to your spouse, who passes away in less than a year with a will leaving the assets to you. The assets will not receive a step-up in basis. Rather, you will inherit those assets with your original basis.

If you intend to make a lifetime gift to your children or other beneficiary, you should, in general, give cash or high basis assets since the gifted asset will not be included in your estate at the time of your death and, therefore, will not receive a basis step-up. In general, better planning would indicate that you should retain low basis assets and make lifetime gifts of high basis assets.

Example: Assume you own the following assets:

	Basis	Value
Cash	$100,000	$100,000
Bonds	500,000	500,000
Real Estate	100,000	500,000
Stocks	50,000	500,000

If you desire to make a lifetime gift of a significant asset, you should consider a gift of all or a portion of the cash or the bonds. There would be no step-up in basis at death for those high basis assets since their basis is already equal to fair market value. In general you would not want to make a gift of the real estate or stocks. Those assets have a very low basis. If you were to pass away owning those assets there would be a step-up in basis. Therefore, from a tax planning prospective, it would be best to die owning the real estate, stocks, and any other low basis asset.

17

Advanced Planning Techniques

Life Insurance Trusts
Leveraging the Exemptions and Freezing the Estate
Family Limited Partnership (FLP)
GRIT, GRAT, and GRUT
Qualified Personal Residence Trust (QPRT)
Private Annuity Contract (PAC)
Self-Canceling Installment Note (SCIN)
Charitable Remainder Trust (CRT)
Charitable Lead Trust (CLT)
Joint Purchase
Sale of a Remainder Interest
Private Foundation
Techniques in Tandem

ADVANCED PLANNING TECHNIQUES are primarily concerned with reducing estate taxes on larger estates. Other goals such as better protecting assets from divorces, lawsuits, and other misfortunes may also involve advanced planning.

As described in chapter 2, in the case of a married couple, credit bypass trusts will avoid tax on only the first $1.25 million for 1998 (increasing to $2.0 million for 2006 and after). Estate assets in excess of those amounts will be subject to substantial transfer taxes unless other techniques are used. Single individuals may pass only $625,000 for 1998 (increasing to $1.0 million for 2006 and after) without incurring transfer taxes unless advanced planning methods are employed.

Life Insurance Trusts

Revocable living trusts (chap. 2) are the basic foundation for many estate plans. In the case of a married couple with combined assets in excess of the lifetime exemption ($625,000 for 1998, increasing to $1.0 million after 2005), the husband and wife will typically each have a revocable living trust containing a credit bypass trust for the surviving spouse and trusts for the children or other ultimate beneficiaries after both spouses are deceased. However, for married couples with a combined estate in excess of $1.25 million for 1998 ($2.0 million after 2005), additional steps must be taken to avoid estate taxes. In the case of a single individual, additional planning will be necessary if the estate exceeds $625,000 for 1998 (increasing to $1.0 million after 2005). After the basic wills and/or trusts are in place, the next most commonly used tool to reduce estate taxes is the life insurance trust, which is designed to avoid estate tax on life insurance proceeds. Life insurance trusts are discussed in chapter 2.

Through the use of credit bypass trusts and life insurance trusts, many estates avoid all estate tax liability. If you have credit bypass trusts in place and your insurance has been removed from your estate but significant estate tax will still be owed, you may need to explore one or more of the advanced planning techniques. Credit bypass trusts and life insurance trusts will only avoid tax on life insurance proceeds, plus $2.0 million of other assets (after 2005). If your net worth is significantly in excess of that amount, additional methods of reducing tax will be necessary.

Example: Assume you and your spouse have the following assets:

Home	$ 500,000
Investments	2,500,000
Insurance	500,000
	$3,500,000

You would probably first adopt credit bypass trusts to avoid tax on $2.0 million (after 2005). You would then probably establish a life insurance trust to avoid tax on the $500,000 of insurance. The remaining $1.0 million of unsheltered assets will result in a $435,000 estate tax.

In the above example, $435,000 of estate tax will be incurred even after credit bypass trusts and a life insurance trust are in place. If you wish to reduce or eliminate that tax, you will need to consider using some additional planning techniques as described below.

Leveraging the Exemptions and Freezing the Estate

Many of the advanced planning techniques involve methods to leverage or amplify the $10,000 annual exclusions or the lifetime exemption. If assets can be valued for gift tax purposes at 50% of their true value, then a married couple could give each child, grandchild, or other beneficiary $40,000 annually. If the asset could be valued at 10% of its true value (which is possible with some techniques), then you could give each child or other beneficiary $100,000 annually ($200,000 annually from you and your spouse combined).

Sometimes advanced planning involves leveraging the lifetime exemption. If a $2.5 million asset could be valued for estate or gift tax purposes at 40% of its true value, then the entire $2.5 million asset could be sheltered by your $1.0 million exemption (after 2005) and could be transferred to your children or other beneficiaries free of transfer tax.

Other advanced planning techniques involve freezing the value of a given asset. The idea here is to arrange assets so that their value for transfer tax purposes is fixed and all future appreciation occurs outside of your estate and free of transfer tax.

> **Example:** Assume you have a parcel of real estate or a closely held business interest or other asset that is expected to appreciate at 7% annually. Assume its current value is $500,000. If that asset does appreciate at 7% annually then in a little over ten years it will double in value. If you are in the 55% estate tax bracket, that additional $500,000 of appreciation will result in an additional $275,000 of estate tax. However, if your interest in the asset had a fixed value and if all future appreciation occurred in your children's estates, then the additional $275,000 of tax would be avoided.

As you review the following advanced planning techniques, you will notice that most are based on the concept of leveraging the annual exclusions or lifetime exemption, or freezing the value of one or more assets. Some of the techniques involve a combination of the leveraging and freezing concepts.

Family Limited Partnership (FLP)

Family limited partnerships are flexible and highly useful tools in the transfer and protection of assets. The primary benefits that an FLP can provide are as follows:

- Reducing gift taxes;
- Facilitating gifts of fractional interests;
- Permitting continued control over gifted assets; and
- Providing creditor protection.

Gift taxes can be reduced through the use of an FLP because gifts of the FLP units can be discounted for gift tax purposes. The value of an interest in an FLP is usually less than its pro rata share of the underlying assets.

Example: Assume I transfer a $1,000,000 rental property to an FLP in exchange for 10 partnership units. I want to sell one of the partnership units to you. If you purchased a single unit, you would have two problems. First, as a minority owner you would not have an effective voice in management. I, as the majority owner, would be able to extract a substantial portion of the partnership's earnings as salary payments to me and I would generally make all decisions concerning the operation of the property. Second, your investment is highly illiquid. There is no market for the partnership units and it would be difficult for you to find a buyer for your 10% interest. Because of those significant disadvantages, you would likely be unwilling to pay me $100,000 for a 10% interest. Rather, you would want a substantial discount. As a result, the value of a 10% interest is worth substantially less than 10% of the underlying asset.

Over the last couple of decades a great number of court cases have addressed the amount of discount permitted for gift tax purposes. The discounts that have been allowed vary from as low as 5% to as high as 80%, but usually range from 30% to 50%.

> **Example:** You transfer a $1,000,000 asset to an FLP in exchange for all FLP units. If you make gifts of the units to your children or other beneficiaries and if the units can be discounted by 40%, then $400,000 will escape the transfer tax.

In many cases you may wish to transfer assets out of your estate in order to reduce transfer taxes, but you may still wish to retain control over the gifted assets. A family limited partnership can help accomplish that goal. An FLP will frequently be structured with a 1% general partner interest and a 99% limited partner interest. The partnership agreement will provide that only the general partner can make decisions concerning the partnership's affairs. If you make gifts of the 99% limited partnership interests, but retain the 1% general partner interest, you will still have control over the gifted asset. Even though 99% of the value of the asset will be out of your estate, you will still make all decisions concerning the operation of the business or investments within the partnership, the liquidation of the investments, and the reinvestment of sale proceeds and similar matters.

Additionally, you may be entitled to extract substantial partnership income in the form of salary or partnership management fees. Of course, the amount of such salary or fees must be reasonable under the circumstances.

A family limited partnership is designed to facilitate the transfer of fractional interests in a business or other investment in a tax-efficient manner while retaining control over the gifted assets. A family limited partnership may also have creditor protection features (see chapter 15).

A family limited partnership may be structured and implemented in a variety of ways. The following is one arrangement that may be appropriate in some situations.

> **Example:** Assume you have three adult children, each of whom is married and has two children, so that you have six grandchildren (nine descendants in total). Also assume you have a large potential estate tax liability. One of

your assets is a $1.0 million parcel of vacant land that you and your spouse are considering giving to your children. A family limited partnership arrangement might be implemented as follows:

You and your spouse create a limited partnership and transfer the $1.0 million parcel to it in exchange for a 1% general partner interest and a 99% limited partner interest. That would generally not be a taxable event since you have simply contributed property to a newly created partnership in exchange for all of the partnership interests.

Assume that it is possible to receive a fair and honest appraisal stating that the true value of the property is $900,000. Real estate values are subjective and there is generally a range of supportable values. Assume that $900,000 is within that range of reasonable values.

Assume that a 40% discount is appropriate to determine the value of the partnership units.

Based on the foregoing, the aggregate value of all 99 limited partnership units, if valued individually, would be $534,600.

Appraised value	$900,000
Partnership units	x 99%
	$891,000
Less discount (40%)	<356,400>
Aggregate value of LP units	$534,600

If there are 99 LP units, then each LP unit would have a gift tax value of 5,400 ($534,600 ÷ 99).

As discussed in chapter 7 (under "Annual Exclusions"), you and your spouse together can give each child and grandchild $20,000 annually without incurring a gift tax or depleting your lifetime exemption. In terms of this example, you can therefore give each child and grandchild 3.7 LP units (3.7 units x $5,400 = $19,980).

If you wish, you could give each child and grandchild 3.7 units each year or 33.3 units in total each year (3.7 units x 9). At that rate, the entire 99 LP units would be transferred out of your estate after three years. No gift tax would be incurred and none of your lifetime exemption would be used. In addition, because you still retain the 1 GP unit, you would have control over the partnership's affairs. The 1% GP interest will permit you to decide when to sell partnership assets and how to invest sale proceeds. It will also permit you to decide whether to issue to yourself reasonable compensation or annual management fees for administering the partnership's properties. Furthermore, it will permit you to decide when distributions should be made from the partnership to its partners.

The above arrangement permitted you to transfer out of your estate 99% of a $1.0 million asset at no transfer tax cost while retaining control over the gifted property. In addition, assume that the transferred property doubles in value over the remaining years of your life; its value at the time of your death would be $2.0 million, only 1% of which will be included in your estate. If you are in the 55% estate tax bracket, the family limited partnership and lifetime gifting program will have avoided nearly $1.1 million of estate tax.

It is possible to make gifts of partnership units directly to your children or other beneficiaries. However, in order to better protect and preserve the partnership units for the benefit of your family, it may be better to make gifts of the LP units to trusts established for the benefit of your children or other beneficiaries. The above example assumes you wish to make gifts to your three children and their six children. In that case, a typical arrangement might be to create three irrevocable trusts to serve as holders of the partnership units for your three children and their descendants.

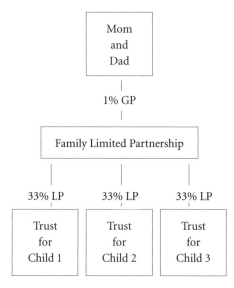

In the above example you will remain fully in control of the partnership assets. You will make all investment decisions and will decide if and when distributions will be made to the limited partners (trusts for your children). If the FLP is properly structured, it may be possible for you or your spouse to serve as trustee of the trusts for the children. In that event, you will have a second level of control. If you do decide to distribute cash from the partnership to the trusts, you or your spouse, as trustee, will then be able to decide whether to distribute the cash on to the children or grandchildren, or whether to retain the cash for investment purposes in the trusts.

GRIT, GRAT, and GRUT

A GRIT is a Grantor Retained Income Trust, an irrevocable trust where the grantor has retained a right to draw income from the trust for a specified number of years. A GRIT will allow you to transfer assets to your children or other beneficiaries at a discounted value for transfer tax purposes.

> **Example:** You have created an irrevocable trust and have transferred $100,000 to the trust. The trust provides that you will receive $6,000 annually for the next ten years. At the end of the ten years, remaining trust principal and accumulated income will pass to your children or be held in trust for their sole benefit.

The above example illustrates a GRIT. The grantor transferred property into trust, but retained a right to income for a specified number of years. When you establish and fund a GRIT you will be making a gift of the remainder interest, which is usually a small fraction of the value of the gifted asset. If you survive the income period, a significant tax benefit will be derived.

There are two basic types of GRITs:

GRAT—A Grantor Retained Annuity Trust pays a specified dollar amount annually or at more frequent intervals regardless of the value of the trust assets.

GRUT—A Grantor Retained Unitrust pays a fixed percentage of the trust assets annually or at more frequent intervals and the payments will vary as the value of the trust assets varies.

Example: Assume you transfer $100,000 to an irrevocable trust and retain the right to receive $6,000 annually for 10 years regardless of the value of the trust assets. That is a GRAT. The amount of the annual annuity is fixed and will not vary.

Example: Assume you transfer $100,000 to an irrevocable trust and reserve the right to receive 6% of the value of the trust assets as valued each year. That is a GRUT. The amount of each year's payment will vary as the value of the trust assets varies.

In general, GRATs provide somewhat less tax benefit than do GRUTs. However, the assets of a GRUT must be revalued each year. Also, the grantor generally cannot serve as trustee of a GRUT. One advantage of a GRUT as compared to a GRAT is that additional assets can be contributed to a GRUT in future years.

A GRIT (whether it is a GRAT or a GRUT) is designed to permit the transfer of assets to your children or other beneficiaries at a discounted value. When you create and fund a GRIT, you will have made a taxable gift of the remainder interest. Using actuarial and present value tables supplied by the IRS, you must compute the value of your retained income interest. That value is then deducted from the total value of the transferred property to determine the taxable value of the remainder interest that you have gifted.

Example: Assume you are age 60 and create a GRAT with $100,000 of bonds. The GRAT provides that you will receive $6,000 each year for the shorter of ten years or your life. At the end of the income period (ten years or your death), remaining principal and accumulated income will be held in trust for your children or will be distributed outright to them as you have directed.

In calculating the value of the remainder interest, you must use prescribed IRS interest rates, which are based on treasury bond rates as adjusted monthly. If the prescribed IRS rate is 6% at the time the GRAT is created, the value of the gift to your children will be $59,141, based on a complicated actuarial formula. If higher IRS rates are in effect at the time of the gift, the value of the gift to children will be greater under the formula.

IRS Rate	Value of Gift to Children
6%	$ 59,141
8	62,639
10	65,690

If the IRS rate is 6% when the gift is made, you will have made a taxable gift of $59,141. You will be required to file a gift tax return to report the gift and your lifetime exemption will be reduced by the $59,141 taxable gift, but $100,000 of assets plus all future appreciation on those assets will have been transferred out of your estate.

The chart above illustrates that as interest rates decline, the desirability of a GRIT increases.

Increasing the number of years of the income interest will further decrease the value of the remainder interest and the value of the taxable gift. If a fifteen-year period to receive income is selected instead of the ten years illustrated above, the following results occur:

	Value of Gift to Children	
IRS Rate	10 Years	15 Years
6%	$59,141	$ 48,523
8	62,639	54,279
10	65,690	59,075

To further illustrate the point, assume a 6% interest rate and a 25-year retained income period. That would result in a taxable gift in the amount of only $38,780. The greater the number of years of income that you retain, the smaller the value of the remainder interest and the smaller the gift. However, when selecting a retained income period, it should be less than your expected or probable life expectancy because if you do not survive the term, the entire trust assets will be included in your estate and will be valued as of your date of death. In that event, your estate will have received no benefit from the GRIT. Your estate will be in no worse position than if you had not implemented the GRIT, but you will not have achieved a tax benefit. Therefore, it is important to select an income period that you have a reasonable likelihood of surviving.

Within certain limits, you may select the level of income payout you would like to retain. The higher the annuity amount you retain, the lower the value of the remainder interest and the taxable gift. For example, assume a 6% IRS rate. Assume income is retained for ten years as above.

Retained Annuity	Value of Gift to Children
$ 6,000	$59,141
8,000	45,521
10,000	31,901
12,000	18,281

The preceding paragraphs illustrate how several variable factors in combination determine the results a GRIT will achieve. Those factors include the following:

- The IRS interest rate in effect at the time of the gift (the lower the interest rate, the smaller the gift);
- Length of time you retained a right to the income (the longer the right to receive income is retained, the smaller the gift); and
- Size of annuity retained (the larger the annuity retained, the smaller the gift).

In some situations, a "zeroed-out" GRAT may be appropriate. Especially during times of low interest rates, it is possible to select income payout rates high enough that the value of the remainder interest and the value of the taxable gift will be reduced to zero or near zero. To the extent that the underlying assets earn more than the retained income stream, the excess will pass to beneficiaries free of transfer tax (assuming you survive the retained income period). In the case of a zeroed-out GRAT, it is imperative to select highly appreciating assets. Stock in a new family business venture or an interest in a prime piece of real estate may be appropriate. The IRS has ruled that GRITs designed to reduce the value of the gift to zero are invalid, but it is still possible to design GRITs that will produce a very small taxable gift.

Prior to implementing a GRAT or GRUT, it is generally necessary to perform the required calculations under various assumptions to determine the optimal structure for the GRAT or GRUT.

In summary, a GRIT may permit you to transfer substantial assets to your children or other beneficiaries free of transfer tax. A GRIT will be most advantageous where the combined income and growth of the transferred assets significantly exceed the prescribed IRS interest rate at the time of the transfer. A GRIT may be especially advantageous where the transferred asset is expected to appreciate greatly.

Qualified Personal Residence Trust (QPRT)

A Qualified Personal Residence Trust, or QPRT, is a particular type of GRIT funded with a personal residence in which you have retained the right to reside for a specified number of years. As in the case of a GRAT or GRUT, you must actuarially compute the value of the remainder interest that is gifted, but special favorable rules applying to QPRT computations can result in substantial tax benefits.

> **Example:** Assume you establish a QPRT and transfer your $1.0 million principal residence or vacation home to it. Further assume that you retain the right to reside in the home for 10 years and that you are age 60. If IRS interest rates are 6.0% at the time of the funding of the QPRT, you will be deemed to have made a gift of the remainder interest in the home in the amount of $455,170. Higher IRS interest rates will yield lower gift values.
>
> | IRS Rate | Value of Gift to Children |
> |----------|---------------------------|
> | 6% | $455,170 |
> | 8 | 377,570 |
> | 10 | 314,270 |

As in the case of a GRAT or GRUT, increasing the number of years of retained use of the home will decrease the value of the remainder interest and the taxable gift. However, if you do not survive the retained use period, then the home will be included in your estate at its date of death value. Although your estate will be no worse off, the QPRT will not have produced any tax benefit. Therefore, as in the case of a GRAT or GRUT, it is important to select a period that you are likely to outlive.

At the end of the period specified in the trust, your right to occupy the home will terminate. The home will then either remain in trust for the benefit of your named beneficiaries or be distributed outright to them, as you have specified in the trust document.

Just before the end of the specified period, you will have several choices:

> If you do not wish to occupy the home in the future, you may permit the period to lapse. The trustee will then proceed according to the provisions you have specified in the trust document: to sell the home and invest the proceeds for the benefit of your beneficiaries, to permit them to occupy the home, or to distribute the home or its sale proceeds to your named beneficiaries.

> If you wish to continue to reside at the home, you may enter into a long-term lease arrangement with the trust. Your rent payments will effectively transfer additional assets from your estate to the estates of your named beneficiaries free of transfer tax.

> As an alternative, you may elect to purchase the home from the trust. That technique can result in an additional benefit, illustrated in the following example.

Example: As in the prior example, assume you created a QPRT and retained a right to occupy the home for ten years. Assume the IRS interest rate was 10% and you were age 60 at the time of the gift. In that event, the deemed gift would have been $314,270 and you would have used that amount of your lifetime credit. Assume the ten-year period is about to lapse and the home is now worth $1.4 million. You may elect to purchase the home from the trust in exchange for a $1.4 million note. If you passed away shortly after that transaction, two tax savings would result:

Although your estate would include the $1.4 million home, your estate would be reduced by the $1.4 million note owed to your children's trust. That asset and corresponding liability would offset each other. In effect, $1,085,730 of value in the home would have been transferred free of transfer tax cost.

Value of home at death	$1,400,000
Gift tax value	<314,270>
Untaxed value	$1,085,730

Because the home is included in your estate at the time of your death, your children or other beneficiaries will receive a step-up in basis (see "Gifts at Death" in chapter 16).

In effect, the best of both worlds will have been achieved:

$1,085,730 of the $1.4 million home passed out of your estate free of transfer tax and yet your heirs received a step-up in the entire basis of the home so that no capital gain will result if the home is sold shortly after your death.

It should be noted that the IRS recently issued a ruling requiring that all QPRT documents must contain a provision prohibiting the sale of the home to the grantor of the trust as illustrated above. If that ruling is upheld by the courts, the sale technique may be limited, although it still may be possible to achieve the desired result.

Q: Are there any limitations as to which properties may be transferred to a QPRT?

A: The property transferred to a QPRT must be either your principal residence or a home that qualifies as a "vacation home" under the vacation home rental income tax rules.

Q: What will happen if we wish to sell our home before the period of the QPRT has lapsed?

A: The sale proceeds may be used by the trust to purchase a substitute home if you wish. If you do not wish to purchase a substitute home or if you purchase a less expensive home, any unused sale proceeds will be invested by the QPRT and you will receive income for the remainder of the QPRT term.

Q: Who may serve as the trustee of a QPRT?

A: Your spouse or any other suitable person of your choosing may serve as trustee. You may serve as trustee only in limited circumstances.

Q: My spouse and I own our principal residence jointly. Would we transfer the home to a joint QPRT or is some other arrangement appropriate?

A: In most cases, the best results will be obtained if the husband and wife each establish a QPRT and each transfers a one-half interest in the home to his or her respective trust.

Private Annuity Contract (PAC)

A private annuity contract, or PAC, involves the sale of an asset to your children or other beneficiary in exchange for a lifetime annuity. The size of the annuity payments will be determined by:

- The value of the asset sold;
- The IRS interest rate at the time of the sale; and
- The seller's actuarial life expectancy.

Example: Assume you have a parcel of real estate worth $500,000 which you wish to sell to your daughter in exchange for a private annuity. Assume that you are age 65. Under the IRS actuarial tables, the annual required annuity payment will be $53,005 if the official interest rate is 6.0%.

According to the mortality tables used by the IRS, a person aged 65 has a life expectancy of approximately 16 years. If you survive to exactly your life expectancy, then a "fair" amount will have been paid. A schedule of sixteen payments at $53,005 results in total payments of $848,080. That is a "fair" amount, since an installment purchase payable over a fixed sixteen-year period at 6.0% would result in approximately the same total payments.

If you died shortly after receiving the first annual payment of $53,005, then your daughter would have received a great tax benefit. The $500,000 asset will not be included in your estate. Rather, only the $53,005 payment received from your daughter is included. The $446,995 difference escaped transfer tax.

On the other hand, if you live five years beyond your life expectancy, then your daughter will have paid an additional $265,025 ($53,005 x 5) to you, resulting in an unfavorable tax result. Your estate was decreased by the $500,000 asset transferred to your daughter, but it was increased by the aggregate annual payments transferred from her back to you over the 21-year period of your remaining life. In this case, the private annuity was disadvantageous. Of course, any appreciation in value of the asset that occurred after the original sale date will have avoided transfer taxation.

As shown above, the private annuity is typically a gamble. If you die within a few years of the sale, substantial value will escape taxation, but if you survive beyond your life expectancy, the private annuity may be disadvantageous.

A private annuity can be highly useful in those situations where it is probable that the parent or grandparent will not survive to his or her life expectancy.

Example: Assume that you have a distinct family history of not surviving to life expectancy or that you are suffering from a terminal illness. In those situations, a private annuity may contribute significantly to avoiding transfer taxes and preserving your family's wealth.

Q: I understand that private annuities provide the greatest tax savings if the person transferring the assets dies shortly after establishing the private annuity. In order to maximize the benefit of a private annuity, should I wait to implement a private annuity sale until I am on my deathbed?

A: In general, the transferred asset will be included in your estate and taxed at its full value if the IRS can prove that at the time of the creation of the private annuity there was less than a 50% chance that you would survive one year. Even in that case, your estate would be in no worse position than if you had not attempted the private annuity transaction.

Self-Canceling Installment Note (SCIN)

A self-canceling installment note, or SCIN (pronounced "skin"), also involves the sale of an asset to your child or other beneficiary. Principal and interest will be paid to you monthly or annually for a set number of years. If you die before all of the payments have been made, all payments due after your death are forgiven. Under the IRS rules, above-market interest must be paid and/or an above-market price must be paid for the asset. That is to compensate you for the fact that not all payments will be made if you die before the pay-off date.

The SCIN, like the private annuity, involves a gamble. If you die shortly after the transaction, then substantial wealth will have passed to the younger generation free of transfer tax. But if you survive to the pay-off period, then your beneficiary will have overpaid (above-market interest or sales price) and the SCIN will have been counterproductive. If you die before the specified period, your estate may have avoided substantial transfer tax; that benefit may be offset to some extent by a rule that requires your estate to recognize all of the capital gain as though your estate had been paid in full.

As in the case of a private annuity, a SCIN is most appropriate where there is a likelihood that you will not survive to your actuarial life expectancy. In that event, a huge estate tax savings may be possible.

Example: Assume that you have a parcel of real estate, a business interest, or some other asset worth $1.0 million and that you wish to pass the asset to your children, or to a trust for their benefit. Assume that you are age 60 and that the current IRS rate is 6.0%. You sell the asset to your children in exchange for a $1.0 million note payable over six years at 6.0% interest. If the note is a SCIN, the IRS rules require a premium in the sales price of $91,000. Therefore, the actual note owed to you by your children will be in the amount of $1,091,000 and the annual payment required to amortize the note at 6.0% over ten years will be $148,000. If you survive the entire ten years, your children will thus pay to you an additional $91,000, plus interest; therefore the SCIN will have been disadvantageous to that extent. However, if you survive only two years from the time of the sale, your children will have paid to you $296,000. The additional $704,000, plus all appreciation occurring after the time of the sale, will have avoided transfer taxation.

Example: Assume the same facts as in the prior example, except that you are age 70. In that case, the IRS rules require a premium in the sales price of $210,000. Therefore, if you survive the entire ten years, your children will have paid an additional $210,000 for the property, but, again, if you do not survive the entire ten years, a very substantial tax savings will have occurred.

Charitable Remainder Trust (CRT)

A charitable remainder trust, or CRT, will benefit one or more charities selected by you. It may also benefit you and your family by achieving significant savings in capital gains tax and transfer tax. Some individuals who establish CRTs do so principally to benefit a particular charity, but most are motivated primarily by the desire to reduce taxes and view the benefit to charity as being of secondary importance.

A charitable remainder trust is most useful where you wish to dispose of a low-basis and low-yield asset. In effect, it permits a sale of the low-basis asset free of capital gains tax so that the total sales proceeds, unreduced by tax, may be reinvested in a higher-yield asset. Also on the plus side, the CRT may provide you with a substantial charitable deduction that can be used to offset income and reduce income taxes.

On the negative side, when you pass away, the remaining principal of the CRT does not pass to your children or other intended beneficiaries. Instead, it passes to a charity or charities selected by you.

> **Example:** 20 years ago, you purchased vacant land for $100,000. It is now worth $1.0 million, but it provides no current income. You would like to liquidate the investment and reinvest the proceeds in marketable securities that will provide a current return. Unfortunately, a sale of the property will result in a $900,000 capital gain and approximately $180,000 of tax will be owed. Therefore, only $820,000 will remain to invest.

> **Example:** As an alternative, assume you transfer the real estate to a CRT, which then sells the property for $1.0 million. No capital gains tax will be owed. The CRT can then invest the entire $1.0 million.

> **Example:** Assume the $1.0 million of sale proceeds unreduced by capital gains tax in the CRT are reinvested in securities producing an 8% yield, or $80,000 annually. Without using the CRT, you would have needed to invest the $820,000 of after-tax sale proceeds in securities yielding 9.8% in order to generate the same $80,000 of annual income.

As in the above example, CRTs are often used to dispose of low-basis real estate. They are also often used to dispose of an interest in a closely held business or where an investor owns a large block of a single security and wishes to diversify his or her holdings.

Charitable remainder trusts must be designed as either annuity trusts (CRATs) or unitrusts (CRUTs). An annuity trust will pay you a set dollar amount annually or at more frequent intervals. A unitrust will pay you a set percentage of the fair market value as determined each year.

Example: You contribute $100,000 to a CRAT that will pay you $6,000 annually regardless of the value of the trust principal.

Example: You transfer $100,000 to a CRUT that will pay you 6% of the value of the trust as measured each year. Therefore, as the value of the trust principal increases or decreases, the amount of the annual payment to you will increase or decrease.

Within certain limits you may select the income payout you desire. Income may be paid for the remainder of your life or for two or more lives. It may also be payable over a set number of years.

The amount of the charitable deduction you will receive will depend upon:

- The value of the property transferred to the CRT;
- Your life expectancy (or the number of years selected);
- The IRS interest rate in effect at the time of the transfer; and
- The size of the annuity payment retained.

Naturally, the larger the annuity selected, the smaller the charitable deduction, because the charity will ultimately receive less.

Example: You are age 65 and are transferring a $1.0 million asset to a CRAT in exchange for a $60,000 annuity to be paid annually for the remainder of your life. If the IRS interest rate in effect at the time of the transaction is 8%, then you will receive a $511,840 charitable deduction. Increasing the amount of the annual annuity payment specified in the trust agreement would cause the amount of the charitable deduction to decline.

Annual Payment	Charitable Deduction
$ 60,000	$511,840
80,000	349,120
100,000	186,400

The amount of the charitable deduction is also a function of the length of the income interest retained. If the income is to be paid for the remainder of a person's life, then the older the person, the greater the charitable deduction.

Example: You have transferred a $1.0 million asset to a CRAT in exchange for a $60,000 annuity to be paid annually for the remainder of your life. The IRS interest rate is 8%. If you are 65 years old, you will receive a charitable deduction of $511,840. If you were older, the charitable deduction would be greater, as shown below.

Beneficiary's Age	Charitable Deduction
65	$511,840
70	$566,860
75	$626,170

A vehicle similar to the charitable remainder annuity trust or unitrust is known as the Pooled Income Fund (PIF). A PIF operates like a charitable remainder annuity trust, except that it is sponsored by a particular charity and many individuals contribute funds to the same pooled income fund. The advantage of the PIF lies in avoiding the cost of establishing your own CRT. A pooled income fund may be useful where the size of the asset to be sold does not justify the cost of establishing and maintaining a customized charitable remainder trust.

The various CRTs all have one decided disadvantage: namely, at your death, or the expiration of the set period of years, remaining trust assets and accumulated income pass to the charity. The asset will not remain to be passed on to your children or other beneficiaries. If it is important to you that the value of the property be available to pass on to your beneficiaries, a Wealth Replacement Trust (WRT) may solve the problem.

A wealth replacement trust is simply an irrevocable life insurance trust (see chapter 2) funded with a policy insuring your life. Upon your death, your beneficiaries will not receive the vacant land, stock, or other asset that you transferred to the CRT, but the insurance proceeds instead. The insurance proceeds will be free of estate tax if the policy is owned through a properly designed insurance trust.

If you had not transferred the vacant land or other asset to the CRT, and if you still owned the asset when you died, then it would be included in your estate and would be subject to significant estate taxes. However, the value of the Wealth Replacement Trust will not be subject to estate tax. Therefore, a CRT used in conjunction with a WRT produces a method of transferring significant wealth out of your estate free of transfer taxation.

Depending on a number of factors, the income tax savings that will result from the charitable deduction may be adequate to purchase life insurance with significantly greater value than the real estate or other asset you transferred to the CRT. Your heirs may, in effect, receive greater value than if you had not transferred the property to the charitable remainder trust.

The above examples assume that you establish a charitable remainder trust and retain an income interest. Alternatively, the income interest may be gifted to another individual or shared with another individual.

> **Example:** You could establish a CRT and designate that your spouse or child will receive the annuity payment from the trust for the remainder of his or her life.

> **Example:** You could establish a CRT to provide that you will receive an annuity payment for the remainder of your life, and upon your death, your spouse, child, or other beneficiary will receive the annuity for the remainder of his or her life.

The above examples assume that the charitable remainder trust is established and property is transferred to it during your lifetime. However, many CRTs are also established by will.

> **Example:** Your will might provide that upon your death, $1.0 million will be transferred to a CRT which provides income to your spouse, child, or other beneficiary for the remainder of his or her life. If properly designed, the value of the remainder interest that would ultimately pass to charity will be deductible by your estate as a charitable deduction. The value of the income interest that you have transferred will be included in your estate and will be subject to estate tax unless sheltered by the marital deduction or lifetime exemption.

Q: Can a CRT be established to benefit more than one charity?

A: CRTs can be designed to benefit any number of charitable organizations and in any proportion you specify in the CRT document.

Q: If I establish a CRT naming one or more specific charities, may I later specify others?

A: CRTs are irrevocable and cannot be amended. However, when the CRT is initially established, you may reserve the right to change the charitable beneficiaries.

Charitable Lead Trust (CLT)

A charitable lead trust, or CLT, is, in a sense, the opposite of a charitable remainder trust. In the case of a CLT, property is transferred to a trust that provides income to one or more charities for a set number of years. After the expiration of the set period, the remaining principal and accumulated income passes to your children or other named beneficiary or continues to be held in trust for their benefit.

At the time you transfer the property to the CLT, you will be considered as having made a gift to your children or other named beneficiaries equal to the value of the remainder interest that they will ultimately receive. The value of that gift will reduce your lifetime exemption, or if your exemption has been totally depleted, then it will result in a current gift tax liability.

Example: You transfer $1.0 million of stocks to a ten-year CLT which pays your named charity $60,000 annually for ten years. At the expiration of the ten years, the remaining principal and accumulated income will be transferred to your children or held in trust for their benefit. Assume the IRS rate is 8.0%. The present value computations result in the following:

Income Interest	$ 402,606
Remainder Interest	597,394
Total	$1,000,000

Based on the foregoing, you will be considered as having made a taxable gift in the amount of $597,394. Your lifetime exemption will be reduced by that amount, or, if you have no remaining lifetime exemption, then a current gift tax will be owed. However, the $1.0 million of stocks and all future appreciation thereon will ultimately pass to your children, even though only $597,394 will have been subjected to transfer tax.

Increasing the period over which payments will be made to the charitable beneficiary will increase the amount of the charitable deduction and will decrease the amount of the taxable gift to your children or other beneficiaries.

Example: Assume the above facts except that 15- and 20-year charitable income periods are selected.

Charitable Period	Charitable Deduction	Gift to Children
10 yrs.	$402,606	$597,394
15	513,570	486,430
20	589,086	410,914

As in the case of a charitable remainder trust, a CLT may be established during your lifetime or upon your death. If it is established during your lifetime, the CLT can be structured in one of two basic ways for income tax purposes. It can be designed so that there is no charitable deduction upon establishment of the trust, but you will avoid paying tax on the future income that passes to charity. Alternatively, it can be designed so that you will receive a sizable charitable deduction upon establishment of the CLT, but will be imputed taxable income in future years as income is earned by the trust (even though the income is flowing directly to the charity). That technique would be appropriate to, in effect, shift a large amount of taxable income from one year and spread it to several succeeding years.

The value of the remainder interest which will eventually pass to your children or other beneficiaries will constitute a current taxable gift that will reduce your lifetime exemption or, if your exemption has been fully depleted, will result in a current gift tax liability. If the CLT is established at the time of your death, your estate will receive a charitable deduction for purposes of the estate tax. The value of the remainder interest passing to your noncharitable beneficiary will be subject to estate tax.

Transferring appreciating assets to a CLT may result in a substantial transfer tax savings, because all of the future appreciation will avoid transfer tax.

Example: Assume you contribute a $1.0 million closely held business interest or other appreciating asset to a CLT. Assume the asset yields current income of 2%, but is also appreciating at 10% per year. Assume the CLT provides that the designated charity will receive $60,000 annually (6%) for fifteen years. At the end of the fifteen-year period, the property will pass to trusts for the benefit of your children. If the current IRS interest rate is 8%, the value of the interest passing to charity is $589,086 and the value of the remainder interest that will pass to your children is $410,914.

In the above example, you may receive a charitable deduction in the amount of $589,086. If the CLT was established during your lifetime, that amount can be used to offset income and any amount not used in the current year can be carried forward for five additional years (of course, you will be imputed income in future years); the $410,914 value of the remainder interest will be considered as a taxable gift. Assuming that the asset transferred to the CLT continues to appreciate at 10% annually and continues to produce current income of 2%, the total tax savings for your family may be nearly $1.6 million.

Projected value of remainder	$ 3,292,463
Taxable value of remainder	<410,914>
Value transferred tax free	$2,881,549
Estate tax rate	x 55%
Estimated tax savings	$1,584,852

Charitable Lead Trust

Year	Beginning Principal	10.00% Growth	2.00% Income	Annual Payment	Remainder
1	$1,000,000	$100,000	$21,000	$<60,000>	$1,061,000
2	1,061,000	106,100	22,281	<60,000>	1,129,318
3	1,129,381	112,938	23,717	<60,000>	1,206,036
4	1,206,036	120,603	25,326	<60,000>	1,291,967
5	1,291,967	129,196	27,131	<60,000>	1,388,295
6	1,388,295	138,829	29,154	<60,000>	1,496,279
7	1,496,279	149,627	31,421	<60,000>	1,617,329
8	1,617,329	161,732	33,963	<60,000>	1,753,026
9	1,753,026	175,302	36,813	<60,000>	1,905,143
10	1,905,143	190,514	40,008	<60,000>	2,075,665
11	2,075,665	207,566	43,589	<60,000>	2,266,821
12	2,266,821	226,682	47,603	<60,000>	2,481,106
13	2,481,106	248,110	52,103	<60,000>	2,721,320
14	2,721,320	272,132	57,147	<60,000>	2,990,600
15	2,990,600	299,060	62,802	<60,000>	3,292,463
Summary	$1,000,000	$2,638,396	$554,063	$<900,000>	$3,292,463

A CLT generally will be helpful only if the total yield on the investment, including appreciation, exceeds the official IRS interest rate at the time of the creation of the CLT. If the investment property yields an amount equal to the IRS interest rate, the CLT would not provide a benefit. If the transferred property yields less than the IRS rate, then the transaction will be counterproductive. Obviously, a CLT should generally be funded only with property that is expected to outperform the official IRS rate.

Joint Purchase

In a joint purchase, two people (typically parent and child) purchase an asset jointly. The older person acquires the income interest in the property for the term of his or her life or for a specified number of years. The younger person purchases the remainder interest. After the period of the income interest has lapsed, the entire asset will be owned by the younger person.

The tax rules now limit the joint purchase technique to certain qualified tangible property which is nondepreciable and non–income producing. The most notable example is artwork. Another possible asset would be undeveloped acreage held for personal use, such as a hunting preserve or land used for camping.

Example: Assume you are age 65 and that you locate a $1.0 million painting that you believe is likely to appreciate in value. You purchase a life interest in the painting and your son purchases the remainder interest. If the official IRS interest rate is 10%, then based on your age, you and your son might pay the following amounts:

You pay	$ 712,130
Your son pays	287,870
Total	$1,000,000

Regardless of when you die, the $1.0 million painting will then be solely owned by your son. In effect, the $712,130 that you paid for the life interest escapes estate taxation. In addition, all appreciation occurring after the purchase will also escape estate taxation.

In the above example, the IRS actuarial tables were used to estimate the division of the purchase price between the life estate and the remainder. However, the actual IRS rules require that you present evidence of the true fair market value of the life estate based on rental rates for comparable property or actual comparable sales of life estates.

The obvious disadvantage of the joint purchase is that you and your son will have substantial cash invested in a non–income producing asset for the remainder of your lifetime. If the artwork does not appreciate in value, the lost earnings on your investment may offset the estate tax savings, depending on the number of years you survive. Therefore, a joint purchase can be classified with the private annuity and self-canceling installment note because it is most suitable if you are not likely to survive for many years. However, for families making sizable investments in artwork regardless of the tax or economic considerations, a joint purchase is a no-lose proposition, with a potentially huge benefit.

Sale of a Remainder Interest

This is similar to the joint purchase described above, except that instead of two individuals jointly purchasing an asset, the older individual already owns the asset and simply sells a remainder interest to the younger person.

All of the rules described above for a joint purchase apply to the sale of a remainder interest, including that it is limited to qualified tangible property which is nondepreciable and non–income producing. Again, the most notable examples are artwork or undeveloped acreage held for personal purposes.

> **Example:** Assume that you are age 65 and own a statue valued at $1.0 million. Assume that the IRS interest rate is 10%. If you sell to your son a remainder interest and retain a life estate, your son will be required to pay you approximately $288,000. Upon your death, the artwork will be owned entirely by your son. In effect, the $712,000 value of the life estate plus all future appreciation in value will pass to your son free of transfer tax.

Private Foundation

Private foundations are established to permit sizable charitable gifts while still retaining a degree of control over the gifted cash or other property. Gifts to a private foundation may provide significant income tax and estate tax benefits.

A private foundation is created by establishing a charitable trust or charitable corporation. Forms and other documents are then filed with the IRS to obtain a ruling that the organization will be treated as a tax-exempt private foundation. If a favorable ruling is obtained from the IRS, then contributions to the private foundation will be deductible for income tax purposes within certain limitations.

A private foundation may also be created as part of your estate plan. Your will or revocable trust could dictate that a private foundation will be created and funded upon your death. In that event, your estate will be able to deduct the value of any property passing to the private foundation.

Q: What are the limitations on contributions to a private foundation?

A: Generally, you may only deduct an amount up to 30% of your adjusted gross income annually. In the case of a contribution of appreciated property, the deduction is limited to 20% of your adjusted gross income.

Q: Is the income tax deduction for gifts to a private foundation equal to the value of the gift or is it limited to my basis?

A: Generally, the deduction is limited to your basis in the contributed asset. However, under current rules, the full value of publicly traded stock may be deducted if the contribution was made before June 30, 1998. This favorable provision may be extended. The various limitations on charitable deductions are frequently revised. It is important to review the current rules before making any sizable charitable contribution.

Q: May I receive compensation for serving as a director, officer, or trustee of my private foundation?

A: Such expenditures by a private foundation are strictly scrutinized and are permitted only to the extent they are reasonable under the circumstances. Similarly, private foundation expenditures for the travel expenses of its executives are also highly scrutinized.

Most private foundations are of the "conduit" type. The private foundation itself does not perform a direct charitable function. Rather, its resources are channeled to one or more public charities, which directly carry out the charitable purpose. Some private foundations are permitted to directly perform a charitable purpose, but that type of private foundation must satisfy an additional array of regulations.

Q: What is the difference between a private foundation and a public charity?

A: Unlike public charities that are financed by the general public or a governmental unit, private foundations have limited sources of funding. Private foundations receive their financing from grants or endowment income from a single individual, family, or company or from a small group of individuals, families, or companies. Although private foundations may receive gifts from friends or associates, they generally do not engage in fund-raising drives. Also, most private foundations channel funds to public charities rather than engage directly in charitable activities.

Q: May I establish a private foundation to provide scholarships to members of my family?

A: No. A private foundation must serve a public purpose rather than a private purpose.

Q: Will my private foundation be exempt from federal income taxes?

A: Depending on the type of grants made by your private foundation, it must pay an annual excise tax equal to either 1% or 2% of net investment income for the year. A number of other more serious excise taxes can be imposed, but those are avoidable if the various operational rules prescribed by the IRS are followed.

Q: Must my private foundation distribute funds for charitable purposes each year?

A: Most private foundations are required to distribute annually an amount at least equal to 5% of the private foundation's assets.

Q: Must my private foundation file annual tax returns?

A: Yes. IRS Form 990-PF must be filed annually. Also, that form must be made available for public inspection and in most cases a notice of its availability must be placed annually in a local newspaper. In addition to the IRS filings, most states have their own filing requirements.

Techniques in Tandem

This chapter has illustrated most of the commonly used methods of reducing estate and gift taxes. In some situations it may be possible to multiply the benefits of two or more planning techniques.

Example: Assume that your $1.0 million closely held business or parcel of real estate is transferred to a family limited partnership (see chapter 15). Assume that the value of the limited partner units can be discounted by 50%. Therefore, for tax purposes, a gift of all of the units to your three children would be valued at $500,000. Assume that the partnership units are not gifted directly to your children, but are gifted to GRATs established for their benefit. Assume you retain a 10% annuity for 10 years and the IRS interest rate is 6.0%. Based on those factors, the value of the remainder interest gifted to children is only 31.9% of the total. Multiplying that 31.9% valuation by the $500,000 discounted value of the limited partnership units results in a total value for the gifts of $159,500. In this example, $1.0 million of property will be transferred to your children while using only $159,500 of your lifetime exemption.

Example: The preceding example achieved in excess of a six-to-one leveraging of your lifetime exemption. For each dollar of exemption used, $6.27 of value was transferred to your children ($1.0 million ÷ $159,500 tax value). In that case, a husband and wife with a total exemption of $2.0 million could transfer $12,540,000 of value without incurring an estate tax.

Example: Assume that you have a large estate and have previously made substantial gifts so that your lifetime exemption has been exhausted and you are now in the 55% transfer tax bracket. Therefore, each additional dollar gifted will result in a $.55 tax. However, if your next substantial gift is made through a family limited partnership in tandem with a GRAT as illustrated above, the value will be reduced to approximately 16% of the true value. Therefore, the effective tax rate will drop to 8.8% (16% x 55%). In addition, all future appreciation on the transferred assets will avoid tax.

Example: Assume that a business asset is contributed to a family limited partnership. However, instead of gifting partnership units to children, the units are sold to children in exchange for an annuity or a self-canceling installment note. Here again, the FLP discount will be multiplied by the private annuity or SCIN discount and may result in a very significant benefit.

18

Business Succession Planning

Transfer to a Child or Other Beneficiary
Transfer to Key Employee
Transfer to Partner or Co-Shareholder
Buy-Sell Agreements
Tax Considerations

AN ESTATE THAT owns a substantial interest in a closely held business will often encounter additional complexities and potential problems. Planning for the orderly transmission of a closely held business is one of the more challenging aspects of estate planning. It is one of the areas where a successful outcome is most dependent on careful analysis, experience, and creativity.

When a large portion of an estate is invested in a family business or a substantial interest in a closely held business, a number of issues arise:

- Who will acquire the business? Will it be transferred to your child or other beneficiary, a key employee, or sold to a third party?

- In what manner will the transfer be accomplished? If the transfer is to your child or other beneficiary, will it be sold to the child, gifted to him or her during your lifetime, gifted at your death, or a combination of the foregoing?

- What is an appropriate valuation of the business? Should some valuation formula be used, or should appraisers or other valuation experts be involved?

- What is the source of any necessary liquidity? If the business is to be sold to your child or key employee, does that person have sufficient resources or will the purchase price be paid entirely out of the future earnings of the business? If the business is to be left at death to your beneficiary, how will estate taxes be paid without a forced liquidation of the business?

- If the business is to be transferred gradually during your lifetime, at what point will operational control pass from you to your successor in interest?
- How will the various income tax/estate tax issues be resolved?
- If you have more than one child or other beneficiary, will they be fairly treated if one is to receive an interest in the business and others will receive other assets?

Business succession cases generally fall into one of four categories:

- You intend to transfer the business to your child, grandchild, or some other family member.
- You intend to transfer the business to one or more key employees.
- You intend to transfer your business interest to your partner or co-shareholder.
- You intend to liquidate the business by a sale to an unrelated third party.

Each of the foregoing transfers can be planned to occur either during your lifetime or after your death.

Example: A transfer to your child or other beneficiary could occur as a sale or gift to that person during your lifetime, or your estate plan could provide that the business interest will be transferred by gift or sale at your death. A sale to one or more key employees can also occur during your lifetime or at your death. Similarly, a sale to your partner or to a third party could be consummated during your lifetime or your estate plan could cause a sale to occur at your death.

One of the most common mistakes that business owners make is waiting too long to relinquish control over the family business through a sale to third parties or a transfer to the younger generation family members. In the case of a sale, the owner may be instrumental in successfully negotiating a sale at a fair price. The owner will be knowledgeable of that particular industry and may be aware of potential purchasers for the business. More than anyone else, the owner will know the strong and weak aspects of the business. In many cases, the full value of the business will be received only if the owner is able to play a major role in the transition of ownership. It may be essential that the owner be able to properly introduce the purchaser to suppliers, important customers, important employees, and other aspects of the business. If the owner is suddenly incapacitated as a result of a stroke or other illness, or passes away suddenly, the family and their advisors will be left to dispose of the business without the owner's experience, input, and guidance. As a result, substantial value may be lost. If the owner is incapacitated, then his or her own financial future may be jeopardized. If the owner has passed away, then the family's financial security may be at risk. One of the most frequent mistakes made by business owners or entrepreneurs is not to recognize when the appropriate time has come to begin a serious campaign to dispose of the business at the most favorable terms.

After twenty, thirty, or more years of operating and nurturing a business, it is understandable that the owner may be reluctant to dispose of it. However, what many owners fail to realize is that a successful sale of the business at its maximum value may be the most challenging and satisfying stage of their business career. The initial creation or purchase of the business and the years of guiding the business may be no more important than the successful disposition of the business. A successful sale of your business may be the crowning achievement of your business career. To wait to undertake that final challenge at a time when your physical and mental faculties may have declined or to pass that responsibility off to your family because you are totally incapacitated or dead may be the most significant mistake of your business career.

Transfer to a Child or Other Beneficiary

Often the business owner wishes to transfer the closely held business to his or her child or other beneficiary. The transfer can be accomplished in several ways. It might involve a sale to the beneficiary during lifetime, a lifetime gift or a testamentary bequest to the beneficiary, or a combination of the foregoing.

Parents often strongly desire to pass the family farm or other business intact to one or more children. However, the children of successful entrepreneurs frequently do not have the requisite ability to successfully continue the business and often have only a half-hearted interest in continuing the business. Therefore, when considering leaving a business to one or more of your children, even a child who has been highly involved with the business, it is most important to objectively and dispassionately analyze whether leaving the business to your child is in his or her best interest. If the child's ability to make the business flourish is questionable, it may be much better to negotiate a sale of the business while it is operating profitably under your control. The proceeds of sale can then be left to your child or other beneficiary in the form of conservative marketable securities which may be more likely to retain their value and future income stream.

The transfer of a business to your child or other beneficiary may be relatively simple or it may become significantly complicated.

Example: Assume your estate consists of the following:

Closely held business	$1.0 million
Marketable securities	$1.0
Total	$2.0

Assume your only heir is your son who has worked closely with you in the business for the last thirty years and is highly talented in, and devoted to, the business. This situation may be relatively problem free. You may simply by will or through your living trust leave the business and your other assets to your son. The marketable securities will be more than sufficient to pay the estate tax and your son will be able to continue on with the business intact.

Example: Assume your estate consists of the following:

Closely held business	$2.0 million
Marketable securities	-0-
Total	$2.0

Here, the estate tax will be approximately $435,000 (after 2005) and will be due nine months after your death. Here, an important question is whether the business has sufficient liquid assets to pay the tax or whether it produces sufficient cash flow to amortize a new $435,000 debt that will be incurred to pay the IRS. As the assumed value of the business increases, the liquidity problem worsens. An estate comprised solely of a $4.0 million business will need to raise $1.5 million to pay the estate tax and may or may not be able to support that level of debt.

Example: Assume that after the payment of estate taxes and other costs, your remaining net estate will consist of the following:

Closely held business	$2.0 million
Marketable securities	$2.0
Total	$4.0

Assume your daughter is highly involved with the business and experienced in its operation and wishes to inherit the business. Assume your son has no interest in the business. Here, the asset values are such that it is easy to treat the two children equitably. Obviously, the business will be left to the daughter and the marketable securities to your son.

Example: Assume the same facts as the preceding example except that your after-tax assets consist of the following:

Closely held business	$4.0 million
Marketable securities	-0-
Total	$4.0

Here, substantial problems may arise. Your daughter who has the experience and inclination to operate the business will be in partnership with your son who has no knowledge of nor interest in the business. That is a classic collision course. Typically, the daughter will be dissatisfied because she will believe that her efforts and sacrifices in operating and guiding the business will never be fairly rewarded because one-half of profits and capital appreciation inure to the benefit of her brother. Your son may be dissatisfied because he is, in fact, a passive investor who may feel that your daughter is not properly exploiting the business or is unfairly benefiting through excessive salaries or other corporate benefits.

Rarely, if ever, should family members who are actively involved in the management of a business be forced into "partnership" with inactive family members. Invariably the active family members feel that their efforts and sacrifices are inadequately rewarded and the passive owners invariably believe that the business should be more profitable or that the active family members are being overcompensated for their efforts.

This situation can arise where one or more children are involved with the business and one or more are not involved. It can also occur where an estate is comprised largely of a closely held business and the owner wishes to benefit his or her spouse and also his or her children from a prior marriage. In that situation, the children who are actively operating the business may be forced into "partnership" with their stepmother. Those types of forced partnerships almost invariably fail, to the detriment of all family members involved. Inappropriate forced partnerships should be avoided if at all possible.

Example: Assume your after-tax net assets will consist of the following:

Closely held business	$2.2 million
Marketable securities	$1.8
Total	$4.0

Assume again that your daughter is actively involved in the business and your son has no knowledge of the business nor interest in it. Your will or trust likely will leave the net assets to your children as follows:

	Daughter	Son
Closely held business	$2.0 million	$0.2 million
Securities	-0-	$1.8
Total	$2.0	$2.0

Here, your son is only a 9% minority shareholder or minority partner. The problem should be manageable. The business should be able to produce sufficient cash flow to buy out the 9% minority owner at a reasonable interest rate over a few years. Depending on the temperament and maturity of your children, it may be sufficient to simply allow them to work out the terms of the buyout of your son's interest. However, in most cases, it would be better to implement a buy-sell mechanism now that will mandate a buyout of the minority interest at reasonable terms that are fair to both children. The pre-establishment of some buyout plan will increase in importance as the size of the minority interest increases.

Example: Assume once again that your after-tax net assets will consist of the following:

Closely held business	$4.0 million
Marketable securities	-0-
Total	$4.0

Assume again that your daughter is involved in the business and your son is not, the classic case destined for catastrophe as outlined earlier. There is no easy solution to this situation. Some possible plans may be as follows:

Consider recapitalizing the business so that a large portion of its value is reflected as debt rather than equity. Assume that after the recapitalization the after-tax net assets in your estate will consist of the following:

Stock in closely held business	$2.0 million
Debt owed by family business	$2.0
Total	$4.0

Now, your daughter can inherit the stock and your son can inherit the corporate debt. Although this situation will be far from problem free, at least your son will have a greater chance of receiving a fair return on his inherited investment in the business. Namely, he will be entitled to interest on his investment at the interest rate you have specified in the debt instrument. The payment of interest and the amortization of the principal will generally have priority over dividend distributions on your daughter's stock. Still, a serious problem may exist since your daughter has inherited the business subject to a major debt. That large debt may preclude normal required business borrowing. Also, if the earnings of the corporation decline to a point that the full interest cannot be paid on the debt instrument owned by your son while leaving sufficient cash flow for your daughter's needs, then a business failure may occur.

It may be appropriate to consider the acquisition of a sizable insurance policy on your life to provide the liquidity needed in this situation. If surplus cash flow from the business could support the acquisition of a $4.0 million life insurance policy, then the problem might be readily solved: the $4.0 million business could be left to your daughter and the $4.0 million of insurance proceeds could be left to your son. In many cases, insurance may be used as a partial solution. If available cash flow could support a $2.0 million policy, then assets could be left to your children as follows:

	Daughter	Son
Family Business	$3.0 million	$1.0 million
Insurance Proceeds	-0-	$2.0
Total	$3.0	$3.0

Here, we still have a forced partnership, but the inactive child is only a

25% partner rather than a 50% partner. Here it may be more likely that the business will produce sufficient cash flow to amortize a buyout of your son's interest over a term of years. Of course, it may be important to have in place a buy-sell mechanism requiring that your son's 25% stock interest be purchased by your daughter or by the business over an appropriate number of years.

In some cases, it may be most sensible to simply mandate a sale of the business. That might be appropriate where the inactive child or children will have a major interest in the business and the anticipated cash flow from the business is speculative and/or there is less than complete confidence that the active child will be able to successfully operate the business so that her interest and her brother's interest are both protected.

Another aspect to consider in connection with a transfer of the family business to a child or other beneficiary is whether a portion or all of such transfer should occur during your lifetime. Lifetime transfers can sometimes be accomplished at a greatly reduced transfer tax cost (see chapter 7). Reduced tax cost will result in reduced liquidity needs, which may inure to the benefit of all heirs. A lifetime transfer of a portion of the business to the active child also may serve other worthwhile purposes, such as providing needed incentive or reward for the active child.

If you decide to transfer interests in your closely held business to your child or children during your lifetime, the issue of control must be considered. Substantially all of a business can be transferred to your child while you still retain full control. In the case of a corporation, nonvoting stock can be transferred to the child or, in the case of a partnership, non-voting partnership units can be transferred, or any one of a number of other mechanisms can be used to maintain control even though a substantial interest in the business has been transferred. The desirability of transferring interests in the business during your lifetime is primarily driven by a desire to reduce transfer taxes. However, the transfer of control is usually dependent on other factors such as your interest in remaining actively involved in the business, your physical and mental ability to operate the business, your confidence in your child's ability to successfully continue the business, and other similar factors.

In some cases, a sale of the business to your child or other beneficiary may be appropriate in lieu of a gift. If a continued income stream is needed from the business, then a long-term installment purchase may provide that cash flow. Various tax and other considerations may also indicate that a sale rather than a gift is appropriate.

Transfer to Key Employee

Often there is no child or other beneficiary who is suitable as a successor to the family business. In that case, a principal concern is to dispose of the business at the most favorable terms for the benefit of the owner and his or her family. In many cases, the most likely successor is a key employee who has worked in the business for many years. If the business is to be transferred to one or more key employees, some of the issues that arise are as follows:

- What is an appropriate and fair value for the purchase?
- How will the purchase price be funded?
- What is the timing of the transfer of ownership?
- When will control be transferred?
- How will the purchase note be secured?
- How can the transaction be structured to produce the best tax result?

The key employee may not have substantial resources. Therefore, his or her buyout of the business may have to be accomplished solely with business earnings. If the key employee will make only a small down payment or no down payment, then, in effect, the purchase is largely accomplished through debt and the business may not be able to support a debt of that magnitude while also providing adequate cash flow to the key employee for his needs. If the transfer is not to occur until your death, then a substantial policy insuring your life may provide the entire needed liquidity or, at least, sufficient liquidity so that the remainder of the buyout price can reasonably be supported by business earnings.

Another issue to consider is the timing of the buyout by the key employee. As discussed above, it may be preferable for the owner, the owner's family, and the key employee to begin the buyout while the owner still has the physical and mental strength to properly transfer the business to the new owner and supervise or oversee operation of the business during the initial critical years to assure that he or she will be able to operate the business successfully and best protect the owner's interest in the business during the buyout period.

Transfer to Partner or Co-Shareholder

If you are a partner or co-shareholder in a closely held business, it will be most important to plan for an orderly transfer of the business. If no plan is in place, in the event of your incapacity or death a serious financial loss may be incurred by your family and/or by your partner or co-shareholder. Here again, it is most important to avoid forced "partnerships."

> **Example:** You and your partner have operated a successful business for many years. You each have a 50% interest. Assume your heirs have never been involved in the operation of the business.
>
> Without proper planning, your spouse, children, or other beneficiaries will inherit your 50% interest and will then, in effect, be in partnership with your partner. Again, the business and your family's security may be headed for disaster. Although you and your partner may have been accommodating, fair, and generous to each other over the years, your partner may not have the same feelings toward your family who are mere passive investors. It is likely that your partner will soon begin to feel that his efforts and sacrifices are not adequately rewarded, since one-half of the company's success is inuring to the benefit of your heirs. Your heirs will possibly feel that they are receiving an insufficient return on their investment and that your partner is extracting excessive profits through salaries and other benefits.

In almost all cases it is important to have in place a mechanism for an orderly transfer of the business to the surviving partner and the transfer to your heirs of marketable securities or other liquid assets that can be used to assure their financial security. In most cases, it would be important to implement a buy-sell agreement between you and your partner. That agreement would typically provide that the survivor will purchase the stock or partnership interest of the first deceased. The surviving partner or co-shareholder will then own the entire business and the deceased partner's or co-shareholder's family will inherit the sale proceeds. An important consideration will be the necessary funding for the buyout.

Buy-Sell Agreements

In almost all cases where there is more than one owner of a business, it is important to have an appropriate buy-sell agreement in place. A properly designed buy-sell agreement will help assure that "forced partnerships" do not occur and that a mechanism exists for the orderly buyout of each owner's interest in the business.

Although there are a great variety of buy-sell agreements, most contain at least six basic provisions:

- **Lifetime restrictions**—Frequently the owners of a closely held business will want to control the admission of new owners. Therefore, typically, buy-sell agreements provide that your stock or partnership interest in the business may not be sold to third parties without the consent of the other owners, or it may provide that the other owners are entitled to a right of first refusal.

- **Purchase at death**—Buy-sell agreements typically provide that upon the death of one partner or co-shareholder the surviving owners will purchase his or her interest. In that way, the surviving owner becomes the sole owner and the deceased owner's family will inherit the sale proceeds.

- **Buyout upon disability**—Many buy-sell agreements provide that in the event of a serious and permanent disability of one owner the healthy owner will purchase his or her interest.

- **Buyout at retirement**—Another common provision is the requirement that an owner who retires from active involvement with the business will have his or her interest purchased by the remaining owner or owners.

- **Valuation**—Virtually every buy-sell agreement will include a stated purchase price or a formula or other mechanism to determine the purchase price. A common procedure is to provide that the partners will meet annually to agree on a purchase price that will be effective during the following year. Another approach is to simply provide that a buyout at death, disability, or other triggering event will be accomplished at the then appraised value. A third approach is to provide a formula for the price, such as some multiple of gross revenues or net profit. If a formula is used, then great care must be taken to assure that the formula is unambiguous and will result in a fair price to all parties under all reasonably foreseeable business conditions.

- **Funding**—It will be important to include a provision to govern the manner in which the purchase price will be paid. Often, a buyout at death will be funded through insurance on the deceased owner's life. Generally, each business owner will own a policy on the other owner's life. Upon the death of a partner, the survivor will receive the insurance proceeds. He will then be obligated under the terms of the buy-sell agreement to pay those proceeds over to the estate or family of the deceased partner in exchange for his or her partnership or stock interest.

If economically feasible, buyouts at death should be funded with insurance. If not, then the financial security of the deceased partner's family may depend on the future success of the business and such success may be in question since one of the principal owners has just recently died.

Occasionally, a buyout in the event of disability may be funded with a disability insurance policy that pays a lump sum in the event of permanent disability. However, such insurance may be expensive and frequently a buyout in the event of disability may have to be financed from the earnings of the business. To the extent a buyout is not funded by life insurance or lump-sum disability insurance, the remaining purchase price will usually be payable over several years at a stated interest rate. During that buyout period, the financial security of your heirs may be dependent on the successful operation of the business. Therefore, it may be appropriate to include certain safeguards such as limits on the payment of salaries to the surviving owner, limits on additional borrowing, limits on the payment of dividends or partnership distributions, and rights for your heirs to inspect the books and records of the business and generally oversee its operation.

Tax Considerations

One of the more complicated aspects of business succession planning is the mass of income tax, capital gains tax, and transfer tax rules that apply. The following are just a few examples of the issues that may be important in a particular case:

Example: Cross-purchase versus redemption—Assume you and I are 50-50 shareholders. If I die first should you purchase my shares (cross-purchase) or should the corporation purchase my shares (redemption)? In either event you will own the entire business, since 100% of the outstanding stock will be owned by you. The buyout can be structured either way, but will have significantly different tax results for the parties involved.

Example: Capital gain versus ordinary income—Should the buyout be structured so that the selling shareholder or partner receives capital gain treatment or should it be structured so that a portion of the seller's profit is taxed as ordinary income? Sellers generally prefer capital gain treatment, but buyers are often better served if the deal is structured to produce ordinary income.

Example: Deductibility of purchase price—It is sometimes possible to structure the buyout so that the purchaser can deduct a significant portion of the purchase price that he is paying to the seller. However, that usually results in ordinary income tax treatment to the seller.

Example: Lifetime sale versus sale at death with step-up—If the shareholder or partner has a very low basis in his interest in the business, it may be preferable, if the particular circumstances permit, to postpone a sale until after death so that the capital gain inherent in the business interest will be forgiven (see chapter 16). That would be particularly true where the sale is being made for a long-term installment note. If I sell my business interest during my lifetime in exchange for an installment note and I die holding the note, my estate will still be taxed on the capital gain from the sale. However, if the sale occurred after my death, there would likely be little or no gain.

Example: Taxability of life insurance proceeds—Life insurance proceeds are generally free of income tax (but not estate tax). However, where an existing insurance policy is used to fund a buy-sell agreement and the policy is transferred between shareholders or other related parties, it is possible to cause the insurance proceeds to be income taxed unless care is used to avoid that outcome.

19

Postmortem Planning

Valuation
Alternate Valuation
Disclaimer
Trust Funding
Estate Equalization
Income Tax Planning

AFTER YOUR DEATH, your executor will have to make a number of elections or choices that may significantly affect the estate taxes and income taxes that will be assessed against your estate. Most strategies to reduce transfer taxes must be implemented during your lifetime. In many cases they are best implemented several years before your death. However, even after your death there is often some opportunity to significantly reduce transfer and income taxes. A few of the postmortem considerations that may be important in a particular case are discussed below.

Valuation

If you have in excess of $625,000 of assets at the time or your death (increasing to $1.0 million after 2005), an estate tax return must be filed. In that case, all assets must be reported at their fair market value. (See chapter 7.)

In the case of marketable securities, the valuation process simply involves checking the market quotes for the day of your death. However, in the case of real estate, closely held business interests, artwork, and other similar assets, the valuation process is much more subjective. For such assets a range of values is possible, and several competent and experienced appraisers may each determine a different value for a particular asset. These types of assets offer an opportunity to obtain a favorable valuation.

If you are serving as an executor, it would be important to discuss your objectives with the appraiser or other valuation expert, and to state whether you prefer an appraisal at the high end or the low end of the range of possible values. Of course, you want a competent and honest appraisal, but within the range of reasonably supportable values, it may be advantageous to report a relatively high or relatively low value depending on the circumstance. Most (although not all) estate plans are designed to avoid tax on the estate of the first to die of a husband and wife. Often, the first $625,000 (increasing to $1.0 million after 2005) is allocated to a credit bypass trust and all excess assets are allocated to a marital deduction trust (chapter 2). If no tax is owed at the first death, then it may be appropriate to seek appraisals or business valuations at the high end of the possible range of values. That will serve to establish a higher tax basis in the assets for the benefit of the surviving spouse, children, or other beneficiaries. As a general rule, since no estate tax is owed on the first death, it is appropriate to attempt to report assets at the highest reasonable value to establish greater basis. An exception to that strategy would be in those situations where the surviving spouse is aged or in poor health and has a short life expectancy. In that situation selecting the highest possible value may have negative consequence.

Example: Assume no estate tax is owed at the time of your death and your personal representative obtains appraisals and valuations at the high end of the possible range of values. Assume that your surviving spouse passes away one or two years later. At the death of your surviving spouse, a substantial estate tax may be owed, based on the value of assets included in his or her estate. If high values were used at the time of your death, it may be difficult to establish lower values at the time of your spouse's death when the estate tax is owed.

Alternate Valuation

The tax rules permit your personal representative to value assets as of the day of your death or as of the date six months after your death. That rule is designed to alleviate hardship in those cases where there is a dramatic decline in the value of an estate shortly after the person's death. The date six months after death is known as the alternate valuation date. If the asset is sold prior to the six-month date, then the date of sale will be the alternate valuation date for that asset.

In most cases, your personal representative will want to value all assets at your date of death and also at the alternative valuation date and select the more advantageous valuation.

> Q: If asset values have increased by the alternate valuation date, can that higher value be elected so that additional basis will be obtained?
>
> A: The alternate valuation date can be elected only if assets have declined in value. It may not be used solely to obtain additional basis in assets.

Disclaimer

One of the more useful postmortem tools is the qualified disclaimer. The disclaimer rules permit a beneficiary to refuse to accept a bequest. That is known as a disclaimer. In that event the asset will generally pass to another beneficiary as though you had predeceased the decedent. Substantial estate taxes may be saved and other family goals achieved through the use of disclaimers.

The disclaimer rules involve several technical requirements. Most notably, the disclaimer must be documented and perfected within nine months of the decedent's date of death. If the disclaimer is properly executed, the inherited asset will never become part of your estate, but will pass to an alternative beneficiary.

> **Example:** Assume you had a will leaving all property to your spouse. Upon your death, all property owned jointly with your spouse passed to him or

her and all property individually owned by you passed to your spouse pursuant to the terms of your will. As a result, your spouse now has a substantial estate and when he or she passes away only your surviving spouse's lifetime exemption will be utilized. Because all property was left outright to your surviving spouse, your lifetime exemption has been wasted. If your combined gross estate is in the 55% bracket, one result of your estate plan will be to cause an additional $550,000 estate tax for your children (after 2005).

In the above example, depending on several factors, your surviving spouse may elect to disclaim a portion of your assets so that they will not pass outright to him or her. Under many estate plans, if the surviving spouse were to disclaim an interest in a bequest, it would then pass to the children. In that case, a disclaimer may be appropriate if the surviving spouse is certain that he or she will have adequate assets for his or her needs without the assets that are being disclaimed. Even if the disclaimed assets may be needed potentially, in some family situations the surviving spouse may be content to disclaim a portion of the assets feeling confident that the children will retain those assets for his or her benefit if needed. Obviously, if there is not that degree of trust and if it is possible that all of the assets may be needed by the surviving spouse, then a disclaimer would not be indicated.

Example: Assume that all assets were left outright to your surviving spouse as in the prior example. Assume that $1.0 million of those assets will not be needed by your spouse and that your spouse disclaims that amount, which then passes to your children under the terms of your estate plan. Since the disclaimed assets will not be part of your spouse's estate, the value of those assets, and future appreciation in value, will not be taxed at the time of your spouse's death and will thereby avoid transfer taxation.

In some cases, depending on the terms of a particular estate plan, if the surviving spouse disclaims an interest in an asset it may then pass to a trust established for his or her benefit. In that case, there may be no disadvantage to the disclaimer, since the disclaimed assets will be available for the surviving spouse's needs by way of the trust and yet substantial estate taxes will have been saved as a result of the disclaimer.

Trust Funding

Many estate plans involve the use of an A-B trust. In that case, assets equal to the lifetime exemption will be allocated to a credit bypass trust and all remaining assets will be allocated to a marital deduction trust. In most cases, both trusts will be established for the primary benefit of the surviving spouse. After the first death, it will be the trustee's responsibility to allocate trust assets between the "A" trust and the "B" trust. Since the unified credit bypass trust will not be subject to estate tax at either death and will ultimately pass to children or grandchildren free of transfer tax, it is generally appropriate to allocate assets with the highest appreciation potential to that trust. On the other hand, the marital deduction trust will be included in the estate of the second spouse to die. Therefore, as a general rule, assets with the least appreciation potential should be allocated to the marital deduction trust.

> **Example:** A large portion of an IRA will be lost to income taxes since all of the IRA must be taxed as it is withdrawn. Therefore, in those cases where the IRA is payable to an A-B trust, you should consider allocating it to the marital deduction trust if possible. Since that trust will be subject to estate tax when your spouse passes away, it will be helpful that it was reduced by the payment of income taxes on the IRA.

Estate Equalization

In most cases of estate planning for a married couple, it is appropriate at the first death to allocate assets equal to the lifetime exemption to a credit bypass trust and to allocate all other assets to a marital deduction trust so that no tax will be owed. However, in those cases where the surviving spouse is aged or in poor health it may be appropriate to elect a smaller marital deduction so that some tax will be owed at the first death. By causing some tax to be paid at the first death, less tax will be owed at the second death. That would be helpful to cause both estates to be taxed in lower brackets. If substantially all of the couple's assets are taxed at the second death, then they may be taxed in a very high bracket.

If the taxation of some assets could be switched to the first death then all assets might, on the average, be taxed in lower brackets. Namely, neither estate may rise to the highest bracket level. Selecting the size of the marital deduction to be claimed may be accomplished through the use of disclaimers or through the use of a partial QTIP election (chapter 2).

Income Tax Planning

Generally, your estate will be required to file its own income tax return and possibly pay income taxes. Similarly, a trust that you may have left may require the filing of an income tax return and possibly the payment of income taxes. There are a number of strategies and techniques to defer, reduce, or eliminate some portion of the combined income tax. A simple example involves the selection of a taxable year. Estates, but not trusts, are permitted to select other than a calendar taxable year. In general, beneficiaries are taxed on estate distributions depending on when the estate's taxable year ends versus their own calendar taxable year. In many cases, by selecting a January 31 year end for the estate, some estate income will receive an eleven-month deferral on taxation.

Another example of income tax planning involves the consideration of estate distributions. In general, distributions from an estate are deemed to carry out taxable income from the estate to the beneficiary to the extent that the estate has taxable income. Any beneficiary receiving a distribution during a taxable year will be considered as having taxable income. If additional distributions in excess of the estate's taxable income are made to a second beneficiary in the following year then his distributions may be received income tax free. Therefore, the timing of distributions vis-a-vis beneficiaries may determine which beneficiary will pay the tax, whether the estate may pay the tax, and the rate at which the tax will be paid.

Example: Assume your uncle passed away on January 5, 1999. His net estate, after the payment of estate taxes, was $2.0 million and he left it equally to you and your cousin. During 1999 the estate earned $200,000 of income on its investments, providing a total or $2.2 million to be distributed.

If your $1.1 million share is distributed to you on December 31, 1999, and your cousin's $1.1 million share is distributed to him on January 1, 2000, you will be required to pay income tax on the $200,000 of estate income. Your cousin will receive his bequest tax free. The distribution to you is laden with taxable income because the estate had undistributed income at the time of the distribution to you. The estate had no undistributed income at the time of the distribution to your cousin, and as a result, his share was not taxable.

The income tax rules involving estates and beneficiaries are rather complex. However, suffice it to say that there are a number of strategies to significantly reduce the combined income tax liability incurred by the estate and the various beneficiaries. If you are ever called upon to serve as an executor or successor trustee, or if you are a beneficiary of a sizable bequest, it would be most important to consult with a competent tax advisor.

Glossary

"A-B" Trust—a trust containing two subtrusts. Typically a credit bypass trust and a marital deduction trust.

"A-B-C" Trust—a trust containing three subtrusts. Usually a credit bypass trust, a marital deduction trust, and a generation-skipping trust.

Administrator—a person who was not named in the will, but was appointed by the probate court to administer the estate of the deceased person. Often used interchangeably with executor or personal representative.

Alternate Valuation Date—the date six months after date of death on which estates are permitted to value estate assets for estate tax purposes.

Annual Exclusion—the amount (currently $10,000) that can be given to any one donee during a given calendar year without incurring an estate tax or depleting your lifetime exemption.

Annuity—a contract that permits you to receive a specified amount annually or monthly for the remainder of your life or a stated number of years. Usually, but not always, obtained from an insurance company.

Asset—anything of value, including real property, personal property, tangible and intangible property.

Basis—the amount you paid for an asset, less allowable appreciation. It is used to compute the capital gain or loss when the asset is sold.

Beneficiary—the person for whose benefit a trust or estate is created. Also used to denote the person who is the object of a gift (donee), or the person named to receive insurance proceeds or the remaining balance of a retirement plan or deferred compensation plan.

Beneficiary Designation—the document that specifies who will receive life insurance proceeds or the remaining balance of an IRA or other retirement account or similar asset in the event of the death of the insured or account owner.

Bequeath—to leave personal property to another by will.

Bequest—a testamentary gift of personal property. Also often used to refer to a gift of real property by will.

Blind Trust—a trust where the trustee is prohibited from divulging to the beneficiary the composition of the trust assets.

Bond—a certificate or evidence of a debt. See surety bond.

Bypass Trust—a trust designed to pay income and/or principal to a named beneficiary without causing the trust assets to be included in the beneficiary's estate for transfer tax purposes.

Charitable Lead Trust (CLT)—a trust that will pay income to one or more named charities for a set number of years with the remainder interest passing to a noncharitable beneficiary, which trust satisfies various IRS requirements so that it is afforded favorable tax treatment.

Charitable Remainder Annuity Trust (CRAT)—a charitable remainder trust that pays a fixed dollar amount annually or more frequently to the noncharitable beneficiary.

Charitable Remainder Trust (CRT)—a trust providing that income will be paid to one or more noncharitable beneficiaries for a specified number of years or for the duration of one or more lives, with the remainder passing to one or more specified charities, which trust satisfies various IRS requirements so that favorable tax benefits will be received.

Charitable Remainder Unitrust (CRUT)—a charitable remainder trust that pays a fixed percentage of the value of the trust principal as valued annually.

Charitable Trust—the generic term for a trust established to wholly or partially benefit one or more charitable organizations. The term includes charitable lead trusts, charitable remainder trusts, and trusts that are established solely to benefit a charity without a noncharitable beneficiary.

CLT—see Charitable Lead Trust.

Codicil—an addition to or modification of a will that is signed with testamentary formalities.

Community Property—a form of ownership of property between a husband and wife that is primarily found in one of the nine states where community property laws prevail.

Corporate Trustee—a bank or an independent trust company that is authorized to serve as an executor, trustee, guardian, or other fiduciary.

Co-Trustee—one of two or more trustees serving concurrently.

CRAT—see Charitable Remainder Annuity Trust.

Credit Bypass Trust—a bypass trust that is intended to be funded with your remaining unified credit equivalent ($625,000 for 1998, but increasing to $1.0 million after 2005). Used synonymously with credit shelter trust.

Credit Shelter Trust—a bypass trust that is intended to be funded with your remaining unified credit equivalent ($625,000 for 1998, but increasing to $1.0 million after 2005). Used synonymously with credit bypass trust.

CRT—see Charitable Remainder Trust.

CRUT—see Charitable Remainder Unitrust.

Curtesy—that portion of a deceased wife's property to which her surviving husband was entitled under common law. Still available in some states, but largely replaced by other statutory elections.

Decedent's Estate—the estate consisting of a deceased person's individually owned property that must pass through probate.

Devise—a testamentary gift of real estate contained in a will.

Devisee—the person to whom real estate is devised or given by will. Modernly, it is often used interchangeably with legatee or beneficiary.

Disclaimer—a renunciation of a devised bequest or other gift, which renunciation will have particular tax results if it follows certain formalities specified by the IRS.

Domicile—that place where you are residing with the present intention of making a permanent home. Often used synonymously with residence.

Donee—the person receiving a gift.

Donor—the person making a gift.

Dower—the portion of a deceased husband's real estate to which his surviving wife is entitled. Dower has been replaced in many states by the elective share.

Dynasty Trust—a trust that is designed to benefit multiple generations without being subjected to transfer taxes.

Educational Trust—a trust established during lifetime, or set forth in a will to be established at death, which provides funds for educational purposes for one or more named beneficiaries.

Elective Share—the share of your estate to which your surviving spouse is entitled regardless of the terms of your will. Used synonymously with statutory share.

Endowment Policy—a life insurance policy designed so that its cash value will eventually equal its death benefit. At that time the policy is said to have endowed.

Estate—the aggregate of all of your property, both real and personal. See probate estate, taxable estate, and gross estate.

Estate Property—that property comprising your estate.

Estate Tax—the tax imposed by the federal government on the value of your taxable estate. Many states impose their own estate tax.

Executor—the person named in your will, and appointed by the court, to administer your probate estate. Often used synonymously with administrator and personal representative.

Family Allowance—that portion of your estate that may be awarded to your surviving spouse or dependent children for their support during the period of the probate proceedings. Usually a minor amount.

Family Limited Partnership (FLP)—a limited partnership owned by family members. Used to transfer assets while reducing transfer taxes and retaining control over the gifted property. Also used as an asset protection technique.

Fiduciary—the person serving as a trustee, executor, or guardian or in another position of trust and who owes the highest duty of responsibility and good faith to the beneficiaries.

FLP—see Family Limited Partnership.

Foreign Situs Trust—a trust formed in, and governed by the laws of, a foreign country. Used primarily for asset protection purposes.

Fraudulent Conveyance—a transfer to a family member or other person that may be set aside by your creditors.

Generation-Skipping Tax (GST)—a part of the transfer tax system that is designed to limit the use of dynasty trusts.

Generation-Skipping Trust—a trust designed to provide income and/or principal to a younger generation beneficiary without the trust principal being included in the beneficiary's estate.

Gift—a voluntary transfer of property for less than full consideration.

Grantor—a person who establishes a trust or transfers property to a trust. Synonymous with settlor and trustor.

GRAT—see Grantor Retained Annuity Trust.

Grantor Retained Annuity Trust (GRAT)—a Grantor Retained Income Trust (GRIT) that pays you a specified dollar amount annually or at more frequent intervals.

Grantor Retained Income Trust (GRIT)—an irrevocable trust from which you have retained the right to receive a specified dollar amount annually or more frequently for a specified number of years or for the duration of one or more lives and which will provide certain tax benefits if specific IRS rules are followed.

Grantor Retained Unitrust (GRUT)—a Grantor Retained Income Trust (GRIT) that pays to you a specified percentage of the principal as valued annually.

GRIT—see Grantor Retained Income Trust.

Gross Estate—the aggregate of all of your property, probate and non-probate, which may be subject to estate tax.

GRUT—see Grantor Retained Unitrust.

GST—see Generation-Skipping Tax.

Guardian—a person appointed by the probate court with the power and duty to care for the person or property of a minor or incapacitated person.

Guardian of the Person—the person authorized and empowered by the court to care for the physical needs of the ward.

Guardian of the Property—the person authorized and empowered by the court to care for the property of the ward.

Guardianship—the entity created when a guardian is appointed to manage the person or property of a ward.

Health Care Surrogate—that person appointed by you to make health care decisions for you in the event of your incapacity.

Heir—one who inherits property from an intestate estate, but frequently used synonymously with devisee or legatee.

Holographic Will—an unwitnessed will written entirely in the testator's handwriting. Not valid in most states.

Income Beneficiary—the individual who is currently entitled to the income from a trust.

Income Interest—the right to receive the current income from a trust.

Individual Retirement Account (IRA)—an investment account that is permitted to accumulate income on a tax-deferred basis, but is subject to a complicated set of tax rules.

Inheritance—the real or personal property inherited from an intestate estate, but frequently used in reference to property received from a testate estate as well.

Inheritance Tax—a tax imposed by some states on the recipients of inherited property.

Insurance Trust—an irrevocable trust designed to exclude insurance proceeds from the insured's gross estate.

Intangible Asset—property that does not have a physical being, but must be represented or evidenced by a certificate or other document such as stocks, bonds, promissory notes, etc.

Intentionally Defective Trust—an irrevocable trust designed to remove the trust assets from your gross estate for estate tax purposes, but to include them in your estate for income tax purposes.

In Terrorem Clause—a provision in a will or trust that provides that any beneficiary who challenges the will or trust will forfeit all rights thereto. In Terrorem clauses are invalid in many states.

Intestacy Laws—the laws of a particular state that specify who will receive your estate in the event that you die intestate.

Intestate—without a will.

IRA—see Individual Retirement Account.

Irrevocable Trust—a trust that, by its terms, is not subject to revocation or amendment.

Issue—children, grandchildren, and more remote descendants of an individual, referred to collectively.

Joint and Survivor Annuity—an annuity payable until both named annuitants are deceased.

Joint and Survivor Policy—a life insurance policy covering two lives and which pays only upon the second death. Synonymous with a second-to-die policy.

Joint Tenants—two or more co-owners of an asset, generally with rights of survivorship.

Kiddie Tax—a federal income tax rule that requires investment income of a child under age 14 to be taxed at his or her parents' marginal tax rate.

Land Trust—a special trust used in many states to hold legal title to real estate for the benefit of the true equitable owners.

Legacy—a gift of money or other personal property by will. Also often used to refer to a testamentary gift of real property.

Legatee—the person to whom a legacy is given.

Letters of Administration—the formal instrument granted by the probate court to the executor empowering the executor to manage the affairs of the estate.

Letters of Guardianship—the formal instrument granted by the probate court to the guardian empowering him or her to manage the affairs of the guardianship estate.

Life Estate—the right to receive the income from a trust or from certain property for the remainder of your life.

Life Insurance Trust—an irrevocable trust designed to remove an insurance policy from your estate so that the death proceeds will be free of estate tax.

Lifetime Exemption—the maximum amount you are permitted to transfer by gift or bequest without incurring a gift tax or estate tax ($625,000 for 1998, but increasing to $1.0 million in 2006).

Lifetime Gift Trust—an irrevocable trust established during your lifetime to serve as the recipient of annual or occasional gifts for the benefit of one or more specified individuals.

Living Trust—a trust, revocable or irrevocable, established during your lifetime, as opposed to a testamentary trust, which is not established until the time of your death.

Living Will—a document expressing your intention regarding the application or withholding of life-prolonging procedures in the event of a terminal illness or vegetative state.

Marital Agreement—an agreement between a husband and wife that specifies their respective rights to each other's property in the event of a divorce or death.

Marital Deduction—that property left to your surviving spouse or in trust for your surviving spouse and which may be deducted from your gross estate and is therefore not subject to estate tax at the time of your death.

Marital Deduction Trust—a trust established for the benefit of your surviving spouse that is intended to qualify for the marital deduction.

Medicaid Trust—a trust designed to provide benefits to an individual without disqualifying him or her from receiving Medicaid benefits.

Minimum Distribution Rules—those IRS rules specifying the minimum amount that may be withdrawn annually from a pension plan, profit sharing plan, 401(k) plan, IRA, or similar qualified retirement plan.

Nonresident Alien (NRA)—a person who is not a citizen of the U.S. and is not considered a resident of the U.S.

Palimony—a court award of support similar to alimony, but between domestic partners who are not married.

Pay on Death Trust (POD Trust)—a bank account that specifies that upon your death the remaining balance will be paid to one or more named beneficiaries. A probate avoidance device, which is not actually a trust.

Personal Property—property or assets other than real property, including tangible and intangible personal property.

Personal Representative—the person appointed by the probate court to administer a decedent's estate. Often used interchangeably with executor and administrator.

POD Trust—see Pay on Death Trust.

Postmarital Agreement—an agreement executed after marriage by a husband and wife to clarify their respective rights to each other's property in the event of death or divorce. Synonymous with postnuptial agreement.

Postnuptial Agreement—a marital agreement executed after the parties are married. Synonymous with postmarital agreement.

Pour-over Will—a will that directs that estate assets be paid to a trust, rather than to an individual named in the will.

Power of Appointment—the authority granted to a person to decide who will ultimately receive the remaining principal of a trust.

Premarital Agreement—an agreement executed before marriage by a husband and wife to clarify their respective rights to each other's property in the event of death or divorce. Synonymous with prenuptial agreement.

Prenuptial Agreement—a marital agreement executed prior to marriage. Synonymous with premarital agreement.

Principal—the assets or property of a trust.

Private Annuity—an arrangement whereby your child or other beneficiary will pay a fixed amount to you annually or at more frequent intervals for the remainder of your life and which may provide significant tax benefits.

Private Foundation—a trust or corporation established to provide charitable benefits.

Probate—the process of administering a decedent's estate or guardianship under court supervision.

Probate Estate—those assets owned by a decedent individually and which must be subjected to probate proceedings. Often used synonymously with decedent's estate.

Property—all assets and other things of value, including real estate and tangible and intangible personal property.

QDT—see Qualified Domestic Trust.

QPRT—see Qualified Personal Residence Trust.

QTIP Trust—see Qualified Terminable Interest Property Trust.

Qualified Domestic Trust (QDT)—a type of QTIP trust designed to qualify for the marital deduction notwithstanding that the surviving spouse is not a U.S. citizen.

Qualified Personal Residence Trust (QPRT)—an irrevocable trust designed to satisfy certain IRS requirements so that a personal residence may be gifted to children or other family members at a significantly reduced gift tax cost.

Qualified Plan—a profit sharing plan, pension plan, Keogh plan, 401(k) plan, IRA, or other retirement plan that is qualified by the tax rules to receive certain tax benefits such as the deductibility of contributions to the plan and the tax-deferred accumulation of earnings.

Qualified Terminable Interest Property Trust (QTIP Trust)—a trust to provide income to a surviving spouse and which may qualify for the marital deduction.

Rabbi Trust—a type of nonqualified retirement plan.

RBD—see Required Beginning Date.

Real Property—land and buildings and other improvements located thereon. Synonymous with real estate.

Redemption—a transaction in which a corporation purchases its own outstanding stock or bonds.

Remainder Interest—that which is left after the expiration of a life estate or a term for years.

Remainderman—the beneficiary who will receive the remainder interest.

Required Beginning Date (RBD)—that date on which you must begin taking distributions from your IRA or other qualified retirement plan. Generally April 1 of the year following the year in which you turn age 70 ½.

Residence—the place of your abode and which is currently inhabited by you. Often used synonymously with domicile.

Revocable Living Trust (RLT)—a trust established during your lifetime for the primary purpose of avoiding probate court proceedings in the event of your death or incapacity, and which may be revoked or amended by you at any time.

Revocable Trust—a trust which by its terms may be revoked or amended by the grantor.

Right of First Refusal—a legal right to purchase an asset before any other person may purchase it.

RLT—see Revocable Living Trust.

SCIN—see Self-Canceling Installment Note.

S Corporation—a corporation that has elected to be taxed in a manner similar to the taxation of partnerships. S Corporations generally do not pay income tax, because each shareholder individually pays tax on his or her pro rata share of the S Corporation's earnings each year.

S Corporation Trust—a trust that has been designed as a permissible holder of S Corporation stock.

Self-Canceling Installment Note (SCIN)—a promissory note received as payment for the sale of an asset and which note provides that all future installments will be canceled in the event of your death and which may provide significant tax benefits.

Settlor—the person who establishes a trust. Synonymous with grantor and trustor.

Spendthrift Trust—a trust containing a spendthrift provision making its principal generally unreachable by a creditor of the beneficiary.

Split-Dollar Insurance—an insurance policy that is owned partially by an employee and partially by his or her employer or partially by some other individual.

Sprinkle Trust—a trust that permits the trustee to distribute income and/or principal among two or more permissible beneficiaries.

Statutory Share—the share of your estate to which your surviving spouse is entitled regardless of the terms of your will. Used synonymously with elective share.

Successor Trustee—that person who will serve as trustee after a prior trustee ceases to serve.

Surety—the insurance company or other individual that guarantees a bond.

Surety Bond—the bond often required to be posted by an executor before receiving letters of administration. The bond must be guaranteed by an insurance company or other approved surety.

Tangible Assets—an asset with a physical being apart from any certificate or document of ownership.

Taxable Estate—that portion of your gross estate which remains after deducting debts, marital and charitable bequests, and administrative costs, and to which the tax rates will be applied.

Tenants by the Entirety—a form of ownership between a husband and wife which is recognized in many states and which may afford protection from the creditors of either the husband or the wife.

Tenants in Common—a form of joint ownership in which each joint owner may individually convey or devise his or her pro rata share of the property without the consent of the other tenant or tenants in common.

Term for Years—the right to receive income or the right to possess property for a specified number of years.

Term Insurance—life insurance that does not acquire cash value.

Testamentary Formalities—the requirements that are mandated by a particular state for the creation of a valid will.

Testamentary Trust—a trust that is set forth in your will and which does not come into being until the time of your death.

Testate—with a will.

Testator—a person who writes or establishes a will.

Transfer Tax—the gift tax, estate tax, and generation-skipping tax combined are referred to as the transfer taxes.

Trust—a formal arrangement whereby one individual or corporation (the trustee) holds legal title to assets (the trust principal) for the benefit of another individual (the beneficiary).

Trust Company—a financial institution empowered to serve as a trustee, personal representative, guardian, or other fiduciary.

Trustee—the person or corporate entity specified in a trust to hold legal title to trust property and to manage and preserve that property for the benefit of the trust beneficiaries.

Trustor—the person who establishes a trust. Used synonymously with grantor and settlor.

Unified Credit—a credit allowed against gift tax or estate tax which equates to a $625,000 exemption for 1998 (increasing to $1.0 million for 2006 and after).

Unified Credit Equivalent—the $625,000 exemption equivalent of the unified credit (increasing to $1.0 million after 2005).

Uniform Gifts to Minors Act (UGMA)—a statute enacted in all states that permits an adult to hold property for the benefit of a minor without the necessity of establishing a formal trust.

Uniform Transfers to Minors Act (UTMA)—a more modern and versatile version of the UGMA that has been enacted in nearly all states.

Universal Life Insurance—a highly flexible policy that permits the owner to change the permiums or death benefit as desired.

Variable Life Insurance—an investment oriented policy that permits the owner to shift cash values among a family of investment accounts.

Ward—the minor or incapacitated person whose property or person is subject to a guardianship.

Wealth Replacement Trust—a trust intended to compensate for the tax-motivated diversion of assets away from your intended beneficiaries.

Whole Life Insurance—a policy designed to accumulate a cash value and to remain in effect throughout your lifetime.

Will—a formal declaration of one's wishes regarding the disposition of one's estate and which requires certain formalities in order to be valid.

Index

for spouse, 41–45. *See also under*
spouse
sprinkle trust, 33–35
testamentary, 19–20, 55
credit bypass trust established in,
46
vs. living, 19–20, 23
Totten, 62–63
transferring assets to, 78–79
improper and incomplete, 78–79
mechanics of, 79–81
tax effects, 83–85
Wealth Replacement Trust (WRT),
209
wills containing bequest to. *See* wills,
pour-over

undue influence, 18
unified credit. *See* lifetime exemption
Uniform Gifts to Minors Act (UGMA), 58
Uniform Limited Partnership Act, 184
Uniform Transfers to Minors Act
(UTMA), 58, 171
universal life (UL) insurance. *See under*
life insurance, types

vacation homes, 203
valuation, 230–31
alternate, 236
valuation process, 234–35
variable life (VL) insurance. *See under* life
insurance, types

variable universal life (VUL) insurance.
See under life insurance, types

"ward," 91. *See also* guardianships
Wealth Replacement Trust (WRT), 209
will contests, 17–19
avoiding, 18, 19
wills, 1–20
absence of, 91. *See also* estate planning, inappropriate or absent; intestate estate
amending, 14–17
assets not governed by, 2
contents, 14
copies of, 15, 17, 167
electing against, 5–7
execution, 14–15
improper, 18
state requirements, 167
invalid, 18–19, 91
location of, 15, 167
pour-over, 20
purposes of, 2, 13–14
revoking/cancelling, 14–18, 168
signing of, 14
witnesses, 14, 15
trust specified in. *See* trusts, testamentary
validity, 14–15, 17–19, 91. *See also* will
contests
videotaping, 18
Wisconsin, 40